BOTSWANA

SAIS African Studies Library

General Editor
I. William Zartman

BOTSWANA

The Political Economy of Democratic Development

edited by
Stephen John Stedman

Lynne Rienner Publishers • Boulder & London

Published in the United States of America in 1993 by
Lynne Rienner Publishers, Inc.
1800 30th Street, Boulder, Colorado 80301

and in the United Kingdom by
Lynne Rienner Publishers, Inc.
3 Henrietta Street, Covent Garden, London WC2E 8LU

Library of Congress Cataloging-in-Publication Data
Botswana : the political economy of democratic development / edited by
Stephen John Stedman.
   p. cm.—(SAIS African studies library)
  Includes bibliographical references and index.
  ISBN 1-55587-305-7 (alk. paper)
  1. Botswana—Politics and government—1966- 2. Democracy—
Botswana. 3. Botswana—Economic conditions—1966- 4. Botswana—
Economic policy. I. Stedman, Stephen John. II. Series: SAIS
African studies library (Boulder, Colo.)
JQ2760.A91B68 1992
968.83'03—dc20   92-25289
                                                           CIP

British Cataloguing in Publication Data
A Cataloguing in Publication record for this book
is available from the British Library.

Printed and bound in the United States of America

The paper used in this publication meets the requirements
of the American National Standard for Permanence of
Paper for Printed Library Materials Z39.48-1984.

Contents

Tables

Acknowledgments

This book began as a series of papers presented at the annual SAIS Country Day Program on Africa, which was funded through the support of the Ford Foundation. In putting together the conference program, I relied on the advice of John Holm and Jack Parson, both of whom made excellent suggestions about possible contributors. I would like to thank Dave Peterson of the National Endowment for Democracy for his help in making it possible for Patrick Molutsi to attend, and our appreciation goes out to Ambassador Botsweletse Kingsley Sebele and his assistant, Mrs. Naomi Majinda, for their interest and participation. I would also like to thank Larry Diamond for serving as a discussant at the conference, and even more for his key role in helping to put democracy in Africa on the agenda of policymakers in Washington and scholars throughout the United States. The manuscript benefited from the keen editorial attention of Benjamin Hardy and Gia Hamilton at Lynne Rienner Publishers. During the editorial compilation of the book, Eliot Posner helped enormously, and Sipho Shezi compiled the index. Finally, the conference could not have taken place without the contributions of I. William Zartman, the director of the African Studies Program at SAIS, and Theresa Taylor Simmons, the administrative assistant for the Program. This was the tenth annual Country Day Program Theresa has managed, and I think it is fitting to dedicate this book to her for her many contributions beyond the call of duty to Country Day and the African Studies Program.

S.J.S.

1

Introduction

Stephen John Stedman

At a time when Africa's dismal economic performance and political corruption and mismanagement have given rise to a new intellectual movement called Afropessimism, when analysts create generic models of African governments that include "lame leviathans," "swollen states," "kleptocracies," and "vampire states," Botswana stands out as an example of economic development, functioning governance, and multiparty, liberal democracy. It is, as I have suggested elsewhere, a country akin to Switzerland, an exception that confounds generalizations, but whose very exceptionality prompts analysts to see it as a hopeful model for other societies.[1]

Consider the following points. From 1965 to 1985, Botswana attained the highest rate of economic growth in the world. From having a gross national product (GNP) per capita of less than $100 in 1966, it now claims GNP per capita over $1,600. It achieved such performance in part due to its excellent bureaucracy, which in terms of norms and capabilities meets the definition of a strong state.[2] Knowing only these three facts—a beginning point in dire poverty, high economic growth, and a strong state—one would predict that Botswana's political system has been highly authoritarian. On the contrary, since its independence in 1966 Botswana has been a multiparty liberal democracy, albeit dominated by one party. Its human rights record has been better than the United Kingdom's.[3]

In Africa, and in less developed countries in general, it is unclear which is more exceptional: that Botswana has a government that governs or that Botswana has a democratic regime. Each deserves explanation. Each creates tensions for the other. Both are relevant to current discussions among policymakers and scholars on the nature of good governance in Africa and its relationship to democracy and development.

■ Development, Governance, and Democracy

Many donor governments and major international aid organizations have recently "discovered" a relationship between governance and economic development. The World Bank, the United States Agency for International Development, and the British government have all commissioned studies that claim to understand how government can help or hinder national development. A recurrent tension in the new thinking about governance concerns the relationship between governance and democracy: Is democracy synonymous with good governance? Is democracy a prerequisite for good governance? Is governance a prerequisite for democracy? Is there any causal relationship at all between the two?

Good governance and democracy are not synonyms. Democracy refers to a specific type of political regime marked by competition, participation, and legal protection of civil liberties.[4] Governance refers to performance by regimes on a set of specified dimensions that relate to the ability of government to control its people (military and civilian) and manage its resources. In a passage that attests to the time-bounded nature of political science's assessment of particular regimes, Samuel Huntington draws the distinction between regime and governance:

> The most important political distinction among countries concerns not their form of government but their degree of government. The differences between democracy and dictatorship are less than the differences between those countries whose politics embodies consensus, community, legitimacy, organization, effectiveness, stability, and those countries whose politics is deficient in these qualities. Communist totalitarian states and Western liberal states both belong generally in the category of effective rather than debile political systems. The United States, Great Britain, and the Soviet Union have different forms of government, but in all three systems the government governs.[5]

This leaves open the question of what constitutes the ability of governments to govern. A brief survey of the literature provides at least three different answers. The first, exemplified by the work of Migdal, centers on the dimension of control: in particular the ability of a state to penetrate and regulate society, extract resources from it, and appropriate them in determined ways.[6] The second approach, that of the World Bank, equates governance with the ability to establish an environment in which capitalism can flourish. Key processes include accountability, transparency, and predictability.[7] The third approach, as exemplified in recent work by Goran Hyden, judges governance by the quality of exchange between government and society in terms of its legitimacy and reciprocity. For Hyden, the dimensions of governance include authority, reciprocity, trust, and accountability.[8]

■ Purpose of the Book

The key question that scholars and policymakers must ask concerns the relationship among democracy, development, and governance. This book does not provide a general answer to this question. It rather seeks to take the experience of one African country, Botswana, as an empirical case study of the conflicts and complimentarities among governance, democracy, and development. We hope that Botswana's experience can provide some substance to what have been largely conceptual, ahistorical, and non-empirical discussions in the donor countries and aid organizations.

This volume examines Botswana's history of economic and political development in light of the following questions:

1. What explains Botswana's impressive economic and political performance since 1965?
2. Do democracy and governance in Botswana reinforce or do they contradict one another?
3. What problems lie in the way of Botswana sustaining its impressive performance?
4. What important international factors have contributed to Botswana's performance?
5. How are changes in southern Africa likely to affect Botswana's development?
6. Can Botswana serve as a model for other countries in Africa? What lessons can be derived from Botswana's experience for other countries?

■ Arrangement of the Chapters

The book comprises three parts: "Botswana's Path to Democratic Development," "Current Problems and Predicaments," and "Botswana in a Changing Southern Africa."

Part 1 examines specific factors that have contributed to Botswana's economic and political performance. In Chapter 2, Stephen Lewis compares Botswana's economic development to that of other African countries, and attributes Botswana's superior performance to a combination of resources, luck, and good choices. He especially emphasizes the good choices: he shows that Botswana's leaders understood the importance of planning for sustaining long-term growth, of good organization for optimal bargaining with donors and foreign corporations, and of discussion and learning for reconciling tradeoffs between political and economic goods.

Lewis's chapter fills an important need in the development literature. Analysts have frequently stressed the need for dialogue between aid agencies and foreign politicians, but as one scholar has recently remarked, all too often the dialogue is between the deaf.[9] Lewis's paper provides us a primer on productive relationships between foreign economists and African politicians. He stresses the need for economists to understand the political constraints that confront African leaders and to work with them in creating a mutual sense of what would constitute good economic choices. He argues that such choices are not predetermined but result from consultation between elites and the mutual creation of interests. Like Lindblom's recent work, Lewis's argument emphasizes the necessity for societal probing to solve social problems.[10] In Lindblom's model, leaders, social scientists, and citizens must create a sense of public interest, rather than "discover" one. As does Lindblom, Lewis stresses the crucial role of debate, consultation, respect for others' points of view, pluralism, and learning in improving public policymaking. Lewis contends that Botswana's democratic openness has been a positive factor in producing good economic decisions.

In Chapter 3, Stephen Morrison investigates what he refers to as Botswana's ethos of state action—the emphasis that political elites place on enterprise, compromise, stability, security, and accommodation. He argues that the seeds of Botswana's statehood were planted in the decade before independence, from 1956–1966. His explanation stresses a number of "Cs": crisis, choice, coalitions, contingency, context, and consensus. Botswana's ethos of state action resulted from a crisis in the late 1950s, when the Bechuanaland Protectorate faced the possible collapse of the regional market in cattle, at that time the country's only major commodity. Colonial and nationalist elites manipulated the crisis to reduce the strength of the Colonial Development Corporation, a private firm that had a monopoly on the export of cattle products. Employing what Morrison calls an "end run" (by choosing a rival entrepreneur from South Africa, Roger Hurwitz), the colonial administration increased its power vis à vis the CDC. The resulting balance of power between state authorities and the CDC led to a class coalition involving black and white members of the cattle-owning elite, the colonial state authorities, and the Colonial Development Corporation. As independence came nearer, the threat that a new political party—the Botswana People's Party (BPP)—might injure the coalition's interests led to the establishment of the Botswana Democratic Party (BDP), the party that has ruled Botswana since independence. While Morrison's story may remind readers of Barrington Moore's analysis of class coalitions and the emergence of democratic politics in Europe,[11] it has more in common with a neglected work from the 1970s: *Crisis, Choice, and Change,* by Gabriel Almond et al.[12] The authors emphasize that class coalition analysis must be wedded to the choices leaders make when crises open new formative possibilities for the development of the country.

Chapter 4 concludes the first section of the book with Patrick Molutsi examining the role of international factors in contributing to Botswana's democracy. He argues that the vast amount of aid funneled into Botswana by international organizations and foreign governments has been crucial to Botswana's economic development. Democracy, he argues further, has been one of the main reasons that Botswana has received so much aid. As he suggests, Botswana's democratic ideology has been one of its most lucrative exports. Yet the equation of international aid and assistance and democracy is not a neat one: a major effect of such assistance has been to strengthen the bureaucracy and its domination of policymaking in Botswana.

Part 2 of the book, "Current Problems and Predicaments," investigates tensions between governance and democracy in Botswana. Botswana's government has accomplished what many others in Africa have not: it governs. Botswana's bureaucracy has made superb economic choices, has been largely free of corruption, and has provided political stability rare elsewhere in Africa. Yet, as the authors of this section point out, Botswana's accomplishments have not been without problems.

In Chapter 5, Jack Parson analyzes the 1989 national elections in order to gauge the continuing strength of Botswana's ruling party, the BDP. As a one-party-dominant state, Botswana has yet to have an election that leads to the turnover of the executive office. Parson suggests that while the BDP may not face defeat at the polls in the near future, some trends point to a greater degree of electoral competitiveness in Botswana. Such competitiveness will provide major tensions for the system and its democratic processes.

Parson's chapter implies a relationship between the challenges that the BDP will face at the voting booth and the viability of continued multiparty democracy in Botswana. Some critics have disparaged Botswana's democratic record precisely because there has been no electoral turnover at the national level. The argument contends that the BDP has tolerated opposition only because the opposition is weak and ineffectual. Yet this thesis could easily be turned on its head: since the opposition in Botswana is so weak and ineffectual, the BDP could have easily established a de jure one-party state.[13]

In Chapter 6, John Holm examines mass participation in Botswana to see whether a political culture supportive of democracy has taken root. Through a comparison of survey data from 1987 and 1989, Holm concludes that while economic development in Botswana is creating a public supportive of democratic structures and values, this public has not participated actively in politics. The failure of Batswana[14] to join organized group politics, Holm suggests, implies a weak foundation for multiparty democracy in Botswana. Holm's chapter supplements his previous work that argues that if democracy is to thrive in Botswana, civil society must be strengthened to counterbalance the bureaucracy and the dominant party.[15]

In Chapter 7, Gloria Somolekae points out existing tensions between bureaucracy and democracy in Botswana. In particular, she contends, while the bureaucracy's autonomy has contributed to Botswana's development, there is an increasing danger that its tendency to make policy will erode citizen accountability and democratic participation. She asks whether bureaucrats might not become corrupt and arrogant (and believe themselves to be infallible) if civil society does not develop means to keep them in check. For their part, the bureaucrats worry about ceding decisionmaking to social groups that might endanger Botswana's developmental success and stability.

Rodger Yeager, in Chapter 8, focuses on another kind of tradeoff between governance and democracy in Botswana: the government and the ruling party have created land-use policies that cause grave ecological damage. In this case, Yeager argues, Botswana's democracy systematically blocks alternative land-use policies from consideration: Botswana's ruling party and bureaucracy have few incentives to change a policy that may benefit the BDP's short-term interests but hurts everyone's long-term interests.

Finally, in most countries the struggle between the state and democracy traditionally has been most acute in matters of national security. James Zaffiro seeks in Chapter 9 to understand how Botswana has balanced the making of foreign policy with its commitment to democracy. In particular he looks at the institutionalization of foreign policymaking and what avenues are open for democratic inquiry and participation.

In Part 3, the book's final section, we look at Botswana's place in the larger region of southern Africa, an area undergoing tremendous change. In Chapter 10, Richard Dale paints in vivid strokes the geopolitical difficulties that have beset Botswana in the twentieth century. As he points out, in the early 1960s Botswana's very survival as a sovereign state was in doubt. For the first fourteen years of its existence, Botswana found itself sandwiched between the white supremacist regimes of South Africa and Rhodesia. Botswana's location insured that it would suffer enormously if it provided direct support for the liberation movements in those countries. As Dale points out, even after Zimbabwe's independence in 1980, Botswana has not been immune from the violent conflicts that marred Zimbabwe's first ten years. An important implication of Dale's article is that Botswana's geopolitical difficulties may not end with the demise of apartheid in South Africa.

Dale's chapter illustrates that Botswana's democracy and sovereignty have flourished in an antagonistic environment, which adds to its accomplishment. Interestingly, while the presence of South Africa as a dominant neighbor could explain why Botswana developed such a strong sense of statehood, it would certainly not predict that Botswana would be a liberal democracy that tolerates open opposition and individual freedoms.

In Chapter 11, Bernhard Weimer and Olaf Claus note that Botswana confronts its problems of reconciling democracy and governance, development and governance, and democracy and ecological health during a time of intense change in southern Africa. Independence in Namibia and the end of apartheid in South Africa, as well as various simultaneous experiments in political and economic liberalization in the region, will create much potential for new regional conflict, but also new opportunities to cooperate. In Botswana's domestic performance Weimer and Claus find possible lessons for the other countries in the region, and suggest that Botswana's history of peaceful conflict resolution could provide an important model for the region as a whole.

■ **Notes**

1. See my review of Patrick P. Molutsi and John D. Holm, eds., *Democracy in Botswana* (Athens: Ohio University Press, 1989), in *Journal of Democracy* 2, no. 3 (Summer 1991): 111–114.

2. John D. Holm and Patrick Molutsi, "State-Society Relations in Botswana: Beginning Liberalization," in Goran Hyden and Michael Bratton, eds., *Governance and Politics in Africa* (Boulder, Colo.: Lynne Rienner, 1992), 83–84.

3. Amnesty International's annual reports on human rights violations have consistently condemned Great Britain's violation of due process in arrests and trials involving Northern Ireland. The organization has also found fault with curbs placed on press freedoms for reasons of state security. Botswana has been criticized occasionally by Amnesty International for its use of the death penalty and for forced repatriation of refugees to Zimbabwe.

4. Larry Diamond, Juan Linz, and Seymour Martin Lipset, eds., *Democracy in Developing Countries,* vol. 2, *Africa* (Boulder, Colo.: Lynne Rienner, 1988), xvi.

5. Samuel Huntington, *Political Order in Changing Societies* (New Haven, Conn.: Yale University Press, 1968), 1.

6. Joel Migdal, *Strong Societies and Weak States: State-Society Relations and State Capabilities in the Third World* (Princeton, N.J.: Princeton University Press, 1988), 4–5.

7. "Managing Development: the Governance Dimension, a Discussion Paper" (World Bank, Washington, D.C., August 29, 1991).

8. Goran Hyden, "Governance and the Study of Politics," in Goran Hyden and Michael Bratton, eds., *Governance and Politics in Africa* (Boulder, Colo.: Lynne Rienner, 1992), 12–16.

9. Thomas Callaghy, "Africa and the World Economy: Caught Between a Rock and a Hard Place," in John Harbeson and Donald Rothchild, eds., *Africa in World Politics* (Boulder, Colo.: Westview, 1991), 65.

10. Charles Lindblom, *Inquiry and Social Change: The Troubled Attempt to Understand and Change Society* (New Haven, Conn.: Yale University Press, 1991).

11. Barrington Moore, Jr., *The Social Origins of Dictatorship and Democracy: Lord and Peasant in the Making of the Modern World* (Boston: Beacon, 1966).

12. Gabriel Almond, et al., *Crisis, Choice and Change* (Boston: Little Brown, 1973).

13. This illustrates the difficulty in two of Robert Dahl's axioms concerning the calculus of tolerating opposition. In *Polyarchy* (New Haven: Yale University Press, 1971), he presents two axioms: "Axiom 1. The likelihood that a government will tolerate an opposition increases as the expected costs of toleration decrease," and

"Axiom 2. The likelihood that a government will tolerate an opposition increases as the expected costs of suppression increase." By the first axiom we expect the BDP to tolerate opposition; certainly the costs of toleration are low. On the other hand, the same factors that account for the low costs of tolerance—the smallness and ineffectiveness of the opposition to the BDP—lead to low costs of suppression. In the Botswana case, Dahl's axioms seem contradictory.

14. "Batswana" is the plural noun for the people of Botswana.

15. Patrick Molutsi and John Holm, "Developing Democracy When Civil Society Is Weak: The Case of Botswana," *African Affairs* 89 (July 1990): 323–340.

PART 1

BOTSWANA'S PATH TO DEMOCRATIC DEVELOPMENT

2

Policymaking and Economic Performance: Botswana in Comparative Perspective

Stephen R. Lewis, Jr.

How does one explain Botswana's excellent, even extraordinary, economic performance, especially in comparison with the rest of sub-Saharan Africa? The basic answer, I believe, is this: While good fortune plays an important role, unusually good economic policy choices were essential to achieving outstanding economic results.[1]

■ Botswana's Record in Brief

In contrast to the rest of Africa and, indeed, much of the rest of the developing world, Botswana has achieved an enviable record:

1. Botswana has the highest rate of economic growth, measured by real per capita income, of any country in the world over the past twenty years. Table 2.1 shows Botswana's growth performance to be a multiple of that of other low-income countries and of the rest of sub-Saharan Africa. The growth rate of employment shows a similarly outstanding record, with formal employment growing approximately three times as fast as the economically active population over the past twenty years. Botswana's debt service is modest and its foreign exchange reserves are the highest on the continent, in months of import cover. Despite a healthy financial balance sheet, government expenditures have risen more rapidly than elsewhere on the continent during the past quarter century.

2. Botswana's performance measured by social indicators, such as those shown in Table 2.2, demonstrates that there has been a substantial spread of the benefits of economic development through provision of health services, education, clean water, and other social services. District planning exercises in Botswana have revealed steady, emphatic demand at

the local level for more and better water, health care, education, communication, and transportation (population is sparse and distance to market is long), and government spending has been directed at those priorities. From the earliest days, the strategy was to develop mining, tax it, and use the revenues to expand public services, develop infrastructure, and diversify investments.

3. Botswana, a multiparty democracy, has held elections every five years since 1965. It has a small but free press, no political prisoners, a commitment to nonracialism in political and civil life, and the best record on human rights on the continent. The ruling Botswana Democratic Party has had large majorities in rural areas, in part due to the attention it paid to the priority demands of those areas for government spending.

Table 2.1 Botswana in Comparative Perspective: Economic Indicators

	1965–1973	1973–1980	1980–1987	1965–1987
Growth rate, GNP per capita				
Botswana	9.3	7.3	8.0	8.2
Sub-Saharan Africa (SSA)	2.9	0.1	–2.8	0.1
All low-income countries (LIC)	3.3	2.6	4.0	3.3
SSA middle-income countries (MIC)	1.9	–1.2	0.3	0.4
Growth Rates, GDP				
Botswana	14.7	10.5	13.0	12.8
SSA	5.9	2.5	0.5	
All LIC	6.0	4.6	6.1	
SSA MIC	5.2	1.4	3.8	
Growth Rate, General Government consumption				
Botswana	5.5	14.3	13.8	10.9
SSA	9.0	7.0	–0.7	
All LIC	7.5	7.2	4.4	
SSA MIC	7.0	8.4	3.5	
Average Inflation Rate				
Botswana	4.4	11.6	8.4	
SSA	7.5	6.8	15.2	
All LIC	9.7	8.9	8.2	
SSA MIC	4.7	14.2	6.8	
Growth Rate of Exports (nominal $)				
Botswana	20.4	18.7	16.2	
SSA	15.1	0.2	–1.3	
All LIC	9.6	2.3	3.5	
SSA MIC	7.2	3.8	4.5	

Sources: World Bank, *World Development Report 1990* (Washington, D.C., 1990); World Bank, *Sub-Saharan Africa: From Crisis to Sustainable Growth* (Washington, D.C., 1989)

Table 2.2 Botswana in Comparative Perspective: Social Indicators

	1965	1989	
Population per Physician			
Botswana	27,450	6,900	
SSA	33,200	23,850	
LIC and MIC	8,270	4,790	
Population per Nursing Person			
Botswana	17,710	700	
SSA	5,420	2,400	
LIC and MIC	5,020	1,900	
Infant Mortality per 1,000 Live Births			
Botswana	112	41	
SSA	160	108	
LIC and MIC	117	67	
	1965	1980	1986
Percent Age Group in Primary Schools			
Botswana	65	91	105[a]
SSA	41	79	73
All LIC	73	93	102[a]
SSA MIC	73	99	95
Percent Age Group in Secondary Schools			
Botswana	3	19	31
SSA	4	16	20
All LIC	20	34	35
SSA MIC	7	17	24

Sources: World Bank, *World Development Report 1990* (Washington, D.C., 1990); World Bank, *Sub-Saharan Africa: From Crisis to Sustainable Growth* (Washington, D.C., 1989)

Note: a. Gross enrollment ratios may exceed 100 percent because some pupils are younger or older than the country's standard primary school age.

4. This record was achieved by a country that was, for the first fourteen years after independence, surrounded by white minority regimes in South Africa, Southern Rhodesia, and Namibia. At great risk to its sovereignty, Botswana has been a haven for political refugees from neighboring states. The wars for independence in Angola, Zimbabwe, and Namibia, and the struggle for freedom in South Africa, have kept open warfare near Botswana's borders for virtually the entire period since independence and have brought repeated armed incursions into Botswana's territory.

5. Finally, Botswana came to independence in 1966 as one of the poorest countries in the world. Over half of its government budget was financed by grants from Great Britain, about two-thirds of its workers had jobs in South Africa, and drought had killed about a third of its total cattle herd, which was then Botswana's only significant asset other than its extraordinary people. Botswana's president, Dr. Quett Masire, often notes that when

the people of what was then Bechuanaland Protectorate asked the British for independence "people thought we were either very brave or very foolish."

Given disastrous beginnings and a dangerous regional context, what explains Botswana's extraordinary record in both economic and political terms? There are two broad categories of factors: luck and management—the latter including economic policymaking.

On the side of luck, Botswana was fortunate in a few critical areas. DeBeers, the managers of the world's diamond cartel, discovered and developed three diamond mines there between 1969 and 1982. Botswana is now one of the top two diamond producers in the world. A rich copper-nickel deposit was discovered; the investment to develop it was over one and one-half times the size of Botswana's gross domestic product (GDP) at the beginning of the project. In agriculture, for most of the first fifteen years after independence Botswana enjoyed the wet phase of a major 20-year climatic cycle in southern Africa. On the political side, Botswana did not have the major tribal differences of other countries in Africa, since a substantial majority of the people come from Tswana-speaking tribes.

The luck was not all good. There were two outbreaks of foot-and-mouth disease; the drought of the mid-1980s was perhaps the most severe then occurring in Africa; there were regional wars; and the history of the protectorate had left a legacy of racism in institutions and practices common to the region. Moreover, for the rest of Africa, countries with mineral wealth have generally done worse, not better, than those without.

The other major category of explanations falls under the heading of "management." Good management explains most of Botswana's sustained political and economic success. Certainly, a look at the record of most oil-producing and hard-mineral-exporting countries demonstrates that mineral wealth alone is no guarantee of sustained economic development.[2] I return to the detailed examination of policy management later in the paper.

■ The African Setting

Botswana provides a striking contrast to the rest of Africa. Indeed, one reason for interest in African economic policymaking is the overwhelming sense that Africa is in an extraordinary economic crisis. Real per capita incomes have been falling for two decades in much of the continent, famine stalks the majority of citizens of a dozen or more countries, many countries are unable not only to pay their debts but even to meet current expenses, and overall the productivity of investment has declined precipitously. While it is clear that many of Africa's economic problems are exogenous, resulting from natural disasters and from changes in the international economy, many are the result of economic mismanagement.[3] Such a conclusion raises the question: What have the policy economists been doing, and why haven't they been able to help African countries achieve more success in the past twenty years?

In searching for tentative answers, one must take note of a number of factors. One of the most obvious in the early years of independence was the lack of trained and educated personnel at all levels of government, and at all levels of the administrative and policymaking process, in the majority of African countries. There is simply no comparison between Asia and Africa in the relative numbers of trained people at the time of political independence.

Then, in the 1950s and 1960s, the major US foundations, particularly Ford and Rockefeller, worked on a trio of actions aimed at improving the rationality of economic decisionmaking in several Asian governments: (1) improved policy formulation and planning in governments themselves, (2) improved training at the university level for local economists, and (3) establishment or upgrading of research institutes to inform policymakers in governments. This enormous undertaking went on for two decades or more in India, Pakistan, Bangladesh, Indonesia, Thailand, Malaysia, and the Philippines. These programs built, in many countries, on a long history of university education and of established bureaucracies capable of performing modern state functions.

In Africa neither the educational systems nor the bureaucracies existed at the beginning. The capacity to turn out enough economists to staff both a government and a university, as well as carry out a modest level of economic research relevant to policy concerns, was simply not available for many years. As a result, the skill levels of government economists were inadequate in many African countries for the first decade or more of independence; in the early days economists were almost by definition foreign economists. For many years thereafter there was no competition for jobs in the government: anyone with the relevant degree was offered a position. If indeed the foundations' three-legged stool for good management was correct, much of Africa limped along with at least one of the legs missing for most of the first two decades of independence.

Other major factors in the lack of development of economic policymaking capacity in Africa have been the relatively high degree of political instability in many countries and a substantial lack of political freedom in many others. These have exacerbated manpower shortages in economics and other professions in two ways. First, instability has often meant that good economic policymaking has a relatively low priority: if there were trained economists, they were unlikely to be heard. Second, the combination of instability and political intolerance has meant that skilled people were often exiled from their own countries. Africa has been called a continent of refugees, and this applies to intellectuals and professionals as well as to the rural poor fleeing starvation, war, or persecution. The inadequate numbers of trained economists produced in Africa have been badly used. In some countries, one found an anomalous situation in which highly trained citizens worked abroad (since they were unable to work at home for political reasons) while expatriates (often of lower quality) filled the vacant places in the bureaucracy.

Another element in the African setting was the postcolonial set of attitudes toward many issues of economic policy. Newly independent African governments were highly suspicious about participation in the international economy, about the role of international companies, and about the role of free markets generally. Starting with the slave trade, the international economy had hardly been beneficent to Africa; and the "free market" often meant the freedom of foreign minorities to exploit local citizens who were prohibited by law from engaging in certain economic activities. Structural rigidities—low levels of response of supply and demand to price changes, single-crop economies—meant that markets cleared only at unacceptable costs in human terms or in terms of economic dislocation. In many cases colonial governments had their own forms of economic intervention and control, whether through marketing boards for export crops or prohibitions on the types of activities permitted to indigenous citizens.

These policies predisposed the postcolonial state to take a major role in controlling and directing economic activities. "Statist" attitudes, combined with very rapid expansion of government's role in African economies, increased the importance of economic planning and policymaking in Africa over what it might have been had the state played a less intrusive role.

This, then, has been the setting in which economists and economic advisers, whether citizens or expatriates, have found themselves in many African countries. On one hand, the capacity to perform good analysis and to create and administer economic policies and plans was hampered both by conditions at independence and by subsequent political disruptions in many countries. On the other hand, the load to be carried by central government economists, policymakers, planners, and economic bureaucrats expanded rapidly.

■ **Economists and Politicians**

In my view, a good portion of the economic wasteland that constitutes the African scene of the past decade can be accounted for by failures of economic analysts (foreign or domestic) to communicate effectively with political leaders. The dominant tendency in economics has been to consider the economist, in the role of policy adviser, as essentially a technician: one discovers the existing government's "social welfare function" and then finds the most efficient policy to deal with the issue at hand in light of leaders' preferences. This is a misleading view of reality.

Fortunately, the view is changing. Economists are moving away from the notion of a single well-defined welfare function for society, to recognize the limits of knowledge, to acknowledge "bounded rationality." We can now see the process of reaching policy decisions as one in which policymakers' preferences become clearer during the search for specific policy alternatives. As Henry Bruton and Paul Clark put it, "there are no 'right' policies independent of the process by which the policy decisions are made."

A number of studies of the policymaking process, as well as several accounts of the role of foreign advisers in developing countries, highlight the critical importance of this interaction between policymakers and technicians. Different authors point to different formulations of the issue, but there are many similarities of approach. Aaron Wildavsky has talked of the need in the policy process to "create the problem"—that is, to reorganize the thinking about issues into a problem that can actually be solved.[4] In countries without foreign exchange (literally), the amount of imagination required to turn the situation into a problem that can be addressed and solved is considerable.

In Africa over the past three decades, the challenge to the economist in government has been significant. In some cases the elected (or the politically appointed) decisionmakers did not have much formal education; even where the political leaders did, the majority of citizens did not. Moreover, until very recently the level of discussion of economic issues in the press of most African countries has been dismal. As a result, there has been a strong tendency to treat economic advice as something of a black box: economists can propose solutions to problems, but it is unlikely that nontechnicians will understand their logic. One result of this treatment has been that economists, and economic analysis, have received an extremely bad name in many countries.

A large share of the problem has been the narrow confines into which economic analysis and advice have often been placed. The very language in which the process is described artificially divides it into a technical element and a political element; these imply, incorrectly, a form of inherent conflict. Economists have often encouraged such a view by taking a kind of morally superior view of "pure" analysis leading to appropriate policies, unsullied by "political" constraints or considerations.

Politicians and economists are susceptible to a vast and dangerous misunderstanding: politicians are left to make fundamental choices without knowing their likely consequences, and economists are likely to give advice without knowing the constraints, potential payoffs, or options facing politicians. This is a common problem for higher-income countries, but in Africa, where resources are scarcer, where the risks may be higher, where the politicians have fewer alternative sources of information and analysis, where the political systems are more fragile, and where the capacity for adjustment in policies may be more limited, the failure of economic analysts to interact in a productive way with political decisionmakers can have disastrous consequences.

In order for this interaction and communication to take place effectively, a great many conditions need to be satisfied. At the most elementary level, political leaders must understand a few basic concepts: scarcity, choice, the likely existence of alternatives, the usefulness of projecting possible consequences of actions, the possible differences between short- and long-run effects, etc. Likewise, economists need to understand something about the relative importance of constituent groups and their leaders; the priorities of these and other political actors; time, money, and other resource constraints; the importance of symbols, including ideology; and the calculus of political tradeoffs. Learning is essential on both sides.

■ Elements of Success and Failure

Providing good economic advice involves the ability to help the client understand and state a problem clearly, and then to present alternatives from which to choose. The ability to be a good policy economist is related to the ability to be a good teacher. I generally blame failures of policy advice mainly on the economists for not being able or sufficiently willing to inform and educate the politicians, or to speak effectively to political concerns. One should not forget the role of the advisees, however; some are much more likely to make an effort to understand technicians than are others, and to help the economist/adviser to understand better the politician's position. Conversation and dialogue are very important.

One measure of successful policy advice is the extent to which, over time, political leaders perceive changes in their options and their constraints. Well-advised politicians participate more and more vigorously in the discussion of economic policy alternatives as time goes on.

Another measure of success is the ability of the advisory process to perpetuate itself through young economists who become better and better at economic analysis for policymaking. Again, the Asian experience shows that one characteristic of successful countries was training to replace people who were promoted or shifted to other assignments. The system must be able to reproduce itself to survive, and it cannot be judged effective if it fails to develop that capacity.

■ Elements of Botswana's Policy Experience

Since independence, Botswana has had an exceptionally close working relationship between elected politicians and government economic technicians (both citizen and foreign). While there has been and continues to be plenty of complaining about the influence of economists in government, there is a remarkable amount of open debate both in and out of Parliament on matters of economic planning and policy. This has raised the general level of economic literacy among politicians, other (noneconomist) civil servants, and members of the business community.

Botswana's leaders developed a clear sense of priorities even before independence. They saw they could not do everything at once, even though everything needed doing. They set priorities (e.g., first achieving financial independence from British grants-in-aid, and developing access to other bilateral and multilateral donors), and then changed them as they achieved some objectives (e.g., a solid start on infrastructure) and could move on to others (e.g., diversification of employment opportunities). Fundamental to setting those priorities was the practice of looking ahead to anticipate problems that would be likely to arise in the future, and preparing ahead of time to deal with them.

For example, as soon as Botswana achieved budgetary independence (which took six years), it established reserve funds to see it through difficult times. Since then it has built up reserves in good years and run them down in bad, enabling its development efforts to proceed almost uninterrupted for nearly twenty-five years.

Perhaps the most dramatic illustration of anticipation in the policy process involved drought. The government (and interested private individuals and organizations) began to think about drought relief measures during the wettest part of the weather cycle. By the time the next sustained drought hit Botswana in the 1980s (arguably the worst in Africa since independence, as Botswana lost more than 80 percent of its crops for five years in a row), measures were in place to run a major drought relief program. In contrast to droughts elsewhere in Africa, not a single life was lost to drought-related causes during Botswana's five-year drought, and relief programs at times fed 60 percent of the total population, a major logistical feat in Africa's most sparsely populated country.

Botswana did not have its own currency and central bank until the pula was introduced as the national currency in 1976. Before its introduction, and for a number of months and even years thereafter, economists from the Ministry of Finance and Development Planning and from the Bank of Botswana held seminars and briefings not only for all cabinet members and senior civil servants from all ministries (and for the Commissioner of Police and the Commander of the Defence Force as well), but also for the entire membership of Parliament (government as well as opposition parties). These briefings covered the basics of balance of payments accounts, how foreign exchange reserves were accumulated and depleted, how they were linked to levels of domestic money and credit, how the foreign rate linked foreign and domestic prices, etc.

While many eyes glazed over during these briefings, the exercise paid high dividends in several respects. Of all African countries, Botswana almost certainly has had the most effective management of the exchange rate as an instrument of economic policy, including several revaluations, several devaluations, and several changes in the currency, or basket of currencies, to which the pula has been pegged. After the first few discretionary changes in the exchange rate there were brief seminars for politicians and civil servants to review the decisions and to discuss their likely effects. The changes were made for a variety of reasons at different times, but in a small and very open economy the ability to adjust the exchange rate without producing major political problems was a notable advantage to the government. It could not have been accomplished had political leaders and senior civil servants failed to grasp what was intended.

When diamond-export earnings dropped by 40 percent in 1981 (there were no sales at all for four consecutive months), the government faced a major stabilization problem. It adopted a package of policies, most of them announced in the February 1982 budget speech, which involved credit ceilings, increased interest rates, a wage freeze (at a time when everyone was expecting a 25 percent increase to catch up with inflation), cuts in government recurrent and development spending, introduction of new consumption taxes, and a 10 percent pula devaluation. Parliament took a full afternoon for a private briefing with economists from the Ministry of Finance and Development Planning. A tripartite government-business-labor group, fully briefed on the entire package, became the source of the wage-freeze recommendation.

It would have been impossible, in my judgment, for the government to deal with the 1982 situation had it not spent the time in basic education for more than five years before the crisis occurred. This was entirely a domestic package, not part of an International Monetary Fund (IMF) or World Bank adjustment program. There have been debates since 1982 about whether the measures were too severe; but the balance of payments improved, reserves came back up, and the February 1983 budget (only twelve months later) was able to be expansionary again.

There are enough stories in the media about the attitude toward stabilization programs in the rest of Africa as well as other areas of the world to make it clear that not all countries have managed to get their economists and their politicians talking together, regardless of how one views the merits of IMF-type stabilization packages. Exchange rate decisions pose frequent problems in Africa; all too often, they become highly politicized because of public statements from presidents, ministers of finance, governors of central banks, etc., about how they will not be pushed around. Meanwhile, economists skulk around governmental corridors trying to avoid talking about the issue, since their own assessments are quite different from what is being proclaimed loudly by their political masters.

In one African country with which I am reasonably familiar, devaluation to deal with extreme overvaluation of the local currency was almost certainly an essential part of adjusting to the realities of the early 1980s. The advice tendered was timely, the arguments persuasive, and the orders of magnitude of the change as near to "right" as one would be likely to get in an uncertain world. However, due to the nature of the local policymaking process, participants were unwilling to discuss the matter either before or after the fact. As a result, there was a great deal of skepticism both among politicians and economists in and outside the government about the nature of the judgments made, the legitimacy of the decisionmaking process, and the efficacy of the accompanying economic analysis. As for the advisory process's ability to reproduce itself, even though the policymaking system had produced a "good" decision, it was sadly lacking in an important dimension: only two or three people understood the underlying analysis and the economic argument. In that dimension, the decision could in no way be considered a success. Indeed it probably damaged future capacity to reach sensible policy decisions.

Another critically important contribution to Botswana's success has been its excellent negotiators and bargainers with outsiders. They have dealt successfully with the South African government (e.g., on revenue sharing in the customs union), multinational companies (e.g., on negotiations with DeBeers that have reserved the lion's share of profits for Botswana and produced seats on the firm's board of directors), the European Economic Community (on access of beef to EC markets), and all the major international donors. In 1981, a small team of Batswana simultaneously negotiated mineral agreements with the three largest companies in the world (measured by 1980 attributable profits)—Exxon, Royal Dutch–Shell, and Anglo-American (parent of the DeBeers group)—and they did it without complaining about the disadvantages of their small size and low bargaining power. In most negotiations Botswana has brought in its own legal, financial, and technical consultants to offset the expertise of larger foreign governments, multinational companies, and foreign banks. Both Botswana's record of success and its attitudes toward the process contrast strikingly with similar negotiating experience in other developing countries.

■ What Explains the Openness of the Process?

Are there underlying qualities in the people and their institutions that explain these operational successes? Tradition and history are of critical importance. Botswana had able traditional leaders for at least a century before reaching independence. Chiefs ruled, but they did so through traditional institutions such as the *kgotla*,[5] where there was an opportunity to express one's view and a need to achieve a degree of consensus. Openness and consultation were always essential. Since independence, in addition to Parliament and elected local governments, there have been frequent presidential commissions on national issues (incomes policy, economic opportunities, tribal grazing policy, and land tenure, to name but a few). Their membership is often broadly based; they hold public hearings and issue public reports that are debated in Parliament. Public education has been a major function of these commissions, as has been consensus-building.

Botswana has a long tradition of using friendly outsiders to help cope with unfriendly ones. The three principal tribal chiefs took the lead in proposing protectorate status for Bechuanaland, but they had help from the London Missionary Society in convincing the British government. Since independence, Botswana has often used external consultants in dealing with foreign banks and companies, and it has used its own diplomatic skills in finding powerful friends outside the region to help cope with the regional powers of southern Africa.

Tradition and culture produced extremely unusual leadership in Botswana. The best examples come from the top: Sir Seretse Khama, the first president of Botswana, was the grandson of Khama the Great, one of the chiefs who first dealt with the British. Sir Seretse, who was president from 1966 until his death from cancer in 1980, gave up claim to his traditional titles and founded a modern political movement, the Botswana Democratic Party. Sir Seretse's chief organizer was Dr. Quett Masire, a farmer from the southern part of the country self-taught as both master farmer and economist. Both men were committed to nonracialism, nontribalism, democracy, and consultation.

Other senior leaders, both at independence and after, have been very able individuals committed to similar values: to education and to developing intelligent, independent people with sound values, a sense of limits, and a respect for others. Young people thrust into positions of responsibility, many of whom in their twenties and thirties are undertaking major assignments in foreign affairs, running major government departments, or negotiating agreements that will affect the whole history of their country, rise to the expectations that others have of them. The process has been able to "reproduce" itself successfully: the cast of characters in senior political and civil service positions has changed almost completely since independence, but the newcomers are a part of the policy process and operate within the same basic systems.

One value important in explaining the success of Botswana and its leadership is openness, tempered with humility. Botswana has always sought to learn from what others have done, both successes and failures. Policies as widely divergent as those on exchange controls, subsidies, health care, and foreign commercial borrowing were developed after study of alternatives used in other countries. Leaders have always been genuinely inquisitive and not afraid to stop a speaker and say: "I don't understand what you just said; please explain it again." This has been a critical element in nurturing an open policymaking process where the economic technicians cannot hide behind (or in) their black boxes, and the leadership is encouraged to participate fully in the economic policy debate.

The traditions and practices of openness and democracy have very practical results. For example, Botswana has lost only a handful of citizens to international organizations, despite enormous pay differentials, so the training investments have paid dividends for Botswana. Most dramatically, perhaps, it is no accident that the drought in Botswana produced no deaths, whereas in Ethiopia it produced countless thousands, though Botswana's drought was more prolonged and more serious. Because elected politicians travel constantly throughout the country, because their elections depend on the welfare of their constituents, and because news is freely printed, there is pressure on government to perform and to produce results.

Finally, it is important to note that Botswana was not afflicted by any rigid ideology regarding economic policy at independence. In many respects development has been Botswana's ideology. Botswana has dealt with mining companies on a pragmatic basis, negotiating agreements that protect national interests; it has used public ownership when that seemed an appropriate vehicle for achieving results; it stood its ground in dealing with South Africa on trading arrangements, refusing both to recognize South Africa's "homelands" and to sign an Nkomati-type defense agreement; and, in the end, Botswana prevailed in reaching its economic objectives without yielding on principles. Some considerable share of Botswana's economic success can be attributed to the government's unwillingness to yield to pressures for ideologically based development policies that produced investment failures in so many other countries.

■ Some Limitations

Lest this seem entirely a praise poem, let me end with a few examples of where I believe the policy process has experienced some problems in Botswana and where the economic and social results might have been significantly better.

Cattle are critically important in Botswana. In rural areas, where perhaps half the people own cattle and the rest aspire to, cattle-owners are the backbone of the Botswana Democratic Party. Most land in Botswana is held communally, so there is a very significant "commons" problem. The issue was addressed in the early 1970s: a commission investigated thoroughly, consultations were held throughout the country, and a Tribal Grazing Land Policy was adopted by Parliament. Nearly twenty years later, it remained at best partially implemented. Highly criticized by both international ecologists and local citizens and politicians, it has yet to deal effectively with issues of land tenure and degradation of the grazing veld that affect the majority of the population. Analysis, decision, and implementation failed to work effectively together in this case. (Politically, dealing with tribal grazing in Botswana is perhaps on a par with energy policy in the United States. Some knowledgeable political observers hold that Congress would have adopted a $1 per gallon gas tax years ago had the vote been taken on a secret ballot!)

Urban housing in Botswana hardly existed at independence, and freehold land was denied Africans during the protectorate era. The Botswana Housing Corporation (BHC), a parastatal organization, was established in 1970 to provide rental housing for civil servants and for members of the small urban private sector. However, the boom conditions of the 1970s, 1980s, and more recently have led to a perpetual shortage of developed urban land and of rental housing, since BHC rents are subsidized by low interest rates on government loans. Rents could not be raised to economic levels for "political" reasons, particularly opposition from civil service groups.

Despite several reports by presidential commissions and other bodies, there has never been a meeting of the minds among politicians, economists, and bureaucrats to design and implement a sensible urban housing policy. Two factors have kept the situation from becoming explosive. First, there has been a highly successful (in numbers of units provided) self-help housing program, as a result of which there has been virtually no squatter problem within Africa's most rapidly growing urban population. Second, the government has had the financial resources to bail out the housing corporation and to continue to fund construction of houses with uneconomic rentals. Urban housing policy has probably been the most expensive failure of the policy process in Botswana, and only the existense of so many successes elsewhere has kept this failure from being a financial catastrophe. In 1992, a major financial fraud in the BHC, perhaps inevitable given the policies on urban housing and land, illustrated the fundamental weakness of government policy in this sphere.

Finally, the jury is still out on incomes policy. Perhaps the most common problem of mineral-rich countries is that of domestic wage inflation, which, combined with currency overvaluation, generally leads to an increasingly uncompetitive position for all nonmineral tradeable goods, and then to stagnation and arrested development. By and large, Botswana has avoided this problem. However, there have been several periods since 1970, particularly since 1990, when the country has come dangerously close to losing control over wages and to developing a completely noncompetitive wage structure.

In some respects, however, wage and income policy may yet become the best long-term success story for the policy process in Botswana. The income policy problems of a growing, mineral-rich country were anticipated, and a major inquiry was conducted less than five years after independence (during the year after the first diamond mine opened). The government's policymaking process attempted to deal with both economic and political realities through resort to debates in the government and in Parliament that were based on the best evidence then available. Since 1971 there has been a seesaw discussion, very public in nature, embedded in the parliamentary process, in a tripartite (business-labor-government) standing commission, and in a continued reassessment of the evidence by "experts," all of which help maintain an ongoing debate about wage policy. The issue is central to the distribution of income in the present, and to the growth of the economy in the future. The debate continues, and the policy changes from time to time—evidence, I think, that policy analysis and formulation in Botswana remain vigorously healthy.

■ Notes

This chapter has many antecedents and has benefited from conversations over many years with colleagues from many countries. The views expressed, however, are those of the author alone, and do not reflect those of any institution or organization with which the author has been associated.

1. Sections on Botswana draw on my experience as a consultant in Botswana since 1975 and my published work on Botswana's development (Lewis and Sharpley, 1988; Harvey and Lewis, 1990). Those on policymaking are based on a variety of pieces of evidence: personal observations of the economic policymaking and policy advising, reports and studies of that process, and reviews of the growing literature on policy analysis in relation to economic development.

2. See Stephen R. Lewis, Jr., "Primary Exporting Countries," in H. Chenery and T. N. Srinivason, eds., *Handbook of Development Economics, Volume II* (Amsterdam: Elsevier Science, 1989), and G. Navkani, "Development Problems of Mineral Exporting Countries" (World Bank Staff Working Paper no. 345, Washington, D.C., 1979).

3. David Wheeler, "Sources of Stagnation in Sub-Saharan Africa," *World Development* 12, no. 1 (January 1984): 1–23.

4. Aaron Wildavsky, *Speaking Truth to Power: The Art and Craft of Policy Analysis* (New Brunswick: Transaction, 1987), 388–389.

5. *Kgotla* is Setswana for "village assembly"; the plural is *makgotla*.

3

Botswana's Formative Late Colonial Experiences

J. Stephen Morrison

Since independence in 1966, Botswana has distinguished itself from the vast majority of states in Africa by sustaining liberal democratic politics and unusually competent state action. The roots of this experience lie at the intersection of the politics and economics existing near the end of Botswana's colonial period. Particularly important is the decade of crisis and struggle that immediately preceded independence, 1956–1966. Then, the major actors in Botswana confronted economic and political conditions so adverse as to create serious doubt whether Botswana could maintain economic growth or vitality, even within the single sphere where there was any hope, namely the cattle export sector. Ultimately, the dynamic of events during this period had a decisive and enduring impact on the character of Botswana's national politics and the future institutional behavior of the emergent Botswana state.

The vulnerability of the Bechuanaland Protectorate (BP) came into full light at the onset of 1956 with the sudden collapse of regional cattle markets. Frustrations among the three partners of the nascent development coalition—elite cattle-owners, the Colonial Development Corporation (CDC, renamed the Commonwealth Development Corporation in 1963), and colonial state authorities—mounted, so much so that in a very short time relations among them became severely frayed, ushering in a period of uncertainty and virtual mayhem.

Yet, quite remarkably, by independence in 1966 the industry and the development coalition attempting to shape it had emerged intact and considerably strengthened. Out of the chaos of the late 1950s there emerged (1) a distinct *ethos of state action:* the primacy of commercial criteria, a high value placed upon compromise, stability, security, and the systematic accommodation of competing interests; and (2) durable *patterns of elite interaction* linking producers, state authorities, and external interests.

Superficially, the emergent independent state, like most others in Africa, wore the garb now so closely identified with decline and failure. The institutional forum selected for management of the nation's major source of wealth was the Botswana Meat Commission (BMC), a nationalized, monopolistic parastatal, which could easily be considered as yet another centralized state entity in Africa likely to become a soft political marketplace. Yet that was not to be the case. Instead, the ethos and patterns of elite interaction already implanted before independence predominated. It then became possible for managerial autonomy to be balanced against accountability to elite ranchers and national authorities. An environment was created in which the industry could, over several years, successfully rebuild regional and international market access while engineering the internal technological transformations required to make such access rewarding.

The crisis itself that resulted from regional market collapse pushed toward, indeed precipitated, a reordering of political relations in elite management of the cattle sector. No less significant to the emergent character of the Botswana state was a simple historical accident: the appearance of the skilled yet ultimately expendable South African entrepreneur Cyril Hurvitz. Had he not succeeded in 1958 in overturning assumptions regarding the possibility for Botswana to penetrate European markets, outcomes could have been quite different.

Most important, however, were those intrinsic features of theBotswana political economy that interacted—quite organically—under severe stress. Three fundamental and highly fluid dimensions of the Botswana political economy were critical:

1.   The behavior of the foreign enterprise positioned at the center of the crisis. Due to its capacity for redefinition, the CDC was able to alter its mode of operation, accepting a loss of final power (over the export abattoir in Lobatse, marketing channels, and massive ranch holdings) while at the same time insisting that its understanding of commercialism prevail in the internal management of the newly established Botswana Meat Commission. In this way, the transformation of the industry's management to a unitary and nationalized corporation proceeded without suffering any real loss of managerial or financial continuity.

2.   The evolving character of the late colonial/early nationalist state, in particular the phasing of its developmental action. The state's late developmental surge, occurring as it did against a backdrop of extreme weakness, and coincident with the advance toward independence, motivated colonial authorities to take an overtly nationalist perspective and to blend its perspective with that of private elite interests.

3.   Two intimately linked aspects of private elite society—the nature of the biracial cattle-owning elite and the independent trajectory of elite

nationalist politics. A community of interest arose in the push toward independence, situated within the elite circles of the Botswana Democratic Party and institutional fora like the BMC, which spanned elite racial categories and successfully merged diverse aspirations (the search for greater private cattle wealth, the desire to live in a cautious, pragmatic independent state).

■ The Mutability of the Commonwealth Development Corporation

How did the character of the CDC positively influence the process of recovery, the change of institutional design, and the alteration of rules governing the development coalition? In what ways did it become dependent, after holding sway over the cattle sector since the early 1950s? In what ways was it able to impose conditions upon governance of the cattle industry after independence?

In the early 1950s the CDC had advanced a claim to nearly monopolistic powers over the cattle economy. Adherence to "commercial" criteria, which the CDC asserted at virtually every turn, guaranteed it wide latitude in the exercise of these powers. It was in this context that relatively unfettered managerial prerogatives steered the CDC toward consideration of a precipitous, final departure from the territory, once its own incompetence, its shortsighted pursuit of narrow self-interest, and the market collapse in the region appeared by the mid-1950s to make its position in the BP altogether untenable. Conflict and the fragmentation of relations with the colonial authorities and the producer elite quickly followed upon the CDC's abrupt, early failures.

In actuality, the CDC's character was far more complex and ambiguous, and far more vulnerable to systematic redefinition, than events of the early period suggested. Initially, circumstances concealed from view the reality that, while always commercial in orientation, the CDC also remained quasi-official. In its first years, the CDC could enjoy virtually unconditional control, but only so long as emergent local and colonial preferences did not seriously intervene or contradict it. As it was, subsequent events seriously departed from CDC expectations, forcing significant modifications in its orientation.

A direct challenge to the CDC arrived when the 1956 crisis exposed its incompetence in guaranteeing markets and prices; soon, the issue of shared participation was at the fore. As debate proceeded, the fundamental order and economic security of the territory stood in jeopardy.

The British government found it intolerable to remain on the sidelines. Soon, colonial officials grew alarmed at the direction events were taking; a new and more aggressive leadership was set in place, equipped with vastly increased developmental resources and an expanded developmental mandate. In 1959, Peter Fawcus moved from the position of government secretary to that of resident commissioner, and Sir John Maud became high commissioner.[1] Well before these changes had been effected, however, there were ample foreshadowings of the direction in which events were to move.

As of 1956, officials were regularly communicating to the CDC their growing impatience over its inability to define an overarching purpose for the firm's massive ranch holdings in the north and the south. The CDC preferred to bypass this larger issue to press instead for permission to separate the ranches functionally, one from the other, and both from the Lobatse abattoir.[2] Exercised in this frivolous fashion, monopoly privilege soon turned impatience into an exasperation that became compounded when the market collapsed.

Perhaps the most telling indicator of the evolution in the colonial government's relations to the cattle industry and the CDC occurred in 1958 when a Mafeking entrepreneur, Cyril Hurvitz, was granted the opportunity to export 30,000 carcasses. An end run around the CDC, this gamble (engineered by Fawcus) relieved immediate pressures while demonstrating to the CDC the colonial state's equal ability to co-opt external interests. Moreover, by strengthening the state's authority and buying time to cope with the regional market crisis, it changed the state's calculus altogether. This showed particularly in its dealings with the CDC, the Rhodesian Cold Storage, South African speculators (the Glazer brothers), and others vying to take advantage of the Bechauanaland Protectorate's dilemma. As subsequent events would demonstrate, Hurvitz, a single and at the time a relatively minor figure in the South African cattle industry, was far more easily manipulated than any of these parties was likely to be. By contrast, however, he was also prepared (and truly able) to assist the industry in breaking out of its regional dependence: first through meat exports and later (beginning in 1961) through production and export of canned products.

Officials' efforts far exceeded the single aim of breaking the market deadlock. The pattern of action seen in the late colonial period revealed an expanding mandate, one that soon blended with the nationalist goal advanced by Seretse Khama and the Botswana Democratic Party (BDP): to preserve the viability of the nation and its sole known source of economic wealth. In practice, hopes were concentrated upon preserving the corporate unity of the biracial cattle-owning elite while also ensuring that there was a continuous role for the CDC, the latter a valuable (and powerful) source of scarce managerial talent and financial capital.

As circumstances shifted, such that the developmental authority of the state (and later of a nationalist elite) expanded, the CDC was forced eventually to yield power in several important respects, accepting partial subordination to the discipline of a (slightly) higher authority. The quasi-official half of the CDC's identity, which theretofore had lain relatively dormant, slowly awakened. Only then did the CDC gradually redefine its institutional role; it began to accommodate systematically the concerns of state authorities and elite producers alike. Under pressure at first from crisis and colonial authority, later from nationalist politics, the CDC's near-hegemony gave way to a new form of elite bargaining far more open to compromise, to defense of a perceived national interest, and to stable management.

The CDC moderated its commercial tendencies and submitted to new rules—remarkably, without generating further dislocations or totally abandoning its commercial influence. The dependent linkage between it and the colonial state made possible an unusually orderly process of adjustment, which gave the state and the nationalists who ultimately came to control it an increasing sway over what had theretofore been the CDC's domain. But also, owing to the CDC's powerful central position in the cattle industry and hence its continuous ability to influence the terms of its involvement, a creative tension emerged within the altered development coalition; this force ultimately guaranteed that during the early independence era the nationalized Botswana Meat Commission would receive ample financial and managerial resources while wrapped in relative political insulation.

The CDC slowly began to sense the shifting political realities after it first advanced the idea in 1957 that shares should be sold to private interests. When CDC General Manager Rendell visited the region in May 1958 to press for immediate formation of a company, a move that would have given the CDC clear advantages by shifting monopoly export rights to an increasingly private concern, he failed. The high commissioner, along with Resident Commissioner Fawcus, rejected his plea. A decision had to await completion of the Ryan study and discussion with the Joint Advisory Council and the Livestock Advisory Council.[3]

Gradually, there emerged a new consensus regarding which principles were to guide CDC actions. Perhaps most significant, agreement was reached that any resolution of the industry's difficulties was to be in *national* terms, brokered by state authorities. This meant at minimum that the CDC would respect the integrity of the territory. It could neither flee nor force a sudden changeover to company status. Free agency was not an option. If outside interests were to be co-opted as an interim solution to the industry's troubles, the colonial government—not the CDC—would select such an actor and define the terms of its involvement. Ample proof of this appeared in the bargain struck with Cyril Hurvitz. So too, if a transition to another commercial basis were to occur—the company status favored by the CDC, or the statutory corporation advocated by Fawcus—it was to happen only after satisfying, even if only minimally, the colonial government's expectations.

Pursuing this logic, Fawcus succeeded in 1959 in promulgating, with London's approval, the Control of Livestock Industry (Amendment)

Proclamation; this barred the creation of an export abattoir, or the sale to outside interests of any share in Lobatse or any future abattoir, without the approval of the resident commissioner. Similarly, the formula advanced in 1958 by the CDC for restructuring the industry was remodeled to reflect colonial and elite producer preferences. Only after the Ryan study had been completed (it argued convincingly that there was no immediate need for a second abattoir) and the 1959 legislation had been passed did colonial authorities finally endorse, in 1960, the plan whereby the CDC limited its ownership (to 50 percent) and profits (to 6 percent), while the remaining half of the industry's ownership was split between a producers' trust and the government.[4]

Over the next five years Fawcus continued to redefine the CDC's role, backed by High Commissioner Maud and in close coordination with Seretse Khama and his emergent (and eventually dominant) national party, the BDP. For their part, the colonial authorities concluded after the 1958–1960 negotiations that their efforts had brought mixed results. Though they had been able to curb the CDC's power in important respects, most importantly by blocking its exit and forcing an open national debate about its restructuring, the CDC for its part had succeeded in insisting that the new institution continue, in effect, to be a commercial company controlled from Johannesburg.[5] By no means had state officials succeeded in subordinating the CDC. Due to the CDC's established and defensible position in the economy, the state had to move unobtrusively, bargaining carefully to obtain incremental advances over time.

Even if now "semi-nationalized," to borrow Michael Hubbard's term, the CDC expected the new arrangements that created the Bechuanaland Protectorate Abattoir Limited (BPAL) in November 1960 to last a decade. In addition, the CDC placed but one-quarter of BPAL's share ownership in the hands of government, which guaranteed that most management authority continued to reside in Johannesburg.

Further elaboration of the tripartite bargain proceeded in several steps. Precipitating much of what followed was the dispute, begun in 1962 and culminating in a March 1963 Legislative Council debate, concerning the contract terms under which ECCO, the joint-venture canning and export company directed by Hurvitz, bought meat from BPAL for export outside the region.[6] Recognizing the broader opportunities the dispute presented, however, Fawcus and Khama also consciously used it as the pretext to postpone planned modernization of the BPAL plant in order to review the industry in full—that is, to stage an open debate on the dual questions of a northern abattoir and the establishment of a nationalized, statutory corporation.[7]

Over the next two years, Khama and Fawcus built upon the momentum of these events with exceptional skill, integrating several related developments: negotiations with the CDC, the legislative steps required to nationalize, internal elections, and the emergence of the BDP as the dominant nationalist political force. These resulted in three quickly successive changes in the cattle industry—the rationalization of the national pricing system, the nationalization of the abattoir, and the exclusion and final buy-out of Cyril Hurvitz—with multiple, positive side effects. In addition, they created manageable financial arrangements that had little effect upon producer prices or the Botswana Meat Commission's ability to deliver annual bonuses. Finally, they made it possible to avoid serious disruption of either the plant's modernization or its industrial workforce.

For the August 1964 debates in the Legislative Council and the Executive Council, the government prepared a White Paper advocating a statutory corporation and advising postponement of a northern abattoir.[8] Once the White Paper had been approved in these bodies and endorsed by colonial authorities, the CDC acknowledged, however bitterly, that its choices had narrowed considerably. After receiving assurances from Seretse Khama that its concerns would be met, the CDC agreed in principle to the proposals.[9]

In early 1965, by which time the BDP had demonstrated impressive strength in the internal elections (winning twenty-eight of thirty-one seats in the Legislative Assembly), Fawcus and Khama further quietly consolidated their position relative to the CDC; the most important advances concerned plant management, bank finances, and draft legislation. The result was that by late 1965, the government was in a position to execute its nationalization plans. By then, these had become established, integral elements of the BDP's national program.

Modeled after Kenyan legislation, the Botswana Meat Commission Act's most significant feature was the assignment of final authority over the industry to Botswana's president: "All control of BMC policy and actions is vested in the President, through his power to hire and fire commissioners, veto any change and issue directives which the BMC is statutorily obliged to carry out."[10] At the strategic level—in terms of final power and ownership—the nationalists had succeeded in achieving their aims.

The CDC, though it had to submit to this reality, hardly did so from a supine position. It possessed significant comparative advantages that it consciously employed to condition the process of change. The CDC's margin of power derived from its half-ownership of the plant (amounting to £320,000, bought out over a ten-year period under the independence agreement), from the managerial expertise provided at Lobatse and from the CDC regional offices in Johannesburg, and from the promise of finance for further development of the cattle industry (and possibly for the Shashe copper-nickel project). Wielding these advantages during the negotiations leading to independence, the CDC insisted that if its public power were to be eclipsed at the same time that the industry looked to it to play an orderly and continuous role—for instance, forbearing to

demand immediate repayment of its investment capital—then the postindependence Commission would have to apply commercial criteria as the CDC
understood them.[11]

In practice, this creed of commercialism had already manifested itself
in several obvious ways. The struggle to wrest authority from the CDC had
stretched across nearly eight years; if authority was to be yielded, it was to
be done bit by bit. Also, throughout this period the CDC had persistently
objected to the establishment of a second northern abattoir. To its mind, to
construct a second plant was to draw resources away from management's
priority—the modernization of Lobatse, critical to market acceptance overseas—and allocate them instead to placate northern constituents. By that
logic, strategic managerial concerns would be subordinated to emergent
nationalist politics. To circumvent such an outcome, Cater, the CDC
regional controller based in Johannesburg, pressed Fawcus hard in 1964 to
see that the Commission's final recommendations and the legislative
debates favored the conversion of the Lobatse plant.

The bargain finally struck during the 1965 negotiations brought additional evidence of what the CDC understood commercialism to mean.
Formal, final authority and management's ultimate answerability, the CDC
eventually conceded, were to rest in the hands of the president, but before
the CDC could fully accept this change, it had to be systematically placat-
ed; in the end, steps that formally blocked political subordination of the
statutory corporation were necessary.

Curiously, certain more personalized placating measures substantially
inflated the CDC Regional Controller's managerial authority during the
succeeding early years of independence. Cater succeeded in assuring, under
the Botswana Meat Commission legislation, that aside from modest taxes
the Commission would have financial independence: no other agency
would be capable of staking a claim to its resources. So too did he require
that involvement by the agriculture ministry (or any other) in the
Commission be precluded and that the Commission be answerable to the
Legislative Assembly in only the most general fashion.[12]

These structural arrangements, while easing certain of the CDC's concerns in insulating the BMC, were still not fully satisfying. What was
required was a device that would somehow placate the CDC and yet also
preserve the fundamental achievement of nationalization. Ultimately, the
solution to this riddle exceeded the CDC's expectations and bound it in a
surprisingly intimate and direct fashion to the newly restructured cattle
industry. In an intriguing twist to events, Seretse Khama eased negotiations
considerably by offering to Cater, in the midst of the debate, the chairman-
ship of the BMC for the first three years following independence.[13]

In sum, once the strategic goal of nationalization had been acknowledged and accepted, however begrudgingly, by the CDC, Seretse Khama
was prepared to concede to Cater increased power against his perceived

internal adversaries, be they veterinary officials of a nationalist bent like Falconer, competitive commercial operators like Hurvitz, or Tswana nationalists demanding significantly expanded access to business opportunities. Paradoxically, this gave rise during the early independence period to a situation in which Cater enjoyed far more managerial autonomy than he had in the period 1960–1965. Presumably, President Khama judged that to be a small, and at worst temporary, price to pay for continuity and assured security of what was at that time the nation's only viable economic sector.

■ The Phasing of State Action

In the period 1955–1966, crisis and individual personalities were hardly the sole factors motivating colonial officials to seek an increasingly higher profile in the management of the political economy. Greater influence came with increased flows of grants-in-aid, which began in earnest in the mid-1950s, in line with broad shifts in colonial policy.[14] Over the next few years, the tie between financial grants and the doctrine that the cattle sector, above all other sectors, had to be actively promoted, acquired ever greater strength and visibility. Supporting it, of course, were capital flows neither intermittent nor insignificant. In the ten years leading up to independence, grants-in-aid exceeding £20m entered the BP.[15] When combined with other forms of development assistance (intercolonial and exchequer loans), these sums made it possible, in the decade 1956–66, for recurrent expenditures to grow fivefold and expenditures for development tenfold.[16]

Conditioned by its protectorate status and the associated possibility that the BP might eventually be integrated into South Africa—a factor always present to some degree until as late, many argue, as 1961—colonial rule for its first sixty or more years was at best a weak, ambiguous, caretaking exercise, performed on a minimalist scale and hence reliant upon an administrative apparatus woefully inadequate, if not outright laughable. Through the years, successive studies documented the continued debility of state capacities.[17]

The final decade of the colonial era, 1955–1966, commenced against this unpromising backdrop. Just what the actual character of the state's enlarged stature would be, and how it would be deployed, however, remained to be seen. Ultimately most influential was the fluid context within which the state first began to act. After a period of prolonged, gross neglect, there suddenly followed a period of developmental activism. Eventually, this dramatic gearing of state ambitions, coupled with peculiar timing—the expansion of the state's role coincident with economic crisis and the advance toward independence—had multiple consequences. Colonial officials had to give preeminent place to urgent tasks—first the market collapse, later a protracted inability to bring cattle disease under control. Officials were thus prompted to defend the BP's territorial integrity, politically and economically, resisting its wholesale subordination to stronger political and economic actors in the region.

Naturally, those colonial officials anxious during the late 1950s to bring evidence of development framed their actions in broad corporatist terms. They placed a premium upon ensuring the integrity of the BP's cattle economy, upon encouraging an inclusionary form of cautious centrist politics for the whole of the BP, and upon answering what were perceived as immediate, national needs. The colonial imagination focused upon finding methods for fusing existing interests into a much stronger, cohesive entity, as defense against chaos.

It was this guiding motivation, backed by a sharply enhanced flow of resources, that first defined the ethos of the late colonial state. It prompted Fawcus and his colleagues not just to assume a larger role but to direct a high proportion of resources toward cattle disease control and water development, while concentrating their political energies upon seeing that the CDC and the cattle-raising elite participated in a new set of stable institutional relationships (eventually formalized as the BMC).[18]

In moving in this direction, the authorities also soon came to acknowledge, however implicitly, a second dimension to the state's historical evolution—their own dependence upon the CDC and the private, cattle-owning elite. Decades of marginality meant that the colonial state had, de facto, conceded considerable economic and political dominion to other interests. In the cattle sector, of course, the CDC stood fast for the early authority that it assumed. Yet no less important, dating back to early in the century, black and white elite cattle-owners, interdependent in the marketing of cattle, had established South African–based market and price relations that, entrenched during the period of extensive smuggling in the 1930s, set the standard against which these interests judged their relations with both colonial officials and the CDC.[19]

As a result, when the colonial state finally moved to enlarge its role in the late 1950s, it began by following in political tracks laid down by others. It may have been motivated by crisis to assert the corporate integrity of the territory, and its authority may have increased with the inflow of greater resources, but since it lacked anything approaching an established form of governance, it was forced by its history to accumulate power by eliciting the cooperation of entrenched interests and by working through established elite forums, however formal or informal. It could only truly become stable and legitimate after it had systematically employed its resources to erect bridges between itself and other actors within the nascent development coalition.

Early state power, then, emerged out of an incremental process of deliberate brokering and accommodation that rearranged and consolidated the status quo within a national format. This implied, most importantly, that the authorities could never fully subordinate the cattle industry to other developmental purposes. Quite the contrary would be the case.

A diversity of allocation modes, some broad and symbolic, others discrete and material, reinforced the state's shifting efforts to create a new national agreement. Various direct gains passed to elite cattle-owners upon the creation of the statutory corporation. The CDC's extractive potential was now permanently curtailed, while its key inputs remained continuous. Nationalization broadened, even if only slightly, the perceived opportunities available to ranchers to wield an increased degree of authority, penetrating what for many of them had been an alien entity with vast power over their individual economic fates.

Curiously, this same maneuver fulfilled important needs of the BDP in bringing symbolic gains to an otherwise mild-mannered party short of political victories in the lead-up to independence. The BMC legislation set in law the president's final authority and made clear that a far fuller form of nationalized control would come in time. In the spare institutional landscape of the period, the BMC stood out as one among very few monuments testifying to the potential reality of an independent Botswana.

The state's most direct and disaggregated allocations were those involving land. Having warehoused for years a huge portion of the nation's land that was neither tribal property nor settler blocs—the Crown Lands— the colonial authorities during the 1950s finally began applying it to economic, and what were ultimately highly political, uses. The unusual phasing of state action in the BP was again manifest: considerable, heretofore underexploited resources such as Crown Lands were still available quite late in the colonial game.[20]

The Ghanzi and Molopo areas were each substantially enlarged out of Crown Land. At the same time, individual holdings roughly doubled in size. Several complementary changes in policy further buttressed production by the white commercial elite: the conversion of British South Africa Company and other holdings from leasehold to freehold tenure; the creation in 1962 of an agricultural bank (later the National Development Bank) geared to increase greatly the availability of finance for water, fencing, and other ranch upgrading; the deliberate underpricing of land; the repeated easing of payment terms; the commitment of resources to the development of trek routes and veterinary services.[21]

Manipulation of land ownership functioned equally well to undergird the colonial state's efforts to lessen the power of the CDC while preserving a role for it. In 1963, Fawcus startled the CDC's regional controller, Cater, with the offer of an exchange of sorts. The state would assume from the CDC full responsibility for the bulk of northern holding grounds (the BECCAT), which had proven such a drain and which remained an embarrassing reminder of the CDC's naive early ambitions to control marketing channels. In return, the CDC would be granted freehold ownership of the vast

(300,000 acres) Molopo Ranch. The CDC itself could not have imagined such a windfall.

Hence, in its evolving relations with both private elites and the CDC, the state in this period orchestrated a process of interlocking adjustments that eventually resulted in a strengthened, state-centered, and deeply inclusionary form of management. Owing to the character of the allocations processes, public power grew at the same time that the recipients of state largesse—the major elite members and institutions in the cattle sector—saw their stake in an independent Botswana grow as the viability of the cattle export sector increased. The end result: a far more solid whole and the beginning of an unusually stable elite politics, its character a complex mix of public and private elements.

Quite soon, a select number of those who embraced the bargain found themselves in a material position wholly unimaginable in prior decades. In the immediate passage to independence, there was the opportunity vastly to enlarge their holdings through purchase both of newly opened state land and of the property belonging to ranchers departing the territory. Over the longer term, there was the added opportunity to share in the management of the industry, enjoy preferential credit (both commercial and concessionary), and derive high profits from a cattle industry that generally presented few obstacles to one's ability to deliver cattle to the BMC.

For their part, Tswana elite enjoyed in this period significant gains in improved water supplies and other forms of infrastructural development (especially veterinary services) financed largely through colonial grants.[22] Moreover, officials made it clear that expansion of the commercial blocs was not to proceed along racial lines; elite Tswana were eligible to buy in. Soon after independence, the reality of that policy became apparent when President Khama and Vice President Masire each purchased land in the freehold areas (in the Tati and Ghanzi, respectively). Thereafter, beginning with sudden speed in the early 1970s, the National Development Bank financed the purchase of numerous Tati and Tuli ranches by prominent Tswana elite members.[23]

Rather than assume an alien, hardened character, the increasingly assertive state, by force of its delayed action, historical ambiguity, and intrinsic weakness, eventually acquired an identity quite different from that of the colonial state elsewhere in Africa. Slowly, it showed itself to be comparatively proximate and flexible, and responsive to local interests. The result: the three concurrent political thrusts of this era—state building, national independence, and promotion of the cattle economy—became fused.

As a consequence, it soon became exceedingly difficult to separate analytically any single concern from the others in the late colonial era. The stability and advance of the cattle sector ceased to be chiefly the concern of private elites and agencies like the CDC. The sector's growth and stability, together with the future development of minerals and the future revision of the customs union rebates with South Africa, presented the sole perceived hope that state revenue deficiencies that grants-in-aid covered would decline. Their fate and that of the emergent state were clearly thus linked. Yet the state-building project could hardly imagine that the cattle sector could be subordinated to a purpose altogether external or antagonistic to itself. Since the state's authority relative to cattle interests was decidedly nonhegemonic, the cattle sector had to be systematically nurtured by the state, its wealth-generating potential not hindered by high levels of extraction. That was essential to guarantee private endorsement of colonial officials' efforts at aggrandizing authority around the state.

Also at play was the metropolitan power's evolving status, specifically its desire, made apparent as the 1960s proceeded, to play a major role in Botswana's political economy extending well beyond independence.

Evidence of the extraordinary responsibilities that Britain assumed in the early years of independence, ones that carried on the modest developmental trajectory set during the previous decade, is manifold. Financially, its "aid provided a crucial supplement to the Government's budgetary resources. Until 1972/73, about half of public expenditure was typically financed from aid sources."[24] Apart from this vital budgetary support, Britain also provided roughly 80 percent of development grants and loans. Administratively, a similar commitment became apparent. As an outgrowth of the Overseas Aid Scheme begun in 1962/63 to upgrade the BP administration (through the subsidization of recruitment and salary costs), the number of South African personnel declined as the number of British expatriate staff rose in the independence era.

Motivating this prolonged involvement, a de facto condominium form of governance integrating British inputs with early national power for the first six years of independence, was an assembly of factors, several closely associated with the phasing issue. Of great importance was the development logic that emerged in the fifteen years prior to independence and asserted the necessity of a long-term British commitment to the independent state's finances. The late surge toward developmental optimism led to the admission, among colonial authorities and nationalists alike, that if outside financial subsidies were withdrawn or reduced sharply at independence, what modest progress had been achieved would likely be nullified.[25] If the cattle export sector, as prevailing doctrine advocated at the time, was to be further favored as a growth center, it had to be exempted from any excessive extractions to satisfy the growing needs of an independent state. What was required, if the British were to honor their responsibilities to this territory, and if Botswana were ever to emerge from its dire condition, made worse by severe drought, was a level of assistance that exceeded locally available revenue.

Also behind Britain's apparent beneficence were geostrageic calculations that, from 1961 onward, significantly strengthened its motivation to assume a role of this sort, consolidating as well the corporatist thrust in colonial officials' thinking. In brief, after South Africa had been expelled from the Commonwealth in 1961, a new foreign policy imperative arose. Gunderson, with slight exaggeration, described the change: "Britain's desire to maintain a sphere of influence in southern Africa under whatever guise increased. . . . [It] sought new forms of rule in Bechuanaland."[26] Subsequently, the search for a regional foothold only intensified once Botswana's other neighbor, Southern Rhodesia, began to move in the direction of its 1965 unilateral declaration of independence.

Under these circumstances, the authorities exhibited a sustained interest in seeing that large British interests such as the CDC continued to be part of the cattle economy, that the sector's growth potential was as secure as possible, that European market access was consolidated, and that biracial elite interests became more stable in the nationalized forum of the BMC.

These events, of course, fit within the overall national context— Britain's hope that it could succeed in cultivating a nationalist movement and an institutional landscape, both amenable to its particular perspective and viable within the tense regional setting. In this context the BMC figured as one element in a larger institutional environment structured by the authorities with the aim of favoring the consolidation of a middle-ground form of elite politics, pragmatic and biracial.

The institutions created for the cattle sector were appropriate companions to those created to facilitate a suitable nationalist politics. Upon its inauguration in 1961, the Legislative Council greatly advanced the institutionalization of the desired form of national politics, a formal process that had begun with establishment of the Joint Advisory Council in 1950.

Soon thereafter, in 1962, it was elites from within these bodies, the mainstream of establishment politics in the Protectorate, who founded the BDP. With the support of the majority of the Legislative Council, and with the subtle encouragement of colonial officials, the BDP leadership initially acted in response to the perceived threat of the Botswana People's Party: "When fully-fledged party politics arrived in Bechuanaland, the impetus came from outside."[27] With its leadership drawn from migrants recently returned from South Africa, the BPP appeared to many to have imported into the BP alien and potentially disruptive doctrines espoused by the banned African National Congress.[28] Prior to its debilitating internal fractures of 1963–1964, the BPP appeared capable of building its strength to a point where it might pose a genuine challenge at the polls. In hopes of precluding that possibility, colonial officials greatly accelerated the schedule for moving toward independence, bringing internal government (under decisive majority control by the BDP) in March 1965, and full independence as of September 1966.

■ The Character of Biracial Elite Society

What factors internal to Botswana's biracial elite society provided it with an eventual cohesion in areas of highest mutual concern? What accounts for the strong community of interest that arose, a political phenomenon that merged aspirations—across racial lines—for a prosperous cattle economy with the shared desire to live under an effective, pragmatic state? What mixture of dependencies and leverages came into play? How did these relate to the formation of the historical bargain that assured the CDC and metropolitan officials a sizeable role after independence?

The contrast between the social reality of the late 1950s and that of the early independent era is striking. The late 1950s were marked by racial, regional, and personal antagonisms that generated various threats of defection. Yet by independence, there were few signs that the perceived interests of the different sections of elite cattle-owning society abraded on one another, or that the national bargain struck with external interests was regarded as anything other than mutually advantageous.

The BMC board that took shape in the early 1960s comprised black and white ranchers from both north and south, under a CDC chair. Thereafter, solidarity within the biracial elite easily withstood its first major test, the BMC workers' strike of late January 1967. This abrupt labor action saw violence directed against white management, and precipitated a Commission of Inquiry whose investigations revealed a spectrum of institutionally racist practices within the Commission.[29] Still, the politics of the period called for diffidence rather than reform. When the findings were debated in the National Assembly, Tswana BDP members came to the BMC's defense, arguing the preeminent value of stability and orderly, incremental change in the industry. Within the cabinet, President Khama's judgment prevailed. There would be no formal apology to the workforce, nor a reinstatement of the 125 workers (of a total of 700) who had been fired.[30]

Before and after independence, the BDP succeeded at establishing a solid rapport with white commercial interests. Halpern wrote in 1965: "The BDP has, in fact, a small number of active white sympathizers and one or two among the Bamangwato Reserve. . . . It was widely accepted that Bechuanaland whites, including Afrikaners, donated funds to Seretse Khama's BDP . . ."[31] By the 1970s, white cattle ranchers held strategic government positions—assembly speaker, minister of commerce and industry—while there was accumulating evidence that the intertwining of black and white elite society had become assuredly self-reproducing. Well after Richard Eaton retired from the assembly, ranchers in Ghanzi continued their regular contributions to the local BDP coffers, underwriting the campaign costs of the Tswana BDP member, Jankie.[32] Once Derek Brink had entered his thirties in the early 1970s and begun his march toward control of a fifth or more of Botswana's marketed cattle, steps were taken, at the behest of the president, to include him on the boards of the BMC and the newly established Barclays Botswana.[33]

This phenomenon emanated from several sources, a few of which have already been noted. The colonial state's several parallel innovations systematically bound the interests of conservative Tswana elites with European elites: its allocation of highly valued resources; its plans for a prolonged metropolitan role that mitigated the perceived transition to full Tswana control, permitting key colonial figures such as Jack Falconer, head of veterinary services, to serve indefinitely as interlocutors between the two populations; its forceful advocacy of an orderly and quick movement toward national independence. In effect, the actions of the colonial state forced settlers to weigh a new set of incentives, to evaluate the true possibilities and associated costs of alternative courses of action. Once it became clear to the ranchers of the Tuli, Tati, Ghanzi, and Lobatse blocs that territorial incorporation of their small areas into neighboring states was not to happen, appreciation of the favorable emergent realities inside Botswana deepened and calculations shifted.[34]

Other compelling forces, endogenous to the community itself, also worked their will upon events. A latent potential for strong concerted action on the part of the Tswana and European elites resided in their historically patterned interactions. Prior decades under weak colonial government had institutionalized a relative balance between white and black elites, one which bred familiarity and policy collaboration while preventing European interests from establishing hierarchical dominance. The manifestations were several: the respect accorded tribal reserves and chiefly authority; the ultimate failure of resident commissioners in the 1930s to subdue chiefly power; the de facto limits placed upon white land purchase beyond allocations of the late 1890s (until the controlled expansions begun in the late 1950s); the creation early in the century of dual advisory councils, African and European; the creation in the 1950s of a Joint Council and a Livestock Industry Advisory Council, each a carefully balanced forum.

As well, interdependent and increasingly competitive marketing channels emerged within this overarching set of arrangements. While 90 percent of the national herd was owned and held by the Tswana elite, long-distance integration into external markets, and later to Lobatse, rested upon the trading role of white freehold farmers. And though speculator prices were often justifiably resented in the reserves, African authorities were far from helpless to moderate speculators' powers. Up to the mid-1960s they were also seldom motivated by the inequities of the national marketing system to attempt to mobilize popular African support around the issue of European trader power, given the other reformist options available, and given their own frequent inclination to benefit from the same activity. In the 1960s elections, ironically, this issue was the select province of opposition parties such as the BPP (and the Botswana National Front, after its founding in 1969), which drew their strength predominantly from urban, not rural, areas.

Structural aspects of the cattle industry further facilitated the establishment of a community of interest within the biracial elite society. Both before and after independence, elite politics was always micropolitics. Despite Botswana's vast expanse of geography, elite interactions were nonetheless significantly colored by the fact that out of an already small total population (roughly one third of a million in the mid-1950s), sizeable cattle wealth rested in the hands of a few individuals, most of whom lived in the eastern part of the country.

There were fewer than 250 European freehold ranches as of the late 1950s, with a total population of 3,500. Judging from Ryan's 1958 report, enormous market power was concentrated among approximately thirty ranchers; a mere 200 European traders were licensed. As regards Tswana producers, Ryan noted in this period: "There are a dozen Africans who speculate on a substantial scale." Only forty-five were registered as traders; in 1956, eight individuals delivered over 200 head to the abattoir, while 116 cattle-owners—those with holdings substantial enough to bypass the services of white traders—sold directly to the abattoir.[35]

These numbers would rise dramatically during coming decades as civil service employment expanded, as African producers received more favorable treatment from the BMC, and as marketing infrastructures improved.[36] Still, even fifteen years after independence (when, according to Gunderson, the BDP's "new men" numbered no more than a hundred), one knowledgeable observer estimated that the dominant African political elite in Botswana totaled no more than 250 members.[37] Within that community, wealth remained highly concentrated, a condition examined in some detail in the 1974 Rural Income Distribution Survey.[38] Hence, while the cattle sector and national politics touched the lives of almost every citizen of Botswana at the time of independence, control at that time and later lay with a tiny number of individuals, black and white, whose respective prospects for increased production and continued power remained bright.

This reality had several important implications, both for management of the cattle economy and for nationalist politics. In each, the community's proportions carried advantages of scale. The assorted tasks of communication, co-option, and establishing consensus were made easier by intimacy within the elite.

However, this is not to assert that smallness in itself reduced the potential for conflict or raised the likelihood of cohesiveness. In this regard, three associated dimensions must also be noted: the evolving imperative of the cattle economy at this time, the dynamic of fear and choice operating among both white and black elites, and the personal choices preferred—and acted upon—by Seretse Khama.

The sudden, drought-induced reduction of the national herd (from 1,352,000 in 1962 to 966,000 in 1966) eased tensions in important, if curious, ways just prior to independence. In this period, elites of all description encountered little difficulty in winning competitive access to the abattoir. The revamping of the plant during the mid-1960s increased its capacity to 100,000 animals per year. This change, in combination with the drought's effects, meant that the prevailing dread was that too few quality, mature animals, not too many, would be offered for sale and export. Under such circumstances a cooperative intra-elite ethos, not an intense intra-elite scramble for shares, could germinate. For the enlarged plant to succeed without imposing undue costs upon one or the other sector of elite producers, there had to be sustained growth in sales to the BMC by all.

In sum, at independence an elite consensus was palpable and indisputable—the cattle industry needed bigger herds, more throughput, more exports, better water, better roads, and other infrastructure. Only later, beginning in the 1970s, did more contentious questions press in—how to distribute scarce quotas at the abattoir, how to reform land tenure to resolve equity and environmental concerns. At independence, realities were far simpler, encapsulated around issues of cattle and national politics, and centered in the emergent biracial elite politics of the victorious BDP.

Second, because members of the ranching elite faced fearful choices, they huddled together, ignoring their other differences; this prompted observers to describe the BDP as "an amazing conglomeration of elements of the society whose respective interests were more incompatible than not," or again as "an amalgamation of a number of localised components."[39]

What precisely drove this dynamic? In the early 1960s powerful Tswana and European cattlemen saw the need to cooperate if they were to succeed in business and in nationalist politics. Neither possessed adequate means to act alone. Each was inherently weak and each foresaw trouble if they did not work together. Circumstances drove these two elites into one another's arms, for to press ahead in isolation was to take unacceptable risks.

An example may help illustrate these points. It was not simply the meager number of "new men" that made the powerful Tswana cattlemen dependent upon colonial authorities, the CDC, and other domestic elites. Equally important, up until the time when nationalist politics and the national debates on the cattle sector intensified, neither the "new men" nor the European cattlemen had shed their assumption that the BP was an unpromising site for an independent nation-state, nor had they attempted to independently move events forward through prior efforts to organize broadly.[40] The consequences were felt acutely by the nationalists as the events of 1960–1963 unfolded—when the BPP, drawing strength from workers recently returned from South Africa, threatened to preempt the political stage. For the "new men," to delay or to bypass alliances with others was to invite disaster. Advancement toward independence had to be accelerated, just as new, viable partners had to be found.

Luckily for the "new men," European ranchers were reaching remarkably similar conclusions: they, too, saw a political threat from the BPP, felt their own relative weakness, and recognized a biracial partnership to be the only realistic solution.[41]

Finally, these beneficial alliances could easily have failed (with incalculably ill effect) had the individual who ascended to the summit of power, Seretse Khama, favored a different course of action. Botswana escaped the destructive pattern of personal rule familiar elsewhere in Africa and embraced an alternative—the installation of a stable biracial elite, bent upon constructing a conservative, pragmatic state linked to the CDC and metropolitan interests—in large measure because of Khama's intrinsic ability to appeal strongly, and simultaneously, to multiple audiences, and because he wanted an inclusionary, technocratic form of governance.

Having had to renounce his claim to the Bamangwato chieftaincy in 1956 in order to return to the BP, he retained enough royal magnetism to appeal to the rural masses. At the same time, however, the renunciation freed him to operate outside the limits of traditional status: to assemble a hundred or so "new men," possessing few claims to traditional privilege, as the elite base of the BDP, and to use the credibility he had established in protracted disputes with the British to strengthen his reputation for moderation, commitment to multiracial democracy, and willingness to cooperate with the British after independence.

Also, by the early 1960s Khama had made clear how he would prefer to govern an independent Botswana. His respect for the limits to his own individual power made it possible to be exceedingly patient, permitting outsiders (including European settlers) to retain their privileges as the short-term cost of moving toward a viable state without incurring the ire of South Africa. No authoritarian, Khama encouraged the delegation of power to the "administrative state" (a point ably argued by Picard). He acted upon no systematic compulsion to undermine the opposition, preferring softer measures. For instance, he opposed trader boycotts in Lobatse and elsewhere in the early 1960s, out of fear that they would be employed to build BPP support and possibly to militarize the abattoir labor force.[42] Luckily for Khama, what threats the BPP and others posed quickly fragmented in the period 1963–1965, making it far easier for him to cajole, co-opt, and enlist potential or actual adversaries. (Negotiations with the CDC, European settlers, and others provide evidence of this.[43]) For the imperatives that Khama consciously embraced at independence were those of state building, the gradual erection of institutions—the BMC among the most notable—to stand against any impulses toward personal rule that might arise after 1966. Hermans aptly summarized Khama's guiding, technocratic passions at independence: "High priority was given to the achievement of budgetary independence. Institutional reforms were carried out within the central administration and outside it. A planning organization was created; statutory corporations were established; a modern system of local government was introduced; the implementation capacity of key ministries was strengthened."[44]

By the time he assumed Botswana's highest office, at independence in 1966, Sir Seretse Khama had demonstrated qualities of intellect and character and pursued clearly defined principles of governance that led directly to wise policy decisions during (and following) his presidency. Struggles over economic policy and economic power during the preceding decade produced new institutions and, more important, a degree of common understanding, shared interests, and mutual cooperation among black and white cattle ranchers that became Botswana's code for political integration, pragmatism, prudence, and foresight—in short, political sanity.

■ Notes

1. "The Resident Commissioner was treated in terms of authority as somewhere between a provincial commissioner and a minor governor. In practice, the passage of time increased the authority of the Resident Commissioner until, in the 1950s he was given the power, and in 1959, the status of a Governor." Louis A. Picard, "Administration Reorganisation: A substitute for policy? The District Administration and Local Government in the Bechuanaland Protectorate, 1949–1966," *Botswana Notes and Records* 16 (1984): 87. See also Richard P. Stevens, *Lesotho, Botswana and Swaziland: The Former High Commission Territories in Southern Africa* (London: Pall Mall, 1967), 139.

2. Botswana National Archive (BNA) File S 536/3 TERGOS Reports: Newsletters, Monthly, High Commission Territories.

3. "Lobatsi abattoir-company formation. Meeting in the High Commissioner's office on 14th May, 1958," Commonwealth Development Corporation (CDC) (London) File 124/101.

4. "Report on HCT Region," EMB 88/59; "Lobatse Abattoir: Transfer to Company," EMB 102/59; CDC (London) File 124/000.

5. This sentiment is conveyed in a letter, dated June 29, 1964, from Fawcus to CDC Regional Controller Cater. CDC (London) File 124/002.

6. Precise details are provided in Michael Hubbard, *Agricultural Exports and Economic Growth: A Study of Botswana's Beef Industry* (London: KPI, 1986), 139–140.

7. Fawcus was quite forthright in explaining his aims in a letter to CDC Regional Controller Cater, dated April 30, 1964. CDC (London) File 124/002.

8. "Conduct and Development of the Livestock Industry," April 1964.

9. "Extract from RC(HCT) August Report Dated 3-9-64 to GM," CDC (London) File 124/002.

10. Hubbard, *Agricultural Exports,* 74.

11. "Extract from Mr. Cater's July Report on SA Region," CDC (London) File 124/002.

12. Fawcus's letter to Cater, dated March 2, 1965, details the manner in which the draft was written to reflect this set of concerns. CDC (London) File 124/002.

13. Letter from CDC Regional Office to London Home Office regarding BPAL, July 1, 1965. CDC (London) File 124/002.

14. Worldwide, funds provided through the Colonial Development and Welfare Acts grew enormously: "In 1945 a total of £120m was authorized and increased to £140m in 1950 and £220m in 1955. By contrast to earlier parsimony these were very large sums. A substantial proportion went to Africa." Cyril Ehrlich, "Building and Caretaking: Economic Policy in British Tropical Africa, 1890-1960," *The Economic History Review* (United Kingdom) 24 (1973): 663.

15. Picard, "Administrative Reorganisation," 86.

16. Quill Hermans, "A Review of Botswana's Financial History, 1900 to 1973," *Botswana Notes and Records* 6 (1974): sec. 3, "1955-72, The Years of Progress."

17. *The Financial and Economic Position of the Bechuanaland Protectorate* (London: HMSO, 1933) (The Pim Report); Lord Hailey, *Native Administration in the British African Territories, Part V, The High Commission Territories: Basutoland, the Bechuanaland Protectorate and Swaziland* (London: HMSO, 1953); H. S. Walker and J.H.N. Hobday, *Report on the Cattle Industry of the Bechuanaland Protectorate and Recommendations for Improving Its Organization and Assisting Its Future Development*, 1939.

18. Regarding expenditures in this period, see *Basutoland, Bechuanaland Protectorate and Swaziland: Report of Economic Survey Mission* (London: Commonwealth Relations Office, 1960), 59 (The Morse Commission); Christopher Colclough and Stephen McCarthy, *The Political Economy of Botswana* (New York: Oxford University Press, 1980), 31.

19. See William Duggan, *An Economic History of Southern African Agriculture* (New York: Sage, 1985), 177.

20. See Gilfred L. Gunderson, "Nation Building and the Administrative State: The Case of Botswana" (Ph.D. diss., University of California, Berkeley, 1971), 373-375.

21. Botswana National Archives, S. 90/6 and 559/6/1-2.

22. See Emery Roe, *Development of Livestock Agriculture and Water Supplies in Eastern Botswana Before Independence: A Short History and Policy Analysis* (Ithaca, New York: Rural Development Committee, Center for International Studies, Cornell University, 1980).

23. Leonard M. Samboma, *The Survey of the Freehold Farms of Botswana* (Gaborone: Animal Production Division, Ministry of Agriculture, November 1982).

24. Colclough and McCarthy, *The Political Economy of Botswana*, 99.

25. See the chapter on Botswana in David Jones's *Aid and Development in Southern Africa* (London: 1977).

26. Gunderson, "Nation Building and the Administrative State," 235.

27. James H. Polhemus, "Botswana Votes: Parties and Elections in an African Democracy," *Journal of Modern Studies* 21, no. 3 (1983): 397-430.

28. See Ranbwedzi Nengwekhulu, "Some Findings on the Origins of Political Parties in Botswana," *Pulu* 1, no. 2 (June 1978): 47-76.

29. "Report of the Commission of Inquiry Appointed by His Excellency the President to Enquire into Certain Matters Relating to the Botswana Meat Commission," National Assembly Paper no. 13, November 1967.

30. Interview with Hugh Murray-Hudson, at BCL offices, Gaborone, November 6, 1984. At the time of the strike, Murray-Hudson served as permanent secretary of the Ministry of Education, Health and Labour. He and Labour Commissioner Mmusi had pressed for a more evenhanded resolution of the conflict, to no avail.

31. J. Halpern, *South Africa's Hostages: Basutoland, Bechuanaland, and Swaziland* (Harmondsworth: Penguin Books, 1965), 294, 329–331. Gunderson, "Nation Building and the Administrative State," 345, also wrote that "At social and fund raising events sponsored by the BDP, the leading members of the European community were present."

32. Interview with Henry Vickerman, Kalahari Arms Hotel, Ghanzi camp, September 13, 1984.

33. Interview with Robert Whyte, Annadale Farm, Pitsani, May 8, 1984.

34. In a letter to the author on August 10, 1984, Margo Russell, author of *Afrikaners of the Kalahari* (New York: Cambridge University Press, 1979), commented on the biracial politics she witnessed in Ghanzi in the early 1970s:

There was great optimism, and a general feeling of everybody's fortunes. The first Herero had just acquired a farm in the midst of the boers. But they felt that the economic future was so good that black neighbours and black ministers was a small price to pay. Re. govt: there was a general satisfaction that sensible local "Bechuana" had taken over from liberal sentimental British, and [there was] a willingness to play along.

35. The Ryan Report, 18–20.

36. By 1980, there were "close to 18,000 employed by the central government or the unified local government services." Louis A. Picard, "The Historical Legacy and Modern Botswana," in Louis A. Picard, ed., *The Evolution of Modern Botswana: Politics and Rural Development in Southern Africa* (London: Rex Collings; Lincoln: University of Nebraska Press, 1985), 21.

37. Ibid.

38. The study estimated that 45 percent of rural households own no cattle, 40 percent own up to 50 head and account for 25 percent of the national herd, while 15 percent, the large cattle-owners with more than 50 head, own 75 percent of the national herd. *The Rural Income Distribution Survey* (Gaborone: Central Statistical Office, 1976). See also Colclough and McCarthy, *The Political Economy of Botswana*, for discussion of the study.

39. Gunderson, "Nation Building and the Administrative State," 259.

40. Gunderson, "Nation Building and the Administrative State," 429, wrote that the form of nationalism

took a different pattern than in other areas of colonial Africa. The majority of indigenous westernized Africans within Bechuanaland did not actively seek political independence from the British. Few Africans dared to believe that Bechuanaland in light of its paucity of economic resources and in the face of its geographic location could achieve viability, if granted independence. Modern Africans realized like the Chiefs in 1895, that for security and stability they must cooperate with the British.

See Polhemus, "Botswana Votes," with regard to the party formation process.

41. Three separate analysts wrote the following regarding the calculations of the European elite and the partnership they eventually forged with the BDP's "new men":

• "The local white community appears to have also seen the formation of the

BDP as a neutralizing factor to the 'extremism' of the BPP and its alleged anti-white attitude" (Nengwekhulu, "Some Findings," 69).

- "For the whites of Bechuanaland and for the governing Nationalist Party, Seretse Khama's victory was the least of three evils" (Richard P. Stevens, "The New Republic of Botswana," *Africa Report* (October 1966): 15–20).
- "It appears that the BDP's policy of building a non-racial state convinced most of them that, if nothing else, this party was the lesser of many evils" (Gunderson, "Nation Building and the Administrative State," 345–346).

42. Halpern, *South Africa's Hostages,* 290.

43. An interesting illustration of this is Khama's treatment of chiefly power. See J. H. Proctor, "The House of Chiefs and the Political Development of Botswana," *The Journal of Modern African Studies* 6, no. 1 (1968); Simon Gillett, "The Survival of Chieftaincy," *African Affairs* 72, no. 287 (1973): 179–185.

44. Hermans, "A Review of Botswana's Financial History."

4

International Influences on Botswana's Democracy

Patrick P. Molutsi

Botswana does not exist in isolation: it has intricate economic, political, and social links to the international community of nations. Botswana is a member of the United Nations, the Nonaligned Movement, the Commonwealth, the Organization of African Unity (OAU), and the Southern African Development Coordinating Conference (SADCC). With Lesotho, South Africa, and Swaziland, it is a member of the Southern African Customs Union (SACU).

As a primary commodity producer of beef and diamonds, Botswana is influenced by interstate relations on the one hand and by the vagaries of international commodities markets, international financial capital, and multinational corporations on the other. For example, as a member of the African, Caribbean, and Pacific (ACP) countries, which have standing trade agreements (Lomé Conventions I–IV) with the European Economic Community (EC), Botswana must abide by certain livestock regulations. To meet the EEC's animal health requirements Botswana has had to design livestock policies and make investments that show the country's utmost concern for disease-free beef production: cordon fences have been erected across the country and in 1988 a vaccine institute was established to provide foot-and-mouth vaccine to Botswana farmers; some of the vaccine is exported to SADCC member states as well.

In general terms these links show that, like other countries, Botswana is influenced by and involved with organizations at regional, continental, and international levels. This chapter focuses on both state-to-state influences and governmental, nongovernmental, and private organizations that affect Botswana's economy, political ideology, and institutions.

Such influence is best analyzed at both the central and local government levels.[1]

This chapter investigates two hypotheses. The first posits that "In supporting Botswana materially and politically, international actors have been vital in both the development and sustenance of a liberal democratic system."

The second hypothesis, which contradicts the first, asserts that "By working closely with and through the central bureaucracy, external actors have weakened or retarded development of national and local representative institutions and popular participation, hence undermining rather than strengthening democracy."

■ Liberal Democratic Ideology and Development

Botswana is famous for its stable liberal democratic system and prosperous economy. Since independence in 1966 Botswana has successfully operated with a Westminister-type constitution. The implementation of that constitution has brought about a liberal, multiparty democratic system, regular competitive elections, an independent judiciary, a small but relatively free private press, adult suffrage, and basic civil and political rights, including freedoms of association, worship, and speech.

The choice of a multiracial, multiparty democracy in the context of a racially troubled Southern Africa of the 1960s was viewed with considerable sympathy by the international community. Botswana's leaders took advantage of the geopolitical situation of their country to project theirs as a democratic experiment on the "doorsteps of apartheid."[2] They appealed for support to the United Nations and its agencies, to foreign governments, and to international humanitarian agencies. The message was fairly simple. Botswana was a young, poverty-stricken nation, but one whose political success could contribute to racial harmony and peaceful transformation in Southern Africa.[3] By the mid-1970s this democratic ideology and the country's geo-political situation had begun to pay dividends. Nordic countries, the United States, Canada, and West Germany responded with multifaceted assistance.

The assistance involved grants and low-interest loans, volunteers, and bilateral technical assistance personnel. Through the latter Botswana received cheap but highly skilled manpower in the areas of health, education, water, road construction, economic planning, and development administration. Private foreign capital and international markets also gave special treatment to Botswana's exports. For instance, the EC paid a premium price for Botswana beef.

■ **Positive Influences**

☐ *Role of International Official Aid and Private Capital*

Economic growth and development are important ingredients for democracy. Political instability engulfing many developing countries has rightly been associated with their economic problems. Botswana has been fortunate to be one of the leading recipients of both foreign financial assistance and private capital investment. These two sources of support contributed significantly to the establishment of a strong economic base. Private capital has been the key to economic growth in both the mining and manufacturing sectors, while official aid went into rural and urban services development to benefit mainly the poor sections of the society. Table 4.1 gives an impression of the flow of private capital into Botswana over the years.

Table 4.1 Net Inflows of Private Capital (pula million)

Year	Long-Term Capital[a]	Short-Term Capital	Total
1976	+14	+21	+35
1977	+15	+21	+36
1978	+45	+26	+71
1979	+91	–6	+85
1980	+97	+4	+101
1981	+94	–5	+89
1982	+54 (61)	+13	+67
1983	+ 58 (59)	+24	+82
1984	+129	+13	+142
1985	+200	—	+200
1986	+187	+48	+235
1987	+127	—	+127

Sources: C. Harvey and S. Lewis, *Policy Choice and Development Performance in Botswana* (1990), 203, and Bank of Botswana annual reports.
Notes: a. Includes retained earnings of foreign shareholders (negative in the case of Botswana Roan Selection Trust).
() These appear to be the correct figures from the Bank of Botswana's reports.

The beneficiaries of this investment have been the mining and manufacturing sectors. The former has been important as a major source of state revenue while the latter remains the key source of employment.

It has been partly through private capital that Botswana's economy transformed from one of the poorest at independence to one of the world's fastest-growing economies in the 1970s and 1980s. An average annual growth rate of 10 percent in real terms was experienced over the larger part of the past twenty years. The gross domestic product per capita also rose from a mere US $40 in 1966 to US $2,330 in the 1989/90 financial year.

Investment has reduced unemployment, which is a major source of political instability in developing countries. The number of people employed in manufacturing industries, for instance, increased from around 14,000 in 1980 to around 26,000 in 1990. Thus manufacturing employment rose from 7 percent to 12 percent of total employment over the same period. The role of foreign investment in both mining and manufacturing has been a direct contributor to Botswana's political stability and democracy in this sense.

Official aid from diverse sources has also been an important contributor both to better income distribution and general economic growth. Foreign aid has been not only reliable but also focused on sectors that tended to benefit a large proportion of the rural and urban poor. Table 4.2 shows sources of and amount of foreign aid given to Botswana during the eleven years from 1976 to 1986.

Table 4.2 Official Development Assistance to Botswana, Gross Disbursements, 1978–1986 (US$ million)

	'76	'77	'78	'79	'80	'81	'82	'83	'84	'85	'86
GFR	1.3	4.3	6.2	22.9	14.9	15.0	24.2	20.1	13.0	13.2	12.5
Norway	7.0	5.1	9.1	9.1	12.8	8.8	7.4	8.0	7.8	11.1	11.7
Sweden	10.2	10.7	19.0	14.8	13.2	15.2	13.2	11.6	11.0	7.3	16.3
U.K.	8.5	8.0	10.4	16.9	20.6	16.6	12.2	13.7	11.0	6.3	8.2
U.S.	6.0	3.0	11.0	6.0	12.0	14.0	17.0	13.0	13.0	11.0	10.0
Others	7.7	7.2	39.4	10.9	13.7	9.8	9.3	8.2	9.1	10.2	23.3
Total	40.7	38.3	95.1	80.6	87.2	79.4	83.3	74.6	64.9	59.1	82.0
Multilateral	7.1	9.4	13.9	26.1	22.7	21.2	18.7	39.1	37.7	37.4	20.4
Grand total	47.8	47.7	119.0	106.7	109.9	100.6	102.0	113.7	102.6	96.5	102.4

Source: Refigured from Per Granberg and J. R. Parkinson, eds., *Botswana: Country Study and Norwegian Aid Review* (Bergen: Chr. Michelsen Institute, Department of Social Science and Development, 1988), 276.

Two points from the above table deserve emphasis. First, Botswana's donors have been diverse. Second, they have been consistent. The improvement in Botswana's domestic revenue since the mid-1970s did not reduce the flow of aid into Botswana. For some donors Botswana became the highest per capita recipient of aid.[4] The impact of this aid becomes clearer when assessed in terms of the sectors that received it. Most of this went into provision of social services, including education and training, health services, water supply, and development of roads. Nordic aid in particular focused on the foregoing sectors and assisted nongovernment organizations and small, village-based manufacturing industries.

The example of Norwegian aid shown in Table 4.3 illustrates the general trend followed by other donors.

Table 4.3 Norwegian Bilateral Aid Disbursements to Botswana by Sector, 1973–1986: Percent Distribution

| | | | | Sectors | | | | |
YEAR	I	II	III	IV	V	VI	VII	SUM
1973	—	—	—	—	—	—	100	100
1974	—	—	—	83	4	—	13	100
1975	—	—	—	61	24	—	15	100
1976	—	—	—	72	19	—	9	100
1977	—	3	43	—	43	—	11	100
1978	1	2	65	—	26	—	6	100
1979	1	5	74	—	12	1	7	100
1980	1	3	—	65	25	1	5	100
1981	1	9	—	35	47	—	8	100
1982	1	6	—	35	43	1	14	100
1983	1	4	—	38	23	—	34	100
1984	2	4	—	37	37	3	17	100
1985	—	3	28	—	40	—	29	100
1986	18	4	26	—	35	2	15	100

Source: Refigured from Per Granberg and J. R. Parkinson, eds., Botswana: Country Study and Norwegian Aid Review (Bergen: Chr. Michelsen Institute, Department of Social Science and Development, 1988), 280.
Note: Column headings are: I—Agriculture, fishing; II—Mining, manufacturing, handicraft; III—Water, electricity; IV—Transport, communication; V—Health, family planning; VI—Education (nonvocational); and VII—other. Discrepancies are due to rounding.

While Norwegian aid focused primarily on health and roads, Swedish aid became the leading contributor to water development (mainly for people and livestock) and rural industries. Aid from the United States focused on provision of primary and secondary education facilities as well as private sector development. The impact of foreign aid on rural development was profoundly illustrated in the Accelerated Rural Development Program (ARDP), which was over 44 percent financed by Swedish and Norwegian aid.[5] Undertaken between 1973 and 1976, this program built several primary schools, about sixty health posts and clinics,

water points, and rural roads. Together with subsequent aid-funded programs, ARDP contributed substantially to qualitative improvement in the
lives of rural people.

In urban areas too, foreign aid has played an important role. The Self-
Help Housing Agency (SHHA) program for the urban poor was started in
1973 with Canadian aid. So far hundreds of thousands of households in
urban areas have benefited from this scheme. SIDA (the Swedish
International Development Agency) has also financed handicrafts and hor-
ticultural activities by low-income urban women. In sum, foreign aid has
averted poverty and misery, improved the quality of life, and (through
investment in social services) helped to legitimate the postcolonial state in
Botswana.

☐   *The Contribution of International Financial Institutions
    and UN Agencies*

International financial institutions, including the World Bank, International
Monetary Fund (IMF), and UN agencies such as UNDP, WHO, UNICEF,
and FAO, have also played and continue to play a distinct role in
Botswana's economy and by implication in the democratic process. These
organizations provide financial and technical aid to Botswana as they do to
other countries. As Table 4.4 shows, Botswana's loans have generally
grown since 1982.

Table 4.4 Public Debts (pula million)

Year	Amount
1982	132.3
1983	199.3
1984	232.4
1985	380.8
1986	409.4
1987	438.4
1988	557.5
1989	739.2
1990	751.9

Source: Bank of Botswana, *Annual Report* (1990), 117.

The external sources of loans included the Commonwealth Develop-
ment Corporation, the World Bank and its International Development
Agency (IDA), USAID, the OPEC Fund for International Development, the
International Fund for Agricultural Development (IFAD), and the UNDP.

□   *Technical Assistance Personnel as*
    an Element of International Influences

One of Botswana's major constraints at independence was the acute short-age of skilled manpower to take up jobs in the new state. Unlike the finan-cial constraint, which was resolved by the late 1970s, manpower require-ments remain a major constraint at all levels of the economy. As a temporary measure to address this problem, government has appealed for technical assistance as part of the aid package. Donors have been keen to attach their own personnel to some of the money they give to Botswana. At present more than 10 percent of Botswana's public officers are foreigners; in some departments the percentage is as high as 40 percent.

The three strategies for the recruitment of technical personnel have been followed with considerable success. First, many relatively skilled personnel have come to Botswana as volunteers from a number of organizations, including the US Peace Corps, Danish Volunteer Service, Dutch Volunteer Service (SNV), German Volunteer Service, British International Volunteer Service (IVS), and United Nations Volunteer Service. In the beginning, the volunteers were concentrated in the field of teaching. Today they include road technicians, economic planners, laboratory technicians, land adminis-trators, and technical trainers.

The second route for expatriate recruitment is through what is called technical assistance personnel. Table 4.5 shows how significant such assis-tance can be.

Table 4.5 **Norwegian Technical Assistance Personnel to Botswana and Their Cost (NOK million)**

Years	Experts	Cost	Volun.	Cost	Total No.	Total Cost
1973–75	33	5.4	34	2.3	67	7.7
1976–80	146	34.6	128	13.1	274	47.7
1981–85	197	82.2	74	18.8	261	101.0
1986	37	21.3	20	6.5	57	27.8
TOTAL	413	143.5	246	40.8	659	184.3

Source: Adapted from Per Granberg and J. R. Parkinson, eds., *Botswana: Country Study and Norwegian Aid Review* (Bergen: Chr. Michelsen Institute, 1988), 281.

Technical personnel play an influential role in decisionmaking in Botswana. In the example of Norwegian-supported experts, a large number are medical doctors posted in rural areas as heads of district medical teams, where they are completely responsible for district health management.

Given its improved financial position, Botswana is now able to recruit expatriates through the third route—directly from the international labor market. Significant numbers have been recruited from elsewhere in Africa and from the Indian subcontinent, Europe, and America.

The influence of foreign technical personnel has been adequately assessed elsewhere.[6] They are part and parcel of Botswana's decision- and policymaking machinery. In a country where the political has become subservient to the techno-bureaucratic sphere, expatriate influence on policy formulation and on the development agenda has been overwhelming.[7] Nevertheless, their policies have tended to be favorable to the majority of the underpriviledged groups.

Botswana's active role in regional political and economic forums has helped boost its international image. In both the Frontline States and the Southern African Development Coordinating Conference (SADCC), Botswana has earned itself a good name and a leadership role. Recent meetings relating to resolution of Africa's economic crisis have put Botswana on a footing with major donors, further proof of its leaders' high international status.[8]

■ Negative Influences

□ The Role of International Press and Pressure Groups

International influence in Botswana has not been entirely positive. Several international press agencies have been critical of some of Botswana's development strategies and its democracy. The South African press, the *New York Times, the Washington Post,* and the *Herald* and *Guardian* newspapers of Britain have in the past critized the government's environmental and wildlife policies.

In 1990 and 1991 four issues attracted widespread international attention and criticism. The first was the government's attempt to remove the nomadic Basarwa people from the Central Khalahari game reserves—their traditional habitat—and resettle them in a new area without adequate water and other resources necessary for their subsistence. This issue was well publicized outside Botswana and to date this resettlement has not taken place.

In the first half of 1990, the government formulated a project to dredge the Okavango Swamps and channel the water into neighboring, water-starved villages. Both the local communities and the Greenpeace movement vehemently opposed the move. They argued that this would disturb the already ecologically fragile Okavango. After several media stories—local and abroad—the government invited Greenpeace to inspect the site, thus yielding to international pressure. This resulted in an even more hostile report from Greenpeace, which has so far delayed the dredging project.

The issue of elephant culling is yet more evidence of international pressure and influence on Botswana's politics and economy. Since 1990 the government has been pressured to discontinue the hunting of elephants despite their excessive numbers in the country. Wildlife and environmental groups outside the country have even threatened to influence the EC against buying Botswana beef if the hunting of elephants continues.

However, the government of Botswana has not yielded to international pressure in every case. For instance, Botswana is one of the few countries that have not yet adopted a number of important ILO labor standards. In late 1991 over 50,000 manual workers went on strike. Government dismissed the workers and returned them on a new employment contract, which stripped them of all previous benefits. International pressure from labor organizations has up to now been ignored and some of the workers were never reemployed.

Several questions have also been raised about income distribution and the real nature of Botswana's democracy. These have provoked criticisms by Botswana government officials, who describe such questions as uninformed and irresponsible.[9] Equally ignored have been questions relating to recent military expansions and resultant expenditure. The government has not taken kindly to these questions. Overall, however, international pressure, the pressure groups, and organizations have done and said things that the local people would not have done or said. They have in this way acted as a watchdog for Botswana's democracy, filling the gap left by local interest groups, which are still weak and at early stages of development.

■ Discussion and Conclusion

International assistance provided to Botswana has gone a long way to create conditions for development of liberal politics in the country. It has helped to create jobs, develop social services, and build infrastructure. These improvements have enhanced the image and influence of the state and helped to legitimize it against the chiefs and opposition parties. The new state has found that it can realize some of its objectives faster than would be the case without aid. In this way it is evident that foreign influences have contributed to the sustenance of democracy in Botswana.

However, the same foreign aid and foreign assistance in general have created conditions that constrain the development of popular participation and sound local government machinery. By its nature foreign assistance works closely with the central bureaucracy. The political arm of the government, the local government, and other institutions/organizations involved with development programs in the country have had little say on where to get aid, and how to use aid money. This is largely because aid and other forms of assistance are channeled through the central bureaucracy, which is then accountable to international donors for how the funds are used.

By collaborating with the central government bureaucracy, foreign influences and aid have undermined the community's own self-help efforts, and set the agenda for development that has in some cases created dependency and therefore cannot be sustained. This has clearly been the case in the programs initiated for women and disabled groups in the country.[10] The withdrawal of aid has caused enormous financial and support problems for these groups.

Botswana remains one of the few stable democracies in Africa today. The international factor has been critical to development of democracy in Botswana. At an economic level, resources and technical personnel have generously been provided by foreign governments and international organizations to assist the efforts to create a democratic society in Botswana. These resources have gone a long way to provide basic necessities of life such as water, food, health, and education to a substantial section of the population, including those in the rural areas. At the same time, the international community has helped to protect civil and political rights. Botswana has been able to build an economic environment conducive to a meaningful political democracy. I have, however, noted the undemocratic role that the bureaucracy plays in society. The dangers that a strong bureaucracy poses to the furtherance of democracy are adequately discussed by Gloria Somolekae elsewhere in this volume.

Botswana's leaders have clearly recognized how valuable a commodity democracy has become internationally. They have as such engaged in a conscious effort to project their country as a political model for the rest of the Third World. In conclusion, then, Botswana gained what it has achieved politically and economically by exporting *three* key commodities: diamonds, beef, and ideology (democracy).

■ Notes

1. The word *influence* in the context of this chapter is used in a neutral way. When judgment is implied, the word *influence* will be prefixed with "positive" or "negative." Positive influence shall be defined as influence that is perceived by national leaders, bureaucrats, and planners as acceptable because it enhances the country's goals and objectives. Negative influence shall be defined as actions and activities of external agent(s) regarded as too critical and hostile to Botswana's development goals and objectives.

2. Gloria Somolekae, "Do Batswana Act Democratically?" in Patrick P. Molutsi and John D. Holm, eds., *Democracy in Botswana* (Athens: Ohio University Press, 1989).

3. Ibid.

4. This has been the case with Norwegian aid. Per Granberg and J. R. Parkinson, eds., *Botswana: Country Study and Norwegian Review* (Bergen: Chr. Michelsen Institute, 1988), 161.

5. Christopher Colclough and Stephen McCarthy, *The Political Economy of Botswana: A Study of Growth and Distribution* (Oxford: Oxford University Press, 1980), 233.

6. Louis Picard, *The Politics of Development in Botswana: A Model for Success?* (Boulder, Colo.: Lynne Rienner, 1987).

7. Ibid.

8. For instance, President Masire was cochairman with Robert McNamara at the first meeting of the Global Coalition for Africa (GCA) held in Maastricht, the Netherlands, on July 2, 3, and 4, 1990. *The Gazette* (Botswana), March 12, 1991.

9. Patrick P. Molutsi and John D. Holm interview with M.P.K. Nwako, minister of commerce, on the Central Khalahari Game Reserve and the resettlement of the Basarwa, Gaborone, April 1988.

10. The School for the Blind in Mochudi village (Podulogong), started by a German Lutheran mission in the 1970s, faced a serious crisis in 1989 when the mission terminated its support and the government was not keen to take it over.

PART 2

CURRENT PROBLEMS
AND PREDICAMENTS

5

Liberal Democracy, the Liberal State, and the 1989 General Elections in Botswana

Jack Parson

In general elections held on October 7, 1989, in Botswana, the fifth such multiparty competitive elections held since 1965,[1] the Botswana Democratic Party (BDP) increased its majority in the national assembly to 31 of 34 seats and took, for the sixth time, the power to govern.[2] In district, town, and city council elections the BDP won 85 percent of all seats and majorities in 10 of the 14 councils. These elections were integral to the most important process in Botswana's postcolonial development, that creating and perpetuating a liberal state. In 1966 Botswana recaptured political independence after seventy-five years as a backwater of the British Empire and slough of the South African economy. During the succeeding twenty-five years Botswana developed a relatively wealthy and increasingly diversified mineral-led market economy. Simultaneously, an imported Westminster-type parliamentary political system took root and, though not unchanged, seemed to thrive. Regular competitive multiparty elections, including those held in 1989, were an important element in that evolution.

The importance of this Botswana experience as a potential "model" for development should not be underestimated, whatever questions may be raised about it. The current era favors the search for such models to be applied elsewhere in Africa, in the South generally, and in Eastern Europe and the former Soviet Union. This chapter develops a limited analysis of a political economy of change through an assessment of the contours of Botswana's electoral history, focused on the 1989 general elections. An analysis of those elections' processes and outcomes in the context of broad changes in social, political, and economic life may provide insights into the processes through which liberal democracy may be created, maintained, and changed.

65

■ The Liberal State and Elections in Botswana

The process that entrenched market relations of production and combined them with liberal democratic political relations in Botswana was led by a successful mining partnership between the government and private firms, mainly the Anglo-American Corporation of South Africa (through its subsidiaries, particularly the DeBeers Diamond Mining Company). A result was the achievement of very high average levels of annual economic growth beginning about 1972. Greatly increased government revenue supported massive expenditures on new physical and social infrastructure as well as support for economic policies, which sustained the private market and the growth of private investment in agriculture and other sectors. Roads, water supplies, health services, and education, provided where none existed before, resulted in an improvement in the quality of life for most citizens. The macroeconomy changed dramatically from one based on agriculture and migrant labor to South Africa to one based upon exploiting the considerable mineral wealth of the country. Government initiatives in agriculture, such as the Tribal Grazing Lands Policy (TGLP), and in other sectors, like the Financial Assistance Policy (FAP) and the lifting of a ban in 1984 on civil servants' participation in private business other than agriculture, had the effect of encouraging the private market. In addition, government policy had the effect of both organizing and controlling the supply of labor required in this market economy. While none too tidy, often contradictory, and chronicled in conflict, this whole process was relatively successful.

Concurrent with these economic changes were changes in the class strata of which society was composed. New class or socioeconomic strata developed and preexisting class strata changed. This socioeconomic change had potentially far-reaching effects on the pattern of political life. Multiparty competitive local government (district, town, and city council) and national assembly elections were crucial in linking the population to the state and mediating the formation of classes and their political struggles. Elections were held throughout the period at constitutionally prescribed intervals beginning in 1965. There was no concrete evidence of systematic manipulation of the election process by the BDP to win majorities.[3] In local government elections, opposition parties sometimes won elected majorities; most dramatic, perhaps, was the elected control of the capital city's council in both 1984 and 1989. These elections mediated the process of social and economic change and provided the indispensable legitimation for the state's direction of that process.

Elections and electoral outcomes are crucial events in liberal democratic systems for two reasons: first, electoral outcomes determine and legitimate the coalition of persons who, for the time being, control the levers of decisionmaking power; second, elections politically mediate the individual and collective experiences of the population. Of these two reasons, legitimation is the more important.

Legitimation through elections provides the state with the moral and practical power to insist upon obedience and with the crucial argument to deny power to those who would oppose it. Discerning the pattern of political elite coalitions and the extent of legitimation are purposes that may be served through an analysis of electoral outcomes. Doing so over time provides one means for evaluating the political economy of change.

The second reason that elections are important is that they may be a means through which the day-to-day experiences of a people are politically mediated. Elections are a process that translates experience into patterns of political thought and action. In class societies, including market societies such as Botswana, this is essential to the process of social reproduction. Class conflict may be played out and understood through elections where elections aggregate and channel—in practice perhaps and as a matter of ideology for sure—this conflict into patterns of apparent cooperation and compromise. This aggregation and channeling takes place while simultaneously reproducing the structure giving rise to the conflict in the first place, the structure of economic relations.

It is for these reasons that multiparty elections are so important to liberal democratic political forms. They present the conflict between those who own and those who do not own property as relations of cooperation. This has the effect of legitimating the domination of the state by those who own, and the exclusion of the propertyless. It has the general effect of representing the political system as an open one available to all and the obligation of the citizenry to accept its authority however opposed the citizenry is to individual actions of the state. It is for these reasons that Ralph Miliband concludes for Britain that the House of Commons is "by far the most important institution in the British political system," not because it is a strong legislative body or is effective in controlling the executive but because it enshrines "the elective principle; nothing, for the containment and management of pressure from below, could be more important than that."[4] The same could be said for the National Assembly in Botswana.

The legitimation and conflict management functions of elections may link the overall development of market relations to the development of liberal democratic, competitive electoral systems. This would be consistent with Charles Lindblom's insight that "liberal democracy has arisen only in nations that are market oriented, not in all of them, but only in them."[5] In Botswana the development of market relations took the form of a state-directed restructuring of the colonial economy to provide a basis for private accumulation. An open multiparty competitive system paralleled this process. Periodic general elections were a method that linked the whole process, legitimating it and, for the time being, sealing the system of class relations and conflict. Thus the study of Botswana's general elections provides one window on the contour of change, legitimacy, and class relations in the political economy of the country.

In this context it is especially important to undertake a critical analysis of this contour of change to avoid conclusions based on the superficialities of both economic and political success measured exclusively in terms of macroeconomic growth rates and the holding of periodic competitive elections. The wide-ranging and persistent research of the Democracy Project at the University of Botswana,[6] for example, raised questions both about the depth of political elite and political party commitment to the idea of competitive politics and about the extent to which there existed an adequate infrastructure of pluralist political competition. The research of the 1984 election study project raised slightly different but related questions about whether the trajectory of economic change and attendant class formation would in the long run sustain the form of multiparty competitive politics.[7] The present chapter seeks to extend this critical approach to the 1989 outcome.

■ The 1989 General Elections: An Overview

The BDP had cause for self-congratulation as a result of the outcome of the 1989 elections. No doubt it assumed a popular mandate to continue the existing path of economic and social policy. It had every right to do so in relation to the functions of elections in a liberal democracy. However, the 1989 elections seemed also to confirm how difficult it was to legitimate permanently the political power of a governing class in capitalist democracies such as that in Botswana. Electoral support for the BDP was shown to be eroding. It won 64.8 percent of the total votes cast, the first time ever it won less than two-thirds of the votes. The Botswana National Front (BNF) in 1989 continued its trend of capturing opposition votes by winning 27.0 percent of the total votes although only 3 seats in the national assembly.[8] While the BDP increased to 31 the number of seats held in the national assembly, 5 of those seats were won on a plurality vote.[9] Had not the opposition split those votes, the BDP majority might have been reduced to 26 out of 34 seats. In urban local government elections, the BDP continued to face declining support. The proportion of urban polling districts won by the BDP declined to 38.8 percent. The BDP won only 12.8 percent of its national vote in urban areas, where nearly 25 percent of the population lived and rapid urbanization was continuing.

The BDP continued to win rural constituencies with impressive majorities except in those regional pockets where opposition parties continued to have a presence.[10] Significantly, however, there was evidence of declining participation in key areas. There were ten constituencies in the BDP heartland where fewer votes were cast than in 1984 despite an increase in the number of registered voters.

Continuity and change also characterized the data on the voting population, including urban-rural and gender differences within that population. In 1989 the registered voter population was 366,179, which was 73.5 percent of the estimated eligible population, an increase of 21 percent.[11] The registered population grew more rapidly in urban (32 percent) than in rural (22 percent) areas, reflecting rapid urbanization. In addition, and in contrast to 1984, the rate of voting participation by registered voters in urban areas was higher than in rural areas.

In 1989, as in 1984, there were more women than men in the eligible and registered populations and men and women tended to register at about the same rate.[12] Women continued to constitute a disproportionate segment of the rural registered voters (nearly 60 percent) while being a smaller part (about 45 percent) of the urban electorate, reflecting again the disproportionate number of men in wage work in the towns.

At a macro level there was a correspondence between the data on registered turnout and gender distribution and electoral support for and opposition to the BDP (see Table 5.2). As in 1984, in 1989 the constituencies where the BDP recorded its greatest support were those where on average the proportion of women in the registered population was highest. Women were 60.5 percent of registered voters in constituencies where the BDP won 80 percent or more of the vote and were 43.5 percent of registered voters in urban areas where the BDP won less than half the vote.[13] In addition, the highest turnout of registered voters was in those constituencies where the BDP won less than half the vote, particularly in urban areas, where the turnout was 73.3 percent. At the same time, it is important to note the small but consistent increase in turnout in constituencies where the BDP won 51 percent or more. The argument that voters became more complacent as the security of the BDP majority increased was not supported by this data.

The data on voter turnout, urban-rural and gender in 1989, raise questions about how to understand the overall electoral pattern and trends. Four processes reflected in the 1989 general elections in particular seem related to the mechanisms of the liberal form of state and the prospects for its reproduction: (1) rapid proletarianization and urbanization, (2) rural changes "squeezing" rural producers and households, (3) the increasingly competitive electoral arena, and (4) a generational change not only in chronological age but also in class strata terms. A survey and analysis of these four areas and issues in 1989 in comparison to earlier elections provides empirical and analytical content to the more general and abstract issues and questions posed earlier.

Table 5.1 Distribution of the Registered Voter Population, 1984 and 1989, by
Gender and Rural-Urban Place of Registration

		Gender			
Place and Year of Registration		Female		Male	
Urban[a]	1984	26,128	(45.2%)	31,714	(54.8%)
	1989	32,522	(44.5%)	40,542	(55.5%)
Rural	1984	144,898	(59.4%)	99,075	(40.6%)
	1989	174,437	(59.5%)	118,678	(40.5%)
National	1984	171,026	(56.7%)	130,789	(43.3%)
registered	1989	206,959	(56.5%)	159,220	(43.5%)
population					
Estimated	1984	235,947	(56.5%)	181,682	(43.5%)
eligible voter	1989	275,758	(55.3%)	222,624	(44.7%)
population					

Note: a. Francistown, Selibi-Phikwe, Gaborone North, Gaborone South, and Lobatse/
Barolong

Table 5.2 Association of Voting Support for the BDP with Gender and the Turnout
of Registered Voters, 1989

Constituencies where the proportion of votes won by the BDP was:	Number of constituencies	Average % of females in registered population	Average % turnout of registered voters
80% or more	8	60.5	67.8
70–79%	9	58.8	67.0
51–69%	8	55.7	66.0
Less than 50%	9	53.3	71.6
Urban only	5	43.5	73.3

☐ *Proletarianization and Political*
Change: Urbanization and Opposition

The mineral-led strategy of large-scale capital-intensive mining through a
partnership between the state and foreign investors generating revenue to
create labor-intensive activities and improve services in rural areas did not
work. Whatever else may be said of it, large numbers of rural dwellers
voted with their feet in the direction of town. Despite significant improvement in the availability and distribution of public and social services such
as roads, schools, water supplies, and health facilities, many persons left
the rural areas. The urban population in 1989 was estimated to be 24.0 percent of the total population, increased from 17.7 percent in 1981, and was
expected to reach 25.3 percent by the time of the 1991 census.[14] While the
drought during the mid-1980s accounted for some of this flow, it could not

account for the continuing exodus of those leaving rural life for life in town.

The more important causes of urbanization, which was also an accelerating process of proletarianization, are relatively well known. In general it became increasingly difficult for the small independent peasantry and sections of the semiproletarianized peasantry (the peasantariat[15]) to remain in small-holding agriculture despite the introduction of such programs as the Arable Lands Development Programme and, in the mid-1980s, the Accelerated Rainfed Arable Programme. The commoditization of the cattle industry during the 1970s accelerated the privatization of grazing land, which continued during the 1980s. Overgrazing in communal areas continued to the detriment of the smallest herds. During the 1980s arable land allocations for new entrants became more difficult as the commercialization of arable farming also accelerated. Large land areas were fenced and arable farming began to encroach on traditional grazing lands in some cases. Many tracts of unused land were already claimed under traditional rights established before the advent of land boards and were, therefore, unavailable for allocation.[16] Combined with the drought, the overall effect by 1989 was to increase the difficulty of remaining in small-scale agriculture even if combined with some other employment; and if you did remain in agriculture, there were limits to the potential for growth and an increase in income. There was a striking disparity between urban and rural incomes. *The Household Income and Expenditure Survey: 1985/86*[17] found that the median income, including cash and in-kind, for rural households was P131.77 per month in comparison to P281.75 in urban areas. The median for cash incomes alone was more skewed, reaching P253.55 in urban areas but only P52.96 in rural ones. In these statistics, women heads of household had the lowest incomes in rural and urban areas and overall. The lowest median cash and in-kind income level was that of women in rural areas (P116.14 per month) while the highest was that of urban males (P382.47 per month).

These realities of life in rural areas made staying there less and less possible and attractive, though most people continued to do so. Those pressured out of agriculture or who decided to abandon it had to become part of, or at least attempt to become part of, the working class in wage employment. There was no practical alternative. For the most part this had to be in unskilled manual work for something around the minimum wage. For construction and building workers that wage was P0.83 per hour in May 1989, up from P0.56 in June 1985, an increase of 48.2 percent, barely ahead of the increase in the urban cost of living index in the period from September 1985 to May 1989 (46.8 percent).[18]

Working-class wage employment was, for the most part, in urban areas. In September 1988 Gaborone, Francistown, Selibi-Phikwe, Lobatse, and Jwaneng accounted for 73.7 percent of all private and parastatal paid employees. Gaborone alone accounted for 45.8 percent.[19] However, with an unemployment rate of 31.2 percent in urban areas, the prospect of finding a job was not good, and if one were found, it likely provided sufficient income for only a limited standard of living given high rents, housing shortages, and the cost of food and other necessities.

Electoral participation rates reflected rapid urbanization. The number of registered voters grew faster in urban areas (32.5 percent) than in rural areas (23.5 percent) between 1984 and 1989. The proportion of total votes cast increased more (27.2 percent) in urban than rural areas, where the increase was 6.9 percent. It was likely that higher participation rates in urban areas reflected the participation of the growing proletariat and lumpen proletariat, who, it could be reasonably argued, continued as in 1984 to vote most often for the opposition, particularly for the BNF, in Gaborone, Lobatse, Jwaneng, and Selibi-Phikwe. In 1989, as noted earlier, the BDP slumped to an all-time low of 38.8 percent of local government seats.[20] A similar decline occurred in support for the BDP in national assembly elections in urban constituencies (see Table 5.3). This trend was most dramatic in Gaborone, the place of greatest growth.[21] As the urban population increased, electoral support for the BDP in urban areas decreased.

Table 5.3 BDP Proportion of Votes Cast in Urban National Assembly
Constituencies, 1965–1989

Constituency	Year and BDP Proportion of the Vote					
	1965	1969	1974	1979	1984	1989
Gaborone/Ramotsw[a]		86.0	56.7			
Gaborone			73.7	54.7		
Gaborone North					42.2	36.0
Gaborone South					45.4	41.9
Selibi-Phikwe					64.5	49.5
Francistown	21.2	34.9	47.4	53.1	45.3	44.8
Lobatse/Barolong	80.2	62.0	80.8	67.2	64.8	65.3

The persistence of conditions causing rural-to-urban migration and the continued inability to absorb the urban population in satisfying and remunerative employment in the structure of the market and government policy were well-established trends in 1990. In the past it was more or less assumed that most of the resulting opposition vote reflected issues faced by working-class strata as such. That vote went to the party (the BNF) that took up working-class issues, at least rhetorically. But in-migration was so rapid during the late 1980s that it was worth asking whether, and what portion of, the urban opposition vote in 1989 was a comment on conditions in rural areas, and what part was more strictly speaking an established working-class vote in urban areas. Some of that vote by recent immigrants to urban areas must have been cast out of opposition to their displacement in the rural economy. Rural departicipation may have been paralleled in urban areas by urban migrants whose ties to the BDP were broken but who were not yet operating politically as a working class even in a limited way. Their alienation from rural life created an inarticulate but firm opposition stance.[22]

Data to identify (let alone systematically analyze) these opposition strata in urban areas did not exist. It is important that it should be sought, for the existence and relative importance of a rural-rooted but urban-located opposition could be quite significant for political parties' organizations and programs. The BDP might be able to target the specific characteristics of this and other transitional urban strata and ameliorate the worst conditions that lead to its polarization toward the opposition. The BNF needed to be sensitive to the differences among the various strata of its supporters if it wished to retain and deepen its urban base.

☐ Rumblings in the BDP Heartland?

This brings us directly to the rural areas and an important outcome of the 1989 elections for the long term. One of the conclusions reached by the 1984 election study was that "any more radical shift in political fortunes of the opposition parties would involve the opposition making inroads into that half of all the seats in which the BDP has more than two-thirds of the votes, and in half of those it has over ninety percent of the votes." The geographical concentration of these seats was primarily in the Central and Kweneng districts. Two developments leading to such a shift, it was argued, were (1) the possibility of a partial "collapse in the traditional base of legitimacy of the BDP," and (2) the possibility of opposition parties "winning over half of the semi-proletarianized majority in those rural areas."[23] In 1984 both possibilities were thought to be unlikely. However, certain outcomes of the 1989 National Assembly election raised the question of whether the former possibility may now be happening while providing new evidence that the latter was not. The result could be some difficulty for the BDP in its heartland for the first time.

In 1989 in eleven constituencies the absolute number of votes cast declined in comparison to results in 1984, although nationally the number of votes cast increased by 10.3 percent. Ten of the constituencies were ones considered safe by the BDP, as many of them were heartland seats.[24] The eleventh constituency was Ngwaketse South, which, although proving the rule, was exceptional because of its electoral history; it will be dealt with later. The ten BDP constituencies included four of the five most strongly held, where the average proportion of the vote for the BDP was 90 percent and seven of the top ten averaged 86.6 percent of the vote. The constituencies in question, rank-ordered by the proportion of the vote accruing to the BDP, were: Serowe North (93 percent), Serowe South (91 percent), Mmadinare (89 percent), Bobirwa (87 percent), Shoshong (86 percent), Kweneng East (81 percent), Boteti (79 percent), Kweneng South (75 percent), Mosopa (71 percent), and Ngami (60 percent). The average vote for the BDP in these ten constituencies was 81.2 percent, 17 percent above the average vote for the BDP nationally.

The abstentious electorate in many BDP heartland constituencies raised the question of whether there had been an erosion in the hitherto traditional bases of legitimacy for the BDP. If so, it also provided some evidence to question the willingness and ability of existing opposition parties to mobilize this disaffection.

Before this analysis can be developed it is necessary to discuss what, after the 1974 election (which produced a low turnout but a large vote for the BDP), became the conventional wisdom about low turnouts and nonvoting: that it expressed satisfaction with the BDP or that since the opposition was so weak there was no incentive to vote. Data from the 1989 elections tended to discredit the arguments of both satisfaction and a weak opposition to explain nonvoting in general in these constituencies:

1. The decline in the number of votes cast was not national, as in 1974; it was specific to these ten constituencies and Ngwaketse South. Until 1989 these constituencies had a voting history similar to all others. Between 1965 and 1969 all constituencies experienced a decline in votes cast. Of the eight constituencies where the total votes cast increased in 1974, two were in the group of ten. In 1979 every constituency experienced an increase in the absolute number of votes cast. The present trend begins to appear in 1984, when two constituencies, Mmadinare and Shoshong, both in the group, experienced a decline in the number of votes cast. In 1989, however, there was an absolute decline in all ten (plus Ngwaketse South) but in no other constituencies, including others safely held by the BDP.

2. Every constituency experienced an increase in the number of people registered to vote, including the constituencies in question. However, the average increase in the number of registered voters in the ten was 10.5 percent (an average increase of 9.4 percent in the number of men and 11.4 percent in the number of women) while the average increase in the other twenty-four constituencies was 25.5 percent. This explains why the figures for the turnout of registered voters were not very different in these ten constituencies as compared to the rest. But it also meant that a large number of eligible voters withdrew from participation long before they could know whether the BDP actually needed their votes; at the time of registration it could not exactly be known how strong the opposition would be. So these

eligible voters withdrew from the overall elections process. The only other explanations were that these rural constituencies, but not others, were discriminated against in the process of registration or were losing population at a much faster rate than other rural areas, but neither of these explanations seemed to be supportable.

3. Elections in Botswana in general—including these constituencies—were becoming increasingly competitive. In 1989, for example, for the first time, no parliamentary seats were uncontested and many fewer district, town, and city council seats were uncontested in comparison to earlier elections. The declining national vote for the BDP indicated a greater competitive elections arena. In the ten heartland seats this was also the case. Although the majority for the BDP was not threatened in 1989, the opposition reduced the proportion of votes going to the BDP in seven cases. At the local government level in these places there was also more competition; the number of unopposed polling districts went down from twenty-four in 1984 to only five in 1989. While the opposition remained relatively weak, it increased and posed a sufficient threat to motivate satisfied and stalwart BDP supporters.

4. Finally, among registered voters in the group of ten there was a tendency to withdraw from actually voting even in the face of more contested seats. Nationally the number of registered voters increased by 20 percent and the number of votes cast increased by 10 percent, a ratio of two new registrants to one new vote. In nearly two-thirds (59 percent) of the remaining twenty-four constituencies this was the case but it was not so in any of the ten. In them there was the double effect of withdrawal from direct participation by not registering and, for some, registering and then not voting.

The accumulated evidence was that nonvoting in at least certain safe BDP seats became in 1989 a means of expressing a political viewpoint short of complete support for the BDP. The idea that such a consistent pattern was explained by satisfaction in the face of no opposition could not be seriously entertained. A working hypothesis explaining this phenomenon was that the traditional bases of support for the BDP had been or were being eroded but that those disenchanted with the BDP were not prepared to vote for the existing opposition; rather, they abstained from electoral participation.

A systematic, empirical explanation of the reasons for this decline would require grassroots research at the constituency level. This has not been done and should become an urgent priority. However, it is possible to speculate on an analysis pointing to certain avenues of further research. The traditional bases of support for the BDP in its heartland lay in a set of powerful economic and political relations between a large semiproletarianized majority (what I have called a peasantariat) and a small elite. For many, patron-client economic relations between large cattle-owners and subsistence-farmers-cum-workers were critical.[25] Where larger cattle-owners also led the BDP, these economic relations were directly translated into political support and votes. Moreover, for many years the economic relations that could have become issues of serious conflict were mediated through the fact that many BDP leaders and candidates also held traditional political status and legitimate authority. Seretse Khama was, after all, chief of the Bangwato (at least by right) as well as president of the BDP and of the Republic of Botswana. This mediation of class through the politics of tradition was important to peasantariat political life.

These material and ideological relations may have particularly predisposed a disproportionate number of women toward more or less automatic support for the BDP. In the traditional political economy women were in a subordinate and exploited situation in terms of controlling the means of production and access to political power. The migrant labor system deepened their dependence with its extraction of males from the household who might otherwise have had easier access to the means of agricultural production. Dependence on male relatives for access to the means of production imbedded women deeply into the patron-client relation and may have created ideological and political relations that effectively coerced a proportion of women into regular voting for the BDP.

In addition, the BDP government did deliver the goods, at least in some respects; roads, schools, clinics, health posts, water supplies, and some agricultural programs were provided. The infrastructure of life improved. Taken together these economic and political relations and services provided a powerful and heretofore unassailable political base for the BDP in its heartland and for many places beyond.

Over the past twenty-five years there may have been an accelerating process loosening these ties. The extension of infrastructural services was important but the benefits to the population were eventually weighed against other issues like unemployment, the ability to grow crops and accumulate cattle, housing, and wages. The latter became more important and could not be handled though patron-client economic and "traditional" political relations. Moreover, the process of proletarianization accelerated, with a larger proportion than ever dependent upon wages for some or all of subsistence needs. While semiproletarianization still characterized the lives of many people (perhaps most) in these rural areas, the process of proletarianization may have reached a point where former political tendencies were not as powerful. For men in this situation, an answer was urban migration as single workers to look for jobs. For probably most, but not all, women it was more difficult, as they had to remain behind managing a household. Those single women with children were less mobile than males. Forced to remain in rural areas but unable to succeed in the rural economy any longer, it may be that such women, and a proportion of men who remained in the rural economy, withdrew from electoral participation; they abstained from this form of political participation.

As a political organization, the BDP also lost some of its automatic appeal to voters in the Central and Kweneng Districts. President Masire could not appeal to voters there in the same way as did Seretse Khama, whatever other leadership qualities President Masire brought to his positions in the party and government. Furthermore by 1989 the party took on a much more technocratic and nontraditional composition, at least at the level of the National Assembly. The primary routes to parliamentary membership and cabinet office were increasingly through the civil service and nonagriculturally based business and professional careers.

This shift in the orientation of the party coincided with a generational change in BDP leadership at the national level. Even as late as 1984, eleven of the thirty-four BDP candidates had also been candidates in the very first election in 1965. Nearly one-third of BDP candidates had held office for twenty years. As of 1989, six of these eleven ceased to be active at the parliamentary level, leaving only five (six if President Masire is included).[26] The torch, as it were, was being passed to a generation that could not claim the more or less automatic allegiance of the peasantariat. The question of generational change is discussed in more detail in a following section.

At the level of peasantariat life these changes were probably inarticulate. But that did not mean that people were unresponsive to the effects of these changes on their lives. If they were increasingly dissatisfied, then one rational political expression of this was to emigrate to urban areas and perhaps vote for the opposition. Another, in rural areas, was to reduce participation in the electoral process. Some persons may have reached a point where they did not wish to vote for the BDP but could not as yet bring themselves to vote against it. Automatic allegiance over the years is not wiped away in an instant. Actually to vote for an opposition party would be an act of such utter disloyalty that it was as yet unthinkable.

This has also to be seen in the context of a rather weak opposition, weak in distinguishing itself from the BDP in the eyes of the peasantariat.[27] The opposition, in particular the BNF, had not offered a concrete alternative vision of the future to the BDP for people in these heartland places. In this situation, abstention made sense.

This brings us to the Ngwaketse South constituency as an exception proving the rule. It was won by Masire for the BDP in 1965 with 95 percent of the vote and was then lost to Bathoen and the BNF until 1989, when the BDP recaptured the seat on a split opposition vote between the BNF and the Botswana Freedom Party (BFP). The slender electoral edge was likely aided by abstentions in Ngwaketse South for reasons not unlike those in the BDP heartland. Unwilling to vote for the BDP (given ex-chief Bathoen's antipathy to it over the years), but with loyalties now divided between the BNF and the breakaway BFP, many people apparently chose not to vote.

If we assume the continuation of the 1989 trajectory, an assumption by no means inevitable, then what of the future in the BDP heartland? There might emerge independent grassroots organizational expressions of this disenchantment, although history would not lead one to predict that. It is also possible that one of the existing opposition parties may be able to present itself in such a way as to legitimize voting for it in opposition to the BDP. There was no reason to believe this was occurring in 1991 looking forward to 1994. The opposition was expending itself on talks of party unity as an elite electoral strategy (see the following section on party competition), which even if achieved would have no impact on the ten constituencies discussed here, rather than in organizing in the rural areas.

What prospect then for the BDP and for the disenchanted in the heartland? The BDP need not worry for the foreseeable (next election, 1994) future. Its electoral hold on these seats was firm and the opposition seemed incapable of breaking that hold by 1994 and perhaps beyond. Departicipation will not cost the BDP any of these seats. But the BDP ignores this tendency at its own long-term risk. The process of departicipation, which in 1989 took some extrapolating to discern, may become obvious and dominant. While the BDP may still win, its legitimacy can quickly erode. The question is whether the "new" men leading the party will be able to find the means to renew the mandate from below in these places.

In the absence of an independent peasantariat political organization or an existing party's attentiveness to their needs, a large portion of the population in the heartland, and perhaps beyond if this tendency spreads elsewhere, may become further alienated from the electoral political process. If so, this will erode the claim to legitimacy by those who continue to be elected. It also may erode whatever grassroots commitment there is to the liberal democratic process. In such a situation, those who control the state may find that coercion becomes more necessary to maintain and reproduce the situation while those who are alienated become increasingly open to the use of coercion to change things. The arbiter of power then is he or she who has the gun—the police and the army. If the situation degenerated to that point, a military coup would not be out of the question. An appeal to the disenfranchised majority against what was perceived to be an exploitive and insensitive ruling clique would provide a popular base for such an event.[28]

These developments are not inevitable. For example, if the rapid urbanization of the country continues and if it leads to full-scale proletarianization, and if this provokes social welfare spending and social-democratic politics, then an alternative scenario is that of developed European-style capitalism and liberal democracy. It is not clear that the economy can support this development. Dependence on diamonds, the absence of a wider and deeper industrial base, and the likely contours of a postapartheid southern Africa militate against it, but it is a possibility. Alternatively, if a peasantariat political organization did emerge and forged political links with its urban counterparts, including the fully dispossessed proletariat—through an existing opposition party or an entirely new one—then the politics of class would not only be on the agenda but could become a reality. A key finding from the 1989 elections here is the need to look carefully at what happened in the rural areas, particularly in the BDP heartland, as well as in town, when assessing likely futures. While the process of proletarianization created rather obvious points of opposition in urban areas, its roots and some of its manifestations were found elsewhere. Perhaps not insignificantly, some of the voices portending opposition and change came importantly, not solely, from the Central and Kweneng Districts, as had been the case in the past.[29]

☐ Competition in the Electoral Arena

Political party competition in both National Assembly and local government elections consistently increased beginning with the 1974 election. For the first time there were no uncontested national assembly seats in 1989. The drop in the proportion of uncontested local government seats was even more dramatic. In 1974, sixty-six seats, or 37.5 percent of the total, were uncontested; this dropped to twelve seats, or 4.7 percent, in 1989. The number of seats having increased from 176 in 1979 to 254 in 1984 made this change appear even sharper.

As in 1984, the trend in contested constituencies was in the direction of multiparty contests, most especially in National Assembly elections. In local government elections the proportion of three-party contests increased from an average of about 6 percent of all seats in 1974 and 1979 to about 20 percent in both 1984 and 1989. In a majority of these cases (15.4 percent of all seats), the election involved the BDP, BPP, and BNF. Two-party local government elections were fought in 70.1 percent of the constituencies, the largest proportion (64.6 percent of the total) between the BDP and the BNF. As in 1984, the BNF demonstrated an increased ability to recruit and field candidates. In National Assembly elections, the tendency to multiparty contests was even more marked. The number of two-party elections declined from 58.8 percent in 1984 to 47.1 percent in 1989, while the proportion of three-party races increased from 32.4 percent in 1984 to 50.0 percent in 1989. These three-party contests in 1989 involved a total of seven parties, although two of the parties (the Botswana Labour Party [BLP] and the Botswana Progressive Union [BPU]) sponsored only one candidate each.

The overall effect of these changes was a greater degree of competition for elected office. The increase in multiparty elections also indicated the increased likelihood of plurality rather than majority elections and a decrease in the correspondence between the proportion of votes received by a party and its representation. In the National Assembly, for example, under a simple system of proportional representation the BNF in 1989 would have won nine seats for its 27.0 percent of the votes instead of the three it actually won, while the BDP would have won twenty-two seats instead of thirty-one. In the present system of single-member-district plurality election, the BDP won five of its thirty-one seats with a plurality, not majority. These facts increased debate among opposition parties about the need for unity in tackling the majority of seats held by the BDP given the current electoral system. If the opposition parties did not split the anti-BDP vote they would win more national assembly seats. That much is clear. Whether this would give a greater voice to the populations dissenting from the BDP is not clear. The contour of the debate among opposition parties in 1990 suggested that it would not necessarily do so, but would merely create local monopolies for opposition parties in specific areas. Each would then be the only electoral outlet for anyone wishing to cast a ballot against the BDP.

The opposition parties' "unity talks," begun in the context of the 1984 election result, were not about the nature and quality of leadership, grassroots organization, the introduction of proportional representation, or programmatic alternatives to the BDP. They were about retaining individual party identification and leadership. They begged the whole question of the sources of opposition to the BDP and ignored the need for a programmatic response to those sources. They sought creation of an election pact such that the existing opposition parties would divide up the constituencies among themselves to enhance each party's ability to win a few more seats in its own area. The talks reflected primarily an elite strategy to avoid competition and in effect to minimize the extent to which the parties individually and jointly came to terms with mass issues. If competition among themselves was avoided, then each opposition party automatically received the votes of those who wished to vote against the BDP. As a result, the likelihood of democratic control of the opposition parties was lessened. Freed again, as in the past, of the need to organize a permanent mass base, party elites could do as they pleased. As long as there was competition for non-BDP votes, then the opposition had to respond to the voices from below.

If this analysis was correct, then the effect on the BDP in the long run was actually a positive one. In the short run the BDP would almost certainly lose several seats, but such an outcome would also minimize the extent to which opposition parties had to organize and respond to the real sources of opposition. While continuing to face a rather amorphous and inarticulate protest vote, the security of the BDP majority in the assembly would be protected at least for the foreseeable future.

The increasingly competitive political arena was indicative of a growing, if not well articulated and defined, opposition to the prevailing dispensation. But this conclusion does not suppose that any political organization was engaged in the process of systematically analyzing the sources of that opposition and responding directly to or organizing those sources. The "unity" talks were one example. The BNF's insistence that it loses elections only because they are rigged was another example of a tendency to look for external causes for failing to win office rather than concentrating on the work of organization and mobilization at a mass level.[30] These responses of the opposition merely interpreted growing electorate dissatisfaction as a vehicle to win office for opposition leaders.

□ *A Changing of the Guard?*

Data on the 1989 elections confirmed trends in candidate continuity from earlier elections: the BDP candidate pool tended to have the most continuity from one election to the next; unchanged qualifications for candidacy meant that the pool of candidates for all parties continued to be drawn from bourgeois strata. But 1989 data did indicate that significant changes were occurring in the leadership of the BDP; the founding generation gave way to a new generation of leaders. This raised the question of who was replacing the founding generation and how this might be related, if at all, to electoral outcomes.

The working hypothesis was that the more recent generation of BDP candidates[31] did not have the same economic and social ties to the peasantariat in rural areas as the founding generation, and this loosened political support for the BDP as a result. This was the most politically significant result of the emergence and increasing prominence of the bureaucratic faction of leadership in the petty bourgeoisie noted by Molutsi, among others.[32] The ruling class continued to be a bourgeois one but its composition evolved over the year; the current phase (say from 1980 on) saw the rise first of a commercial faction, and the late 1980s saw the emergence of a more powerful bureaucratic faction not only in the public service itself but also in political life, as senior civil servants crossed the line into electoral politics and cabinet-level office.

There was one datum from the analysis of electoral outcomes in the heartland constituencies of the BDP that supported the view that this development may have weakened support for the BDP. Let us call those ten constituencies the "A" constituencies. The "B" constituencies were those nine remaining relatively safe BDP constituencies.[33] I have assumed that the founding generation of the BDP (those who stood for the National Assembly) were those candidates in 1965 and 1969; I have further assumed that their social and economic relations with constituents were close, leading to continuity in political relations. Working with these assumptions, I discerned that "A" constituencies were those where the closer and more personal ties had been disrupted, for whatever reason. In the results of the BDP primaries in 1989 only 2 "founders" from 1965 through 1969 continued to represent the BDP in the 10 "A" constituencies, while they did so in 5 of the 9 "B" constituencies. Moreover, in the "A" group from 1969 through 1979, 7 of the 10 constituencies had seen a turnover in candidacy while in none of the "B" constituencies had candidates changed. The "A" group had a total of 24 different candidates (an average of 2.4 per constituency) from 1965 to 1989 compared with an average of 1.6 (or 14 different candidates) in the "B" group.[34] The question was whether and in what ways the different candidate pools linked the rural population to the party and whether this was related to a possible erosion of support for the BDP. The hypothesis is that there was a greater social and economic distance between the rural population and the new candidates as compared to the old, and that this led to political discontinuity.

If this is the case, then certain avenues of speculation about the future become evident. One is the fact that there was a significant turnover of BDP candidates in "B" constituencies in 1989.[35] As more founders leave the scene in 1994 there may ensue a process similar to that which occurred in the "A" group. Second, if this discontinuity existed it meant that the character of the BDP as an organization changed. Whereas the founders (around whom the national party was built) came out of the social context of their constituencies, with their feet firmly planted there, now a larger pool were coming from backgrounds in the national realm with reduced ties at the grassroots level. This would explain why the BDP introduced party primary elections (the first by any party) in 1984 and institutionalized them in 1989: party primaries helped to manage the difficulties encountered in a generational changing of the guard. On the one hand the primaries provided an institutional means for the newcomers to intrude in the nominating process, particularly in constituencies where the old guard was deeply entrenched. Second, the primaries aided the creation of constituency-level legitimacy for candidates who did not automatically have that. Their selection through primary election in the constituency helped confer legitimate status within the party at that level. The primaries provided an organizational means through which these processes, often of conflict, could take place. The success of this process was not guaranteed, as the case of Mochudi showed: Ray Molomo failed to dislodge Greek Ruele in the 1984 BDP primary but did so in 1989 only to face a decrease in the number of votes cast in the rural parts of the constituency, where Ruele's "roots" were located. A key to the repeat election (mandated by the High Court in 1990), therefore, was the extent to which Ruele actively campaigned in those places, having not done so, I am informed, in the original election campaign. Ruele was prominent at the time of the launching of the repeat election campaign and was given every encouragement to "do the right thing" by getting out the vote. The increase in the BDP vote on June 30 and Molomo's slender majority of 104 votes may owe much to this.

Finally, it may be commented that this analysis also raised important questions about the opposition parties, particularly the BNF. Its "founders" always operated in the national context and only with difficulty found candidates willing and able to run for office. So it did not automatically benefit from closeness to the rural grassroots except in the narrow regional context offered by ex-chief Bathoen. The loosening of ties with the grassroots in the BDP began to level the playing field, creating new opportunities for the opposition to organize in those areas and field viable candidates. They would do well to pay close attention to this in those seats where the BDP was strongest.

☐ The 1989 Elections in Perspective

For the most part, election outcomes in 1989 were consistent with trends from 1984: increasing political party competition, the growth of the BNF as the main electoral opponent of the BDP, continuity in the class composition of the candidate pool, the loss of support for the BDP in urban areas. Two outcomes in 1989 were consistent with trends in 1984 but were inchoate at the time: the generational/factional changing of the guard in the BDP leadership and some erosion of its support in key rural areas. This continuity reflected a continuous core trajectory in the political economy of Botswana: the evolution of a mineral-led peripheral capitalist economy and polity in southern African conditions.

The analysis of the 1984 elections argued that crucial to understanding the electoral outcomes was an appreciation of (1) the underlying economic structure and attendant class relations, and (2) the political mediation of class forces that took place in the organization and process of elections. The former determined the parameters and practice of class conflict; the latter determined the directness by which class and cultural relations were reflected in the election. The organization of political parties and their activity combined with the perceptions of the electorate in its various social situations resulted in the outcome of the election event.

This perspective remained an appropriate one in reflecting back on the 1989 elections and in thinking about the future. The state's partnership with foreign mining capital continued to generate revenue, which underpinned a process of private accumulation. Incentives promoting the commoditization of production in agriculture were deeply part of state policy; the organization of state policy promoting private accumulation in the nonagricultural economy was also prominent and growing. These policies were congruent with the material interests of factions within the BDP and beyond to the governing class as a whole.

The assumption lying behind these policies continued to be that the resulting private economy, while enriching a minority, would create jobs and therefore the benefits would trickle down to the majority, so in the long run everyone would be better off. In the meantime sufficient revenue existed to extend the public infrastructure of roads, schools, water supplies, and health services to ameliorate the social impact of existing inequalities. In this way the class content of this trajectory was partially marginalized. In 1989 as in 1984 the BDP continued through these economic and political means to attract the support of crucial numbers of the growing capitalist class and important strata of the exploited classes. In rural areas, patron-client relations and the ideological and cultural subordination of women also continued to be important underpinnings for a favorable election outcome for the BDP. The BDP organization continued to be more effective than its rivals and the appeal of opposition parties to the working class and peasantry remained ambiguous. As a result the BDP continued to win, overall, substantial majorities in National Assembly elections.

The fact that the BDP continued to win electoral majorities at the national level in 1989 did not mean, however, that it had resolved the conflicts resulting from the contradictions inherent in the trajectory of change. It only meant that the BDP had been successful in managing those conflicts through a political process of mediation. In fact, this chapter highlights the continuing conflict arising from the trajectory of developing capitalism: proletarianization leading to urbanization; the continued reliance on a narrow range of minerals as the fuel for the economic engine; continuing, probably widening, gaps between the bourgeoisie and working classes. For example, the *Household Income and Expenditure Survey: 1985/86,* already referred to, reported an overall Gini coefficient of 0.556 and described an income distribution where the bottom 40 percent of households shared 10.7 percent of the total income while the top 20 percent shared 61.5 percent of the total income.

Despite good management by the BDP, electoral opposition to it increased. The BDP was on the verge of losing all of the urban areas. The only seat it won on the Gaborone City Council was the one in North East, the polling stations for which were Thornhill and Northside Schools, rather exclusive and expensive English medium schools located in an area where only the long and well established and relatively wealthy could afford to live. Urban political polarization along class lines was evident although it was not well organized or very articulate. In rural areas there was some decline in votes cast for the BDP and some evidence of a withdrawal from participation in elections in key areas of support. The conclusion I reached for the 1984 election, that "the BDP continued to cement its relationship to the peasantariat," could not be reached in an unequivocal way for 1989.[36]

What then of the multiparty system in Botswana? It remained alive and well in 1989. Given the trend toward greater electoral competitiveness, it was best to describe it not as one party and a bit, as in 1984, but as one party and a third. The combined opposition vote accounted for slightly more than one-third of the total votes. However, the BDP remained the most effective, best organized, and richest party, enjoying in addition the advantage of being a successful incumbent. While unable to eliminate the sources of opposition to it, the BDP did not give up trying to persuade opposition voters to vote for it.

The opposition parties benefited from the votes cast by those who wished to express, through that means, their unhappiness with the BDP. While opposition parties maintained a critical stance toward the BDP, they remained unable to offer a clear and consistent alternative to the organization and program of the BDP. The BIP and BPP continued their electoral decline begun in the 1974 election. These two, together with the BPU, mobilized voters largely around issues of social and economic inequality but did so through the use of regionalism and ethnicity. As a result, there continued to be limits to their ability to field candidates and attract votes beyond a narrowly confined area and population. Even within their natural constituencies, the ability of these parties to deal with the real issues of poverty, jobs, and agriculture was limited by this overlay of ethnicity and regionalism.

The BNF, on the other hand, strengthened its national position in relation to the total votes cast and in terms of some kind of national organization and program. However, its internal contradictions—seen in the leadership and in factions—absorbed a great deal of energy and limited the ability to concentrate on creating an efficient organization and consistent strategy. The split in the party in Kanye was an example, a split that probably cost the BNF at least one and possibly two seats in 1989. It is also reasonable to conclude, as evidence in this chapter suggests, that the BNF had yet to tackle systematically the question of organizing the opposition in constituencies where the BDP was strongest. Until it, or another party, did so, the likelihood of an opposition majority was slight. The "unity" talks among opposition parties did not suggest that this organization would be forthcoming.

In general, then, the social and political conditions that sustained Botswana's multiparty system in the past continued to do so during 1989. Some of the revenue from mining was used to alleviate the most destabilizing effects of the trickle-down policy. Despite inequalities, conditions for the majority in Botswana were arguably better than in most African countries and the process of accumulation did not directly depend upon the taxation and explicit repression of the peasantry, peasantariat, and proletariat. Factional struggles within the BDP showed no sign of breaking into open political warfare. The nonbourgeois classes remained without an independent political organization.

The most important potential development on the horizon seemed to be the likelihood of either stagnation or much slower growth in mineral revenue during the next few years, warnings about which were persistently made. This happened earlier, during 1981–1982, resulting in a cutback in government spending and mild contraction generally in the economy. Some of the social consequences of that reduction in revenue were arguably reflected in opposition voting in 1984. If this should again happen the political consequences could be even more drastic. As of 1991, the difference was that considerable foreign exchange reserves, built up in the intervening good years, would allow a continuation of existing expenditure levels for some time—but not indefinitely. Even during the good years, the mineral-led economy was unable to absorb the demand for employment and reasonable incomes, the drought of the mid-1980s notwithstanding. A process of wider and deeper industrialization seemed also to be unobtainable in existing circumstances. If such a decline in revenue were to materialize in the next few years, then conditions might exist for a rapid buildup of social pressure resulting in a more spontaneous and explicit politicization of the population for which the political parties would be organizationally and programmatically unprepared.

The struggles resulting from processes at work in the political economy of Botswana will shape the future just as they define the present and reflect the past. These processes of private accumulation, sustained by the state, had immediate and disadvantageous consequences for direct producers and workers and those who straddled those situations. In the past the "institutions and processes of political mediation—dominated by bourgeois class strata" were able to "blunt the otherwise sharp edge of class politics."[37] Whether these would be able to do so in the future remained, as in 1984, to be seen.

■ Notes

The research on the 1989 elections was supported by a Fulbright grant during the period May–August 1990. That research was preceded by a yearlong Fulbright research grant in 1984–1985, during which I collaborated with a team of researchers at the University of Botswana doing a study of the 1984 elections. A follow-up research trip in 1987 was supported by a research grant from the College of Charleston. I would like to acknowledge the support of these agencies. The description of 1989 elections outcomes is substantially based on a paper written in Botswana in 1990, some of which may appear as a postscript in an as-yet-unpublished manuscript on the 1984 general elections.

1. The first Legislative Assembly election was held in 1965. District and town council elections were first held in June 1966 shortly before independence in September. The national assembly election of 1969 was called earlier than the constitutionally prescribed maximum interval of five years. The cabinet decided to hold elections for local government simultaneously with National Assembly elections in 1969. The practice of holding these elections simultaneously continued in all subsequent elections in 1974, 1979, 1984, and 1989.

2. Unless otherwise noted in this chapter, the data on candidates and elections outcomes were compiled and calculated from the following sources: Botswana National Archives, "Botswana General Elections"; Office of the President, I/10/3086, H 4/10 I; Central Statistics Office; Ministry of Development Planning, *Statistical Abstract 1967* (Gaborone: The Government Printer, n.d.); W.J.A. Macartney, "The General Election of 1969," *Botswana Notes and Records* 3 (1971): 32–37; Supervisor of Elections, *Report on the General Elections 1969* (Gaborone: The Government Printer, 1970); Supervisor of Elections, *Report to the Minister of State on the General Elections, 1974* (Gaborone: The Government Printer, n.d.);

Supervisor of Elections, *Report to the Minister of Public Service and Information on the General Election, 1979* (Gaborone: The Government Printer, n.d.); Supervisor of Elections, *Report to the Minister of Public Service and Information on the General Elections, 1984* (Gaborone: The Government Printer, n.d.); and Supervisor of Elections, *Report to the Minister of Presidential Affairs and Public Administration on the General Election, 1989* (Gaborone: The Government Printer, n.d.).

3. The Botswana National Front consistently claimed that the BDP rigged elections and on several occasions took results to court. On a few occasions, often on technical irregularities, results were overturned and reelections held, but in none of these cases was evidence presented that the elections were systematically manipulated. On rarer occasions the BDP went to court complaining of irregularities in local government seats where it had lost.

4. Ralph Miliband, *Capitalist Democracy in Britain* (New York: Oxford University Press, 1984), 20.

5. Charles Lindblom, *Politics and Markets: The World's Political Economic Systems* (New York: Basic Books, 1977), 5.

6. Summarized in part in the collection of papers presented at the symposium on democracy in Botswana held in 1988 and sponsored by the Botswana Society and the University of Botswana. John Holm and Patrick Molutsi, eds., *Democracy in Botswana* (Gaborone: Macmillan Botswana Publishing Company on behalf of the Botswana Society and the University of Botswana, 1989).

7. See Jack Parson, Lionel Cliffe, and Ranbwedzi Nengwekhulu, eds., "The 1984 Botswana General Elections: Class Politics and Competitive Elections," the 1984 University of Botswana Election Study Project (manuscript).

8. The BNF won Gaborone North, Gaborone South, and the Okavango constituencies. The other two historically important opposition parties, the Botswana People's Party (BPP) and Botswana Independence Party (BIP), continued to decline, reaching in 1989 their lowest proportion of the vote. The BPP won 4.3 percent of the total votes and the BIP won 2.4 percent. The Botswana Progressive Union, formed in 1984, won .9 percent of the vote. The Botswana Freedom Party (BFP), formed by Leach Tlhomelang in Kanye as the result of a split in the BNF there, won .5 percent and the Botswana Labour Party (BLP) won .02 percent of the total vote.

9. Francistown, North East, Mochudi, Kanye, and Selibi-Phikwe. The BNF successfully challenged the Mochudi election in the High Court on the grounds that the hours of voting had been extended to accommodate the long line of prospective voters, in contravention of the electoral law. The seat was declared vacant. The reelection was held on June 30, 1990. Ray Molomo of the BDP won with a majority of 104 and 50.9 percent of the vote. The BDP successfully petitioned the High Court in the cases of two local government seats won by the BPP and BNF. In the case of the seat won by the BNF (Woodhall in Lobatse), the basis for the BDP petition was the illegal extension of voting hours, the same grounds brought by the BNF in Mochudi.

10. The Okavango region, North East region, and in and around Kanye in the Ngwaketse District.

11. The estimate of the eligible population in 1989 is necessarily a rough one. It is based on the projected age distribution contained in the *Statistical Bulletin*, vol. 14, no. 3, September 1989 (Gaborone: The Central Statistics Office, 1990), 2. The figure was arrived at by adding to the number of persons 25 years and older 80 percent of the 20–24-year-old age group. The number of registered voters reported here is 890 less than figures published in the report of the supervisor of elections. In

compiling the data on the gender distribution of the registered electorate, a small number of addition errors was found in the published figures. The difference had no effect on the elections' outcomes or on the voters' roll itself but marginally affected the published turnout figures in certain cases.

12. The raw data for Table 5.1 was compiled by the author and Mr. Fathazia Lenyatso and is archived with the Democracy Project at the University of Botswana. The cooperation and help of Mr. M. M. K. Molefe and his staff at the Office of the Supervisor of Elections is enthusiastically acknowledged.

13. There were rural exceptions to the rule in the Okavango and the North East, where the BDP received less than half the vote. An interesting urban example was the North East polling district in Gaborone, the only one won by the BDP, where 60.5 percent of the registered voters were female, while only 38.6 percent of the registered voters in the Gaborone South constituency as a whole were women.

14. *Statistical Bulletin,* September 1989, 1. Results from the 1991 census indicated that the total population had grown to 1,325,000 and that the population of Gaborone had grown to 134,000, or just over 10 percent of the population. The population of Gaborone in 1981 was 59,660 and the total population was 941,000. Gaborone in 1981 accounted for about 6.3 percent of the population. The 1991 census results were reported in *Mmegi/The Reporter,* vol. 8, no. 38, October 4–10, 1991, 2.

15. A discussion of this term in this context is found in Jack Parson, *Botswana: Liberal Democracy and the Labor Reserve in Southern Africa* (Boulder, Colo.: Westview, 1984), and Jack Parson, "The Peasantariat and Politics: Migration, Wage Labor and Agriculture in Botswana," *Africa Today* 31, no. 4 (1984): 5–25.

16. See Ornulf Gulbrandsen, *When Land Becomes Scarce* (Bergen, Norway: Bergen Studies in Social Anthropology, no. 33, 1984).

17. (Gaborone: The Central Statistics Office, 1988).

18. *Statistical Bulletin,* September 1989, 29 and 37.

19. *Labour Statistics 1988* (Gaborone: The Central Statistics Office, 1989), 22.

20. In Francistown, the BDP won a majority of 8 out of 13 seats but half of these seats were won on a plurality vote. The BDP lost 4 seats out of 10 in Selibi-Phikwe and lost its majority in Lobatse. In the capital, the BDP lost all of the 13 seats except for one. This was a dramatic reversal from a decade earlier when in 1979 the BDP won 7 of the 8 seats on the Gaborone Town Council.

21. In Lobatse Town Council elections, the BDP won only 50.3 percent of the vote. The inclusion of the rural Barolong Farms, historically an area of strong BDP support, in the constituency diluted opposition voting. This was a situation that would have to be looked at after the 1991 census and subsequent redelimitation of constituencies.

22. On these grounds alone, it is very difficult to entertain the assertion of Harvey and Lewis that urban opposition voting reflected a significant and successful rural bias and urban neglect in government programs: "The government's commitment to programmes and policies which benefited the rural majority, the Botswana Democratic Party's principle constituents, was critical. Indeed, the policies were carried out with sufficient purpose that the BDP began losing seats in urban areas, both in Parliament and in town councils, by the 1980s." Charles Harvey and Stephen R. Lewis, Jr., *Policy Choice and Development Performance in Botswana* (London: Macmillan and OECD, 1990), 47.

23. Parson, Cliffe, and Nengwekhulu, *The 1984 Botswana General Elections,* 171.

24. I include Kweneng East here although the number of votes cast there

increased by 23, or .5 percent. No other constituency had an increase of less than 3 percent. The Kweneng East result fits most closely the pattern of decline.

25. The resulting hierarchy was one of several tiers reaching down to the poorest of the poor, those currently called Remote Area Dwellers, or San, usually referred to with the more derogatory name Basarwa. "Inequities in the overall political economy of Botswana reproduce the structural deprivation of a rural underclass deprived of a market for its labor, thus of the means of exchange necessary to achieve balanced household budgets. These inequities, themselves a modern legacy of the history of deprivation we have witnessed, have brought about current poverty at CaeCae and throughout those areas called remote." (Edwin Wilmsen, *Land Filled With Flies: A Political Economy of the Kalahari* [Chicago: The University of Chicago Press, 1989], 303; see particularly Chapter 7, "What It Means to Be Excluded").

26. The five were: O. I. Chilume, L. Makgekgenene, M. P. K. Nwako, G. K. Koma, and E. S. Masisi.

27. I do not wish to underestimate the financial problems of opposition parties operating in rural areas. They are at a distinct disadvantage in relation to the BDP. See Mpho Molomo, "The Political Process: Does Multi-partyism Persist Due to the Lack of a Strong Opposition?" *Southern Africa Political & Economic Monthly* 3, no. 7 (May 1990): 9.

28. These speculations will remain just that, speculations, without additional research, which needs to be done at a grassroots level, in electoral terms in the polling districts and constituencies. Systematic research on the parameters of peasantariat and proletariat life in rural areas (and in urban areas for that matter) is time-consuming and requires extended residence, but is necessary to deepen analysis of political life. Elections' outcome data, government reports, visits during elections, and onetime surveys—the kind of data upon which this book is based—are important, but given the direction of the resulting analysis, they lead to the conclusion that in-depth constituency research is an urgent priority.

29. See, for example, Neil Parsons, "The Idea of Democracy and the Emergence of an Educated Elite in Botswana, 1931–1960," in *Botswana—Education, Culture and Politics,* proceedings of a conference held at the Centre of African Studies, University of Edinburgh, December 15–16, 1988 (Edinburgh: Centre of African Studies, University of Edinburgh, n.d.), 175–197.

30. The BNF continued to call for an all-party mechanism to conduct elections and blamed rigging for its defeat in 1989. See *Botswana Guardian,* July 20, 1990, 1 and 4.

31. For example, Mmusi, Mogwe, Kedikilwe, Magang, and Sebego, joined in the cabinet by specially elected members such as Merafhe and Mogae.

32. See Patrick Molutsi, "The Ruling Class and Democracy in Botswana," and his "Whose Interests Do Botswana's Politicians Represent," both in Holm and Molutsi, *Democracy in Botswana,* 103–114 and 120–131, respectively. See also Ranbwedzi Nengwekhulu, "Class, State, Politics and Elections in Postcolonial Botswana: The 1984 General Election," in Parson, Cliffe, and Nengwekhulu, *The 1984 Botswana General Elections,* for an analysis of the composition of the governing class.

33. These were Maun/Chobe, Sebina and Gweta, Nkange, Tonota, Tswapong North, Tswapong South, Mahalapye, Molepolole, and Kweneng West.

34. A pattern of candidate turnover similar to the "A" group existed in the eight constituencies where the BDP has consistently faced significant opposition. There, the average was 3.6 candidates per constituency from 1965–1989. Those constituencies were: Okavango, North East, Francistown, Mochudi, Ngwaketse

South, Kanye, Ngwaketse West, and the Gaborone/Ramotswa-Gaborone–Gaborone North and South constituencies. The "new" candidates in the "A" group were: G. Masusu, P. Kedikilwe, W. Mosweu, J. Mauratona, Roy Blackbeard, G. Chiepe, Ester Mosinyi, David Magang, and Peter Mmusi. The "old" candidates in the "B" group were: D. Monwela, M. Maswikiti, O. Chilume, L. Makgekgenene, M. Nwako, G. Sebeso, G. Koma, and D. Kwelagobe.

35. The new candidates were K.B. Temane, R. Ndwapi and P. Seloma.

36. Jack Parson, "The 1984 Botswana General Elections: Outcomes and Issues," in Parson, Cliffe, and Nengwekhulu, *The 1984 Botswana General Elections*, 93.

37. Ibid.

6

Political Culture and Democracy: A Study of Mass Participation in Botswana

John D. Holm

Democratic government in modern societies means that open and tolerant discussion of issues results in decisionmaking with significant responsiveness to the opinion expressed. Critical to making this system work is energetic and substantial citizen participation in voting, political parties, and interest groups. The degree of such participation required or possible is a debatable issue,[1] but students of African politics generally agree that most if not all states on the continent need more citizen involvement, and that this goal will not easily be achieved nor will it be extensively accomplished.[2]

The prevailing perspective in political science is that a general process of social mobilization accompanies the expansion of citizen participation. In the process citizens develop more sophisticated levels of political cognition, increase their commitment to democratic values, and expand influential activities directed toward the political elite.[3] Critical to this transformation is the proliferation of organized groups that inform their members on public affairs and socialize them to become active in politics.[4] Economic growth sustains group proliferation by providing a wider distribution of education, mass communication, and income to the mass of the population, thus making individuals available for mobilization and capable of participation.

Two basic questions are raised by this perspective. One is whether social mobilization is the only means by which a participant culture can be created to sustain a liberal democracy. Is it necessary that social and economic modernization provide a resource and skill base? Might not political circumstances be sufficient to mobilize a citizenry to participate in terms of voting and involvement in parties and interest groups? A second question is whether social mobilization leads to political liberalization without certain other relatively autonomous transformations also taking place. For instance, could development of a sense of nationhood or the emergence of a universalistic as opposed to a personalistic state be necessary before the socially mobilized see the necessity of becoming politically active?[5]

This chapter explores these issues in the context of Botswana, which has experienced over two decades of substantial social mobilization but has concomitantly enjoyed a sustained period of multiparty electoral politics. At first glance this country would seem an ideal environment for the process of social mobilization to work its effect on citizen participation. Since independence in 1966, Botswana has experienced rapid economic growth (over 10 percent per annum in real terms), a steady expansion of the formal educational system (from one with only a scattering of primary schools to the point where most children attend school free for ten years), and a blooming of public and private mass media (in 1991 there were five weekly newspapers at the national level). In Africa, Botswana's record of combined social and economic mobilization over the last twenty years is probably unmatched. According to the theory, in this country of all on the continent social mobilization should bring an expanding participant stratum committed to democratic ideals and acting upon their commitments.

The increasing voter turnout in Botswana over the last two decades would seem to support this conclusion. Among eligible voters turnout has gone from 21 percent in 1974 to 37 percent in 1979, and then to more than 50 percent in both elections in the 1980s.[6] However, such a correspondence of aggregate data on social and political change does not in itself establish that mobilization is working at the individual level to promote the new citizen behavior. Effective political party mobilization at the grassroots is an alternative possibility; traditional leaders may use their prestige to spark the turnout of their followers; or highly emotional political issues may galvanize citizens to take part in the voting process.

Many political observers in Botswana have been skeptical that the increase in the percentage of people voting is reflective of the emergence of a socially mobilized participant stratum capable of influencing elected officials. Following various forms of logic, they conclude that social mobilization in Botswana has yet to have much behavioral impact. Their arguments reflect a number of prominent hypotheses on the forces preventing the rise of a participant culture in the Third World.

One hypothesis is that the development of organized group life outside of politics creates a participant political culture regardless of the extent of social mobilization.[7] From this perspective, I have suggested that in Botswana interest groups lack the resources, organization, and motivation to become active in various aspects of politics, from elections to lobbying with politicians.[8] In such a context, where group politics is underdeveloped, it is likely that those belonging to organized social groups, even if they are socially mobilized, will not show any more support for or involvement in the new democratic institutions than the rest of the population.

Some political scientists have long held that democracy requires institutions of socialization to inculcate democratic norms.[9] In Botswana, the leaders of the major parties have taken this idea very seriously and invested considerable time and effort in training seminars on various aspects of democratic government, particularly for those associated with their organizations. Some political observers, including most prominently Rwendezi Nengwekhulu, contend that this effort has been a failure in terms of both party cadres and the general membership, let alone in terms of the effect on the general public.[10] From this perspective, political parties are elite organizations that benefit themselves but have not educated their followers. The parties may have created partisanship, but this loyalty has not been accompanied by a transformation of the political culture.

A prominent thesis in recent analyses of the Third World is that political elites offer no incentives for mass involvement. Rather they promote the exit of the citizenry from politics and government.[11] Some have attributed this absence of incentives to government policies that so frustrate producers that they avoid all aspects of modern government; alternatively, the political elite may adopt a strategy of departicipation actually to stifle citizen political action.[12] In Botswana, the contention has been that citizens are not motivated to participate in mass political structures because politicians do not debate or decide important issues; instead, top bureaucrats perform this function through secretive interministerial conflicts.[13] Since politicians tend to be unconcerned with policies, they do not mobilize attentive publics with respect to political issues. Thus there is little or no association between awareness of and concern about political issues, nor between citizen support for and participation in democratic political structures.

Still another school contends that economic growth does not bring citizen mobilization but rather political alienation of those impoverished by the social change taking place.[14] Since the state supports this process, the alienated withdraw from the political system. With respect to Botswana, Jack Parson argues in Chapter 5 and elsewhere that those remaining in the rural areas have "become alienated from [electoral] participation."[15] In the urban areas, on the other hand, he thinks participation has not declined significantly because there are articulate opposition parties to voice the feelings of the alienated.

There are students of political development who argue that some local cultures will sustain citizen involvement in modern political systems regardless of the degree of social mobilization.[16] Many in Botswana agree with this perspective. Thus, it is argued that Tswana culture, particularly the *kgotla* (the traditional village forum for communal decisionmaking), has led to the public being able to adjust easily to participation in the new liberal democratic structures established at independence. Leonard Ngcongco reflects this perspective when stating that Botswana's traditional culture teaches "the people the necessity of observing and participating in their own governance."[17] If this is the case, then those most likely to be active in the traditional system (i.e., those who are older or who participate in the *kgotla*) should be the ones most inclined to support and to participate in the new democratic institutions.

The analysis that follows has two objectives. First, it explores the extent to which social mobilization in Botswana has resulted in the development of a mass participant culture supportive of a liberal democratic system. Second, it examines whether the alternative hypotheses for the promotion or retardation of a participant culture help to explain present levels of citizen perception and activity in Botswana.

The argument presented is as follows: Social mobilization has succeeded in promoting a cognitive awareness of the new democratic polity and in stimulating an acceptance of the new system, but it has had almost no impact on behavior except for stimulating some engagement with autonomous groups. Rather, traditional culture, partisanship, and an attentive public have been critical factors supporting behavioral involvement in politics. Some exit from politics takes place among the socially mobilized who have no desire to return on a permanent basis to their home villages. Finally, alienation reduces participation only with respect to party membership but mostly in urban areas.

■ Data

No one has collected a data set explicitly designed to test the above hypotheses; however, two recent large-scale surveys by the Democracy Research Project include questions at least somewhat related to all the variables involved. Project staff administered the first survey in August and September 1987 and the second at the same time in 1989.[18] The former focused on all aspects of political involvement, from information about and support for the democratic system to various forms of participation. The 1989 survey concentrates on participation, particularly with respect to the October elections that followed later that year.

The sample for the 1987 survey came from the three southern districts (Kgatleng, Kweneng, and Ngwaketse) and from the capital city of Gaborone. A quota of persons within randomly selected census enumeration districts was interviewed. The total sample is 1,297.

The 1989 survey is more extensive in terms of geographic coverage, involving the sampling of fourteen of the country's thirty-four election districts. The districts chosen represent varying degrees of partisan competition, ethnic composition, and urbanization. Interviewers were given quotas of various socioeconomic groups to contact. The sample numbers 2,874.

Generally the socioeconomic distributions of the samples correspond to those of the populations from which they were drawn.[19] However, both surveys have limitations. The 1987 survey concentrated on Tswana areas, though it does have at least 100 remote area dwellers. The 1989 survey sampled more minority areas, but it probably underrepresents the remote areas.

■ Operationalization of Variables

□ Independent Variables

The 1987 survey taps social mobilization with the following variables: urban residence, years of education, ability to speak and write English, employment status, reading a newspaper the previous week, and access to water (i.e., whether indoor plumbing, a nearby standpipe, or a borehole). In the 1989 questionnaire, social mobilization indicators included education, reading the *Daily News* at least occasionally, mention of reading one of the private newspapers, listening to political radio programs, urban residence, and employment status.

Variables contained in the hypotheses explaining the lack of social mobilization or the traditional foundations of participation are operationalized as follows:

1. Organized group membership is measured by respondents indicating their involvement in a list of groups mentioned by the interviewer. In 1987 those delineated were cooperatives, agricultural extension groups, churches, trade unions, parent-teacher associations, women's groups, borehole syndicates, or others recalled by the respondent. The 1989 list, more limited, included trade unions, the Botswana Christian Council, the YWCA, cooperatives, and any other group named by the respondent.[20]

2. Traditional political culture indicators in 1987 were attending meetings at the *kgotla* (often, sometimes, not at all), having spoken at the *kgotla* in the last year, still living in the district of birth, and age; in the 1989 survey there were only *kgotla* attendance (always, very often, often, once in a while, never) and age.

3. Partisanship in 1987 included engaging in one of a number of party activities, party membership (attending party meetings regularly or sometimes), and expression of support for one of Botswana's parties; in 1989 the items were party membership, attendance at freedom squares (the name given to political party rallies in Botswana), and having been helped by the local member of Parliament (MP) with some problem.

4. The attentive public was tapped in the 1987 survey by whether respondents could name a specific difference between the BDP and the

BNF, and whether they could name an issue that was presently being discussed or had been raised recently either in Parliament or in their local council. In 1989 the indicators were two questions asking whether the respondent could name important local or national problems.

5. Alienation, measured only in 1989, was based upon whether the respondent thought government development programs benefited the people, and whether the upcoming elections would benefit either his/her household or community.[21]

□ *The Participant Culture*

The 1987 survey probes three aspects of citizen participation: political awareness, support of the new political system, and behavioral involvement in politics. Political awareness is covered with three questions asking the names of the respondent's councillor, member of Parliament, and local council president (or in the case of Gaborone, the mayor). Support for the liberal democratic system is examined by asking respondents whether they think politicians are better problem solvers than chiefs or bureaucrats, whether they prefer a multiparty system to one party or none, whether they like elections more than the chieftaincy as a form of government, whether they see groups as the best method of influencing elected officials (as opposed to the *kgotla* or patrons), whether they believe that the chiefs listened to the people more in the past than the politicians do today, and whether they believe minorities and youth have a right to speak up at the *kgotla*. As participation indicators, the 1987 survey counts party membership, involvement in party activities, support of one party over the others, and membership in a politically active group.

The 1989 data set contains only participation indicators: registration for the upcoming election, voting in 1984, and party and group membership.[22]

■ Data Analysis

The data analysis focuses on the extent to which each of the above six sets of independent variables (social mobilization, organized group membership, attentive public, partisanship, alienation, and traditional political culture) are associated with the three sets of participation indicators (political information, democratic preferences, and mass participation). The discussion proceeds by examining separately each of the three groups of dependent variables.[23]

All the data are ordinal or have been recoded to be so. The preferred measure of strength of association for such data is the correlation coefficient called Kendall's tau.[24] Tau varies between plus and minus one, with zero being no association.[25]

☐ Political Information

Table 6.1 is based on the 1987 survey and presents the correlates of the three political information variables (knowledge of the name of respondent's MP, councillor, and council president/mayor) with indicators for five of the independent variables. There is evidence of a strong social mobilization effect with respect to ability to name one's MP and council president. In addition, these two information indicators have some association, though nowhere near the social mobilization level, with the attentive public variables. Traditional culture also has an impact in terms of its most

Table 6.1 Correlates of Political Information (Tau B or C), N = 1,186

	Know MP	Know Councillor	Know Council Pres. or Mayor
Social Mobilization			
Urban resident	.10	−.23	.48
Education	.29		.46
Speak and write English	.25		.42
Employed	.16		.36
Read newspaper previous week	.22		.54
Access to water	.20		.38
Traditional Participation			
Born in district		.11	−.33
Age			−.12
Attend *kgotla*			
(regular/some/none)	.18	.15	.10
Speak at *kgotla*	.14		.20
Attended *kgotla*			
where councillor spoke	.16	.20	
Attentive Public			
Name issue being discussed			
in council or Parliament	.15		.20
Know difference between parties	.11	.12	.22
Interest Group			
Group membership	.14	.20	.13
Partisanship			
Political activist		.16	.12
Party member		.12	.15
Party supporter		.11	

Note: All correlations in this table are significant at p <= .001. Correlations below .10 have been omitted to improve the readability of the table.

intense level of involvement: those who speak up at the *kgotla* are also informed about their MP and council president.

Knowledge of the councillor, on the other hand, is related to a more locally based cluster of variables, specifically participation in a party organization, the *kgotla,* and organized groups. This knowledge is much stronger in the rural areas than in the towns, especially with persons still living in the villages of their birth.

The 1987 data suggest there are at least two separate information acquisition systems in Botswana, one focused on the national polity and the other attuned to village networks. The former is very much based on skills resulting from social mobilization and shows an awareness of political figures who interact with the national government. The village information system, on the other hand, depends on the more personalized contacts of local party organizations and traditional participation forums, particularly the *kgotla,* and is attentive to the elected official most in personal contact with the local citizenry (i.e., the councillor).

□ *Democratic Preferences*

Table 6.2 reports on citizen attitudes of support for a democratic approach to government as it has taken shape in postindependence Botswana. The first six columns reflect a choice between aspects of the new system of competitive elections and a noncompetitive or traditional Tswana approach. All six show a strong association between support for the democratic system and the social mobilization indicators. The partisanship and the attentive public variables reflect some connections with the six democratic support items as well, but much less than with that of social mobilization. Without question social mobilization is bringing a change in support from the traditional system to the postindependence liberal democracy.

According to theory, social mobilization entails increasing geographic movement by those affected by its processes. If this is the case, it seems likely that the various indicators of social mobilization might have a stronger impact on preference for the modern system among those residing outside their home district than those still living in it. The former would have much less opportunity to obtain political advantage through the traditional system, which operates on the basis of long-standing personalistic ties. This hypothesis proves very powerful in terms of the impact of social mobilization on preference for a group approach to political influence (columns 4 and 5 of Table 6.2). Table 6.3 reports the results. The two indicators of preference for group politics indicators (one concerning the MP and the other the councillors) are only related to social mobilization among respondents living *outside* their home districts (columns 2 and 5 of Table 6.3). Those who have not moved (columns 3 and 6) show almost no association of social mobilization with believing the best way to influence one's leaders is through organized groups. This same pattern did not occur with respect to the connection of the social mobilization variables with any of the other democratic preference items.

In contrast to social mobilization, traditional culture factors (in terms of living in one's home district and age) have a consistent negative association to the democratic preference items in Table 6.2. Thus, those who are regular participants in the traditional system have not come to accept the new liberal democracy as legitimate. In this context, the government's

Table 6.2 Correlates of Democratic Preferences (Tau B or C), N = 1,186

	Best Problem Solver: Pols/ Bureaucrats/ Chiefs	Prefer Multi-Party System	Prefer Elections to Chieftaincy	Prefer Group Approach MP	Prefer Group Approach Councillor	Chief Listens More Than Pols	Allow Youth or Minority to Speak in *Kgotla*
Social Mobilization							
Urban resident	.10	.25	.19	.17	.13	.16	
Education	.12	.31	.26	.21	.23	−.20	
Speak and write English	.12	.30	.26	.19	.21	−.27	
Employed		.23	.20	.16	.15	−.19	
Read newspaper previous week	.10	.34	.24	.17	.18	−.19	
Access to water		.28	.11	.14	.14	−.12	
Traditional Participation							
Born in district		−.19	−.12	−.13	−.12	.15	
Age		−.10	−.21	−.10	−.11	.14	−.12
Attend *kgotla* (regular/some/ none)	.10						
Speak at *kgotla*		.21	.12				−.19
Attend *kgotla* where councillor spoke							
Attentive Public							
Name issue being discussed in council or Parliament	.10	.16	.13				
Know difference between parties		.14	.16			-.13	
Interest Group							
Group membership	.12						
Partisanship							
Political activist				.10	.13	−.10	
Party member		.10	.12	.15	.15	−.24	
Party supporter	.10	.10				−.10	

Note: All correlations in this table are significant at p <=.01. Correlations below .10 have been omitted to improve the readability of the table.

Table 6.3 Correlates of Preference for Groups: Controlling for Residence Inside or
Outside Home District (Tau B or C)

	MP Best Influenced by Group Politics			Councilor Best Influenced by Group		
	Total Sample[a] N=1,186	If Living Outside Home District[a] N=400	If Living Inside Home District N=782	Total Sample[a] N=1,186	If Living Outside Home District[a] N=400	If Living Inside Home District N=782
Education	.21	.40	.03	.23	.41	.08
Speak and write English	.19	.30	.05	.21	.32	.10
Employed	.16	.32	.00	.15	.31	.00
Read newspaper	.17	.24	.05	.18	.27	.05
Access to water	.14	.29	-.03	.14	.31	-.03

Note: a. All correlations in these columns are significant at p <=.001.

persistent use of traditional political structures, particularly the *kgotla,* to
approve the implementation of new national policies in a local area makes a
lot of sense in terms of mobilizing the acceptance of this traditional segment of the population.

The only strong support for the new system among traditionalists is
that those speaking up in the *kgotla* prefer the multiparty system. This is
not surprising in that often supporters of the traditional polity in Botswana
turn to opposition parties to express their rejection of the national government and its policies.

The variable reported in the last column in Table 6.2 is different in
kind from the others. It concerns the right of minorities and youth to speak
up in the *kgotla.* Neither the socially mobilized, the partisans, nor the attentive public are more inclined than other citizens to give a democratic
response. As has been shown in developed countries, willingness to grant
political rights to low-status groups is often not related to education, commitment to general democratic principles, or high-status employment.[26]
Thus, that the democratic value reflected in the last column is not related to
social mobilization, let alone to the other correlates of democratic support,
is not surprising.

One independent variable in Table 6.2 does show a definite association
with rejecting participation of youth and minorities in the *kgotla.*
Respondents who speak up in the *kgotla* tend to feel that members of these
two low-status groups should not also have the right to voice their opinions
(correlation = -.19). Thus, while the *kgotla* has become a critical vehicle
for village discussion of local policy questions, those who have dominated
it resist applying the principle of freedom of speech, supposedly the principle enshrined in *kgotla* tradition, to any but those who have traditionally
been included. In this respect, the *kgotla* political culture is not democratic.

In summary, with respect to commitment to the new democratic struc-

tures, social mobilization has a powerful effect. At the same time, traditional prejudice against certain excluded groups participating in politics
remains, at least with respect to the *kgotla*. This is probably one reason that
the socially mobilized who are living outside their home districts, and who
are also not especially welcome in the *kgotla,* develop a strong preference
for a group approach to politics. Whether they act on this preference is, as
we shall see, a different matter.

☐ *Mass Participation*

Tables 6.4 and 6.5 present correlates of the six sets of the independent variables with mass participation indicators in the 1987 and 1989 surveys
respectively. Both tables show the same basic pattern: social mobilization
has little relation to political activities, ranging from the more high-

Table 6.4 Correlates of Mass Participation (1987) (Tau B and C)

	Group Member[a]	Party Activist	Party Member	Party Supporter
Social Mobilization				
Urban resident	.10			
Education				
Speak and write English	.13			
Employed	.17			
Read newspaper				
previous week	.10			
Access to water	.12			
Traditional Participation				
Born in district				
Age				.10
Attend *kgotla*				
(regular/some/none)			.13	.13
Speak at *kgotla*	.11	.15		.11
Attend *kgotla* where				
councillor spoke		.17	.16	.12
Attentive Public				
Name issue being				
discussed in				
Parliament or council	.14	.11	.13	.10
Know difference				
between parties	.15	.20	.22	.27
Interest group				
Group member[a]			.29	.11

Notes: All correlations in this table are significant at p <=.001. Correlations below .10
have been omitted to improve the readability of the table.
     a. This variable has been made roughly equivalent to the group variable in Table 6.5. See
footnote 20 for details.

Table 6.5 Correlates of Mass Participation (1989) (Tau B or C)

	Registration N=2,874	Voted '84 N=2,357	Party Member N=2,874	Group Member N=2,874
Social Mobilization				
Education				.18
Read daily news				.19
Listen to political program (radio)				
Employed		−.10		.17
Read private newspaper				.18
Urban				
Traditional Culture				
Attend *kgotla*	.21	.21	.20	
Age	.22	.29	.19	
Attentive Public				
Concerned about local issue				.11
Concerned about national issue				.11
Interest Group				
Group member		.10	.13	
Partisanship				
Party member	.22	.19		.13
Helped by MP	.13			
Attend freedom square	.21	.18	.29	.11
Alienation/Satisfaction				
Development doesn't benefit people				
Election won't bring change to household			−.13	
Election won't bring change to community			−.11	

Note: All correlations in this table are significant at p <= .001. Correlations below .10 have been omitted to improve the readability of the table.

Table 6.6 Correlates of Participation: Controlling for Desire to Build in Home Village (Tau B and C)

	Education	Read *Daily News*	Read Pvt. Newspaper
Registration			
Total sample N=2,874	−.08	−.04	−0.4
Will not build at home[a] N=849	−.16	−.15	−.15
Will build at home N=2,120	−.04	.01	.00
Voted in 1984			
Total sample N=2,281	−.08	−.07	−.06
Will not build at home[a] N=675	−.16	−.15	−.12
Will build at home N=1,547	−.04	−.03	−.03
Party Member			
Total sample N=2,874	−.03	−.02	−.04
Will not build at home[a] N=835	−.12	−.13	−.12
Will build at home N=1,865	.01	.02	.01

Note: a. All correlations in these rows are significant at p <= .001.

intensity items like party support, membership, and activism, to such low-involvement forms as registration and voting. Those Batswana whom we identified as socially mobilized, while informed about national politicians and strongly valuing liberal democratic government, show no more inclination than the rest of the population to get involved in the new system. The only exception to this generalization is that social mobilization does produce in both samples a definite inclination to join politically oriented groups. In effect. social mobilization has supported the expansion of organized interest groups that act as representatives of citizens, but these groups have not yet motivated their socially mobilized members for political involvement.[27]

An important finding of the previous section was that among those who did not reside in their home districts, the socially mobilized had a strong preference for a group approach to politics over involvement with traditional structures. It would thus seem likely that in this same subgroup social mobilization would have a particularly strong effect on group membership. No such result appeared. The average increase in association of the six social mobilization variables with the group membership indicator was only .03 higher for those living outside their home areas than for those living inside.

The most consistent finding revealed in Tables 6.4 and 6.5 relative to mass behavior in Botswana is that political participation in terms of registering, voting, and various partisanship dimensions is associated with participation in the traditional system (i.e., those who are older and are participants in the *kgotla*). The 1987 survey shows also that the attentive public, i.e., those aware of issues being discussed in Parliament and the councils and those aware of the differences between the parties, are very much party activists, members, and supporters. Finally, the 1989 survey provides strong evidence that partisanship correlates with registration and voting. In summary, the overall picture that emerges from the two Democracy Research Project surveys is that traditional culture, partisanship, and attentiveness to political issues drive grassroots political participation in Botswana, not social mobilization.

The gap between value preferences of the socially mobilized and their actual behavior is striking. It may be that satisfaction of the socially mobilized with the political system, given the steady rate of economic growth (among other things), is such that members of this group do not feel inspired to participate. Almond and Verba, for instance, have offered such an explanation for low participation in Western democracies.[28] If this is the case, indicators of satisfaction with the new Botswana political system should show some negative relation to participation. Parson, it will be remembered, hypothesizes that the reverse is the case, namely, the alienated participate less in the case of registration and voting. Parson, to be sure, only makes his case with respect to rural people who are the most disadvantaged (i.e., the least socially mobilized).

This issue of the impact of alienation and satisfaction on political behavior is addressed in the bottom section of Table 6.6. Neither a satisfaction nor an alienation effect appears to be present. The two associations that are present support the idea that party membership is related to a belief that the elections will bring positive change to the respondent's household and community. This confirms Parson's hypothesis (and rejects the satisfaction thesis) but only with respect to party membership. Interestingly, however, these two alienation indicators have a much stronger connection with party membership in the cities than in the countryside.[29] Thus, the 1989 data only show compelling evidence of alienation in the cities, and then only with respect to party membership.[30]

If neither satisfaction nor alienation explains the lack of a social mobilization effect on mass participation, there is a need to probe further for what could be the blocking factor(s). Since traditional participation is important, one possibility is that an interaction effect exists between traditional culture and social mobilization. We saw in the previous section that only the socially mobilized who live outside their home districts have a clear preference for a group approach to politics over the traditional one. This same segment of the population may actually reject the idea of getting involved in grassroots aspects of democratic politics because of its highly traditional or communal character. To explore this possibility, a control (whether the respondent had built or intended to build a house in his or her home village) was introduced into the 1989 survey. It seemed possible that persons not wanting to return home on a permanent basis and socially mobilized would be looking for forms of participation less likely to be dominated by traditional community leaders than the election process. They thus might tend to turn their back on registration and voting.

The results are consistent with this explanation. As shown in Table 6.6, the socially mobilized who do not want to return to their home districts are inclined not to register, not to vote, and not to become party members, whereas among those who have built or want to build in their home villages, almost no association exists. Botswana thus shows some evidence of a special kind of "exit" from politics occurring in its villages. The socially mobilized who do not want to return home to live tend to stay out of grassroots politics.

■ Summary and Conclusions

Botswana is in transition to a more participatory culture. Social mobilization is changing the perceptual political world of the citizenry. Those who experience education, mass communications, and employment in the market economy are much more aware than their fellow citizens of the national polity and supportive of the new structures that have been

put in place. The postcolonial state is acquiring a new basis of legitimacy.

This socially mobilized group is not, however, more active in the mass
level politics of the new system than the rest of the population, except for
having some proclivity to join organized interest groups. There are several
reasons for this lack of political mobilization. One, which we did not
explore above, is that a considerable segment of socially mobilized is
employed by government directly or in parastatals. By law, government
employees cannot run for office or engage in most partisan activities.
Moreover, many employees of government, including those in parastatals,
believe that BDP politicians will seek to damage their careers if they participate in opposition politics.[31] If the state did not employ large numbers,
probably over 50 percent of those with more than a junior certificate (nine
years of school), this demobilization would not be so critical. In effect,
massive expansion of the state over the last two decades has left civil society with a small pool from which to obtain political activists.

Also important in explaining this gap is the hypothesis relative to organized groups (i.e., that they do not socialize their members to participate in
politics). This effect was documented in the preceding section in that membership in groups had little noticeable association with other forms of mass
political participation. This apolitical nature of organizational life in
Botswana is explicitly fostered by group leaders. For instance, the
Botswana Trade Union Federation has a policy of not taking sides in
national elections, even though only one party, the Botswana National
Front, openly opposes the anti-union sections of the Trade Union and
Employers' Act. In part this avoidance of politics stems from the fact that
political parties in Botswana are organized primarily on an ethnic basis.
Interest groups whose memberships cut across ethnic lines are hesitant to
anger a segment of their constituency by siding with one party. Also, interest group leaders who sympathize with opposition parties fear that if they
show their true colors they will anger the ruling party, whose tenure in
power does not seem likely to end soon. To make things still worse, many
groups in one way or another receive substantial government funds, which
could be endangered by involvement in politics.[32]

Yet another factor fostering the gap between the commitment of the
socially mobilized to liberal democratic politics and their lack of actual
participation is the communal basis of grassroots politics in Botswana. The
socially mobilized who do not reside in their own communities and do not
intend to do so are inclined to exit electoral politics. They look to organized
groups to represent their interests through intervention with civil servants
and short-circuiting elected officials. They may prefer the new system but
they are hesitant to become entangled in the web of social relations that
interweave with local politics, which in Tswana villages include *makgotla,*
weddings, funerals, and paying respect to traditional leaders.

It will be recalled from the introduction to this chapter that two of our hypotheses specified that politicians were not doing enough to promote citizen participation. Specifically, party leaders were not socializing their members to become involved, and they were not debating the issues publicly and thus creating interest in politics that would lead to more citizen activism. The foregoing data analysis indicates that while partisanship and citizen attentiveness to politics play a secondary role to social mobilization relative to political information and support for the democratic structures, both variables are important in the absence of social mobilization in promoting mass participation. Also important in explaining this participation is the hypothesis on traditional culture. Particularly significant is *kgotla* attendance and participation.

These three factors—partisan socialization, the attentive public, and traditional participation—need not have an inevitable positive effect as far as the development of democratic politics. They could, and do in many African countries, work in the opposite direction. Even in Botswana, the data used in this study revealed that those who speak most in the *kgotla* reject the idea that minorities and youth have an equal right to participate in their meetings. It is very possible that the political elite could encourage application of this traditional Tswana principle of politics to various aspects of political life from selection for leadership positions to policy outputs.

The parties could turn their educational programs from supporting multiparty politics to advocacy of a one-party system. The Democracy Research Project survey of party elites found that all but one of those interviewed favored a multiparty system. This could change if the level of trust between the BDP and the opposition parties were to decline.

The attentive public could become alienated by politics if the economic situation were to deteriorate, which is almost inevitable after twenty years of steady growth. Political leaders could then respond to the resulting discontent by encouraging the attentive public, through the mass media, to put their faith in an authoritarian leader. This elite survival technique has been typical in African states, particularly when the public becomes disillusioned with its plight.

Mass participation in Botswana's democracy thus rests on a fragile foundation until the social mobilization process begins to support the development of more organized groups prepared to mobilize their members for political action. Some things could be done to speed the process along. Government could loosen its laws governing the formation of groups, particularly with respect to trade unions. Foreign aid organizations might have an impact if they were to provide some start-up funding for interest groups. For the most part, however, the groups themselves must decide that more direct political action is necessary to secure their goals. In some interviews the Democracy Research Project staff conducted in the latter half of 1991, only a minority of the leadership in the groups surveyed indicated any inclination to make such a strategic change.

Thus far our discussion has related to the specific hypotheses being tested. There are some general implications of this research that should also be noted. First, the lack of social mobilization with respect to political participation may help to explain the stability of Botswana's democracy over the last twenty-five years. Had the socially mobilized been more active, as in the case of other African countries such as Nigeria and Uganda, popular demands on the ruling BDP and the civil service would have been much greater for such things as higher wages and expanded social services. The absence of activity may have given the regime time to gain sufficient legitimacy to survive the inevitably more intense political conflicts to come.

Second, this study points to the need for other social forces to support democratization in the absence of social mobilization producing a participant stratum. However, these alternative forces in the form of political parties, an attentive public, and traditional political structures can become severe threats to elected leaders. The hope of many is that constitutional structures can be erected to prevent such antidemocratic tendencies from leading to a regime breakdown. Botswana's experience indicates that leadership is equally important. The political elite, most especially those members who have led the BDP, has been assiduous in fostering the three forces identified as crucial to citizen involvement in Botswana's democratic politics. Thus, while the BDP leaders could have rejected the *kgotla* as a means to communicate with the people, they have made it one of government's principal channels for interaction with villagers. The BDP leaders have also worked hard at building their party organization at the grassroots level, and, possibly more important, they have not actively hindered the growth of opposition parties. With regard to policy debate, the parties have not been very aggressive in challenging each other on important issues. Nevertheless, they have mobilized an attentive public that supports multiparty politics and participates in local groups and party organizations.

Finally, the prevailing thinking in Western academic and foreign policy circles is that construction of democratic polities requires the emergence of autonomous groups that both represent civil society vis-à-vis government decisionmakers and socialize their members to take part in elections and party activities. Botswana illustrates another option in which the political elite uses existing political structures to encourage democratic participation. Such a regime provides an opportunity for citizens to learn about and become involved in democratic structures before social mobilization has created a wide range of organized groups to demand such structures at the mass and elite levels. This Botswana approach is probably more tenuous in terms of offering a long-term chance of success; however, it may be the only viable alternative for many African countries.

■ **Appendix**

Below are three tables giving the cross-tabulation frequencies for the first row of correlations in Table 6.1. The number in parentheses is the case count on which the column percentage in the cell is based. The Total rows and columns contain total case counts for the appropriate response and the table as a whole. Below each table is the Tau.

Know MP	Urban	Rural	Total
Correct Answer	82% (n=207)	71% (n=630)	857
Incorrect	18% (n=46)	29% (n=265)	311
Total	253	915	1,168

Tau = .10

Know Councillor	Urban	Rural	Total
Correct Answer	40% (n=86)	68% (n=606)	692
Incorrect	60% (n=129)	32% (n=289)	418
Total	215	895	1,110

Tau = −.23

Know Council Chair/Mayor	Urban	Rural	Total
Correct Answer	71% (n=174)	18% (n=168)	331
Incorrect	29% (n=71)	82% (n=710)	781
Total	245	867	1,112

Tau = .48

■ **Notes**

A Research and Creative Activities Grant from the Graduate College of Cleveland State University partially supported the data analysis undertaken in this chapter. I most appreciate both this support and the critical reading that Robert Charlick, Rodger Govea, Kenneth Grundy, Victor LeVine, and Donald Rothchild gave earlier drafts of the manuscript.
    1. Some emphasize that this rational activist model of citizenship must be combined with "passivity, trust and deference to authority and competence" if a stable democracy is to be achieved. Gabriel A. Almond, "The Intellectual History of the Civic Culture," in Gabriel A. Almond and Sidney Verba, eds., *The Civic Culture Revisited* (Boston: Little Brown, 1980), 16. Others perceive that the definition of participation should be less constrained and include forms that will do more to enhance the influence of those below the middle class. See for instance, Carole Pateman, "The Civic Culture: A Philosophic Critique," in Almond and Verba, *The Civic Culture Revisited,* 57–102.

2. See, for instance, Larry Diamond, Juan Linz, and Seymour Martin Lipset, eds., *Democracy in Developing Countries*, vol. 2, *Africa* (Boulder, Colo.: Lynne Rienner, 1988).

3. Daniel Lerner, *The Passing of Traditional Society: Modernizing the Middle East* (New York: Free Press, 1958); Karl Deutsch, "Social Mobilization and Political Development," *American Political Science Review* 55 (1961): 493–514. On the modernization process in general, see Alex Inkeles and David H. Smith, *Becoming Modern: Individual Change in Six Developing Countries* (Cambridge, Mass.: Harvard University Press, 1974). On the more recent literature related to the development of political participation, see Joan Nelson, "Political Participation," in Myron Weiner and Samuel P. Huntington, eds., *Understanding Political Development* (Boston: Little Brown, 1987), 103–159.

4. Norman H. Nie, G. Bingham Powell, and Kenneth Prewitt, "Social Structure and Political Participation: Developmental Relationships," *American Political Science Review* 63 (June and September 1969): 361–378 and 808–832.

5. See John Holm and Patrick Molutsi, "State-Society Relations in Botswana: Beginning Liberalization," in Goran Hyden and Michael Bratton, eds., *Governance and Politics in Africa* (Boulder, Colo.: Lynne Rienner, 1992), 75–95.

6. The 1974, 1979, and 1984 turnout figures are found in John D. Holm, "Elections in Botswana: Institutionalization of a New System of Legitimacy," in Fred M. Hayward, ed., *Elections in Independent Africa* (Boulder, Colo.: Westview, 1987), 124; those for 1989 in Jack Parson, *The 1989 Botswana General Elections' Results and Selected Issues of Botswana Political Economy* (Charleston, S.C.: by author, n.d.), 2. The turnout for 1965 was 56 percent, but this high rate is probably best explained by the fact that it was the first national election in Botswana and the outcome would determine the nature of the postindependence government.

7. On the importance of organized group membership for the development of a participant political culture, see Nie, Powell, and Prewitt, "Social Structure and Political Participation," and Robert Bianchi, "Interest Group Politics in the Third World," *Third World Quarterly* 8 (April 1986).

8. John D. Holm, "How Effective Are Interest Groups in Representing Their Members?" in John D. Holm and Patrick P. Molutsi, eds., *Democracy in Botswana* (Athens: Ohio University Press, 1989), 142–153.

9. See the discussion of agents of political socialization in Jack Dennis, ed., *Socialization to Politics* (New York: John Wiley & Sons, 1973), 321–409.

10. Ranbwedzi Nengwekhulu, "Political Parties as Facilitators of Democracy in Botswana," in Holm and Molutsi, *Democracy in Botswana*, 203–209.

11. Albert Hirschman, *Exit, Voice, and Loyalty* (Cambridge, Mass.: Harvard University Press, 1970); Goran Hyden, *Beyond Ujamaa in Tanzania: Underdevelopment and the Uncaptured Peasantry* (Berkeley: University of California Press, 1980).

12. Nelson Kasfir, *The Shrinking Political Arena* (Berkeley: University of California Press, 1974).

13. Patrick P. Molutsi, "The Ruling Class and Democracy in Botswana," in Holm and Molutsi, *Democracy in Botswana*, 103–114; and Mpho G. Molomo, "The Bureaucracy and Democracy in Botswana," in Holm and Molutsi, *Democracy in Botswana*, 237–242.

14. See, for instance, Samuel P. Huntington and Joan M. Nelson, *No Easy Choice: Political Participation in Developing Countries* (Cambridge, Mass.: Harvard University Press, 1976), 50–51. Scholars have generally had a difficult time actually documenting alienation. For example, see David B. Hill and Norman R. Luttbeg, *Trends in American Electoral Behavior* (Itasca, Texas: F. E. Peacock, 1980), 109–147.

15. See Parson, *The 1989 Botswana General Elections' Results*, 10.

16. See, for instance, Gabriel A. Almond and Sidney Verba, *The Civic Culture* (Boston: Little Brown, 1963).

17. L. D. Ngcongco, "Tswana Political Tradition: How Democratic?" in Holm and Molutsi, *Democracy in Botswana*, 47.

18. I worked with the members of the Democracy Research Project at the University of Botswana on development of the 1987 questionnaire and its administration. They created the 1989 questionnaire, and I helped with its administration. This chapter would not have been possible without my colleagues' contributions of ideas, time, and energy. I am most indebted to each of them. Funds to support our endeavors came most generously from the Social Science Research Council of New York, the Swedish International Development Agency, the University of Botswana, Cleveland State University, the National Democratic Institute for International Affairs, and the Swedish Agency for Research and Co-operation.

19. A comparison of the 1989 survey with population norms is provided in Patrick Molutsi and Balefi Tsie, "Report of the 1989 Election Study" (Paper presented at the Democracy Project Workshop, Gaborone, December 8 and 9, 1990), chap. 3.

20. While the 1987 list was more inclusive than the one used in 1989, both encouraged the respondent to say whether he/she was a member of a group. The 1987 measure also asked about the regularity of attendance at meetings. The lack of comprehensiveness of both measures means that they are only a valid group measure with respect to the groups mentioned.

21. Parson speaks of rural alienation as coming from an economic change that involves the decline in the viability of small farmer agriculture, the rise of wage labor on larger farms, and the erosion of patron-client relations. In short, small holders lose economic resources and cannot find relief from personalized coping mechanisms. The 1989 survey questions ask whether the benefits from government development programs reach the people and whether the forthcoming elections will have personal or communal payoffs. The first question specifically and the latter two in a more general way focus on the sense of economic helplessness with which Parson is concerned. See Parson, *The 1989 Botswana General Elections' Results*, 16.

22. In order to make the 1987 group indicator as a dependent variable roughly equivalent to the one in the 1989 questionnaire, only the four most politically active types of group choices were included, specifically, membership in trade unions, cooperatives, women's groups, and the other groups response. Thus the independent variable of group membership for 1987 includes more groups (eight) than is the case for this dependent variable.

23. Gloria Somolekae provides an analysis of the 1987 data with respect to political information and democratic preferences in "Do Batswana Think and Act as Democrats?" in Holm and Molutsi, *Democracy in Botswana*, 75–88. Her discussion permits the reader to examine some of the cross-tabulation tables on which the correlations in this chapter are based.

24. Tau B is reported for square tables and Tau C for rectangular ones.

25. While some readers would find percentage frequencies more understandable, using a correlation coefficient allows for many relationships to be reported in one table, thus making possible analysis of the relative importance of each hypothesis. To obtain a rough approximation of the frequencies on which the correlations in the following tables are based, the reader should consult the appendix, where the frequencies for the correlations in the first row of Table 6.1 are displayed.

26. See, for instance, Mary R. Jackman, "General and Applied Tolerance:

Does Education Increase Commitment to Racial Integration?" *American Journal of Political Science* 22 (May 1978): 302–324.

27. The only exception to this generalization is the connection of group membership with party membership (.29) in Table 6.4. This high correlation very likely results from the fact that the question on party membership was asked in connection with a series of questions on other forms of group membership. Thus the response may have been contaminated by a spillover effect from the other membership items. The absence of equivalent correlations for group membership with the other participation variables in the 1987 survey points to such a conclusion.

28. Almond and Verba, *The Civic Culture*.

29. In the urban areas, the correlation of the belief that elections will not benefit one's household goes up to −.23 with party membership and that for not benefiting community goes up to −.15 with the same variable, while for the rural areas both associations decline to -.09.

30. At the suggestion of Gloria Somolekae, a number of other controls were tried to see if in certain contexts a stronger association could be obtained between the alienation variables and the various participation items. None of the controls, including those for education, being born outside of one's village, and being non-Tswana, made any difference.

31. See, for instance, Bphraim Molema, "Whither Public Service," *Mmegi*, March 15–21, 1991, 11.

32. For a more elaborate discussion of these problems see John D. Holm, "How Effective Are Interest Groups?"

7

Bureaucracy and Democracy in Botswana: What Type of a Relationship?

Gloria Somolekae

Botswana has earned admiration from many as a shining model of democracy in Africa. While many African countries that adopted liberal democracy at independence soon abandoned it, Botswana's has survived and continues to thrive today. As a result, the country has attracted much study aimed at explaining why Botswana's democracy has survived, as well as addressing the controversial issue of whether Botswana provides a model for other African countries.

Botswana has remained an exception to most of Africa in another important aspect: its outstanding governance. First, Botswana has maintained a strong and relatively autonomous bureaucracy, while in other countries such as Zambia, Kenya, Mozambique, and many others, the bureaucracy lost this autonomy shortly after independence. In addition (and possibly as a function of its autonomy), Botswana's bureaucracy has been one of the most effective in Africa. As a World Bank team put it in 1984, "Public sector management is performed in Botswana with commendable attention to detail, discipline and dedication by the civil service. It is considered one of the most successful in Africa, if success is measured by the capacity of a system to formulate and implement effectively strategies and programs for economic and social development."[1] Finally, Botswana's bureaucracy has remained relatively free of corruption.

This chapter aims to explain why Botswana's bureaucracy managed to retain its autonomy when the contrary occurred elsewhere in sub-Saharan Africa; highlight the role this bureaucracy has played in the development of democracy in Botswana; assess the implications of bureaucratic autonomy for democracy in general; and provide some suggestions on how best to achieve a balance between democratic control and bureaucratic autonomy.

This chapter argues that Botswana's bureaucracy is both a boon and a threat to democracy in Botswana. Its good policy implementation record has enabled the political leadership to translate policy goals into successful programs. However, this has not been without cost to democracy. The power of the bureaucracy has grown so great that, if unchecked, it could undermine the ability of the political representatives to control government policymaking. Already, the bureaucracy tends to dominate policymaking, which runs contrary to the fundamental democratic value of having political representatives formulate policy. The bureaucracy has not been easy to control, either; hence, it is not uncommon in Botswana to hear complaints from political leaders (especially at the local level) that the bureaucracy has become too powerful and difficult to control. Unless effective bureaucratic control mechanisms are put in place, it may be difficult to ensure future bureaucratic accountability.

■ Bureaucracy and Democracy: A Theoretical Overview

The relationship between democracy and bureaucracy has become the subject of much research and writing in both political science and public administration. Theoretically, the nature of this relationship should be straightforward: politicians formulate policy and administrators implement it. At best, the administrator provides impartial advice, but is personally removed from any final decision. However, most academics agree that this image does not reflect the relationship as it exists in practice.

The politics/administration dichotomy has been discredited in both scholarly and popular literature. Most analysts share the view that "even if civil servants wanted to merely follow orders, . . . that is practically impossible. Politicians lack the expertise, the information and even the time to decide on all the thousands of policy questions that face modern government each year. . . . [M]inisters are largely, if not wholly, dependent on their official advisors."[2]

We must caution that while this may be true of most parliamentary systems that have followed the British model, countries such as the United States may be exceptions. In the United States as well as some other Western countries, politicians are much better informed and better educated than are their counterparts elsewhere. The study by Aberbach, Rockman, and Putnam provides empirical evidence to support this thesis.[3] This means that while in presidential systems the civil servant might still be critical in assisting the minister with information, the degree of dependency may be far less than in a parliamentary system where ministers are not (and are not expected to be) experts in the policy domains they oversee.

Recent observers argue that "this presumed separation of administration and politics allows [administrators] to engage in politics without the bother of being held accountable politically for outcomes of their actions

. . . and without the interference of political actors who might otherwise make demands for the modification of these policies."[4] The presumed separation is also alleged to benefit politicians by "permitting many of the difficult decisions of modern government to be made by individuals who will not have to face the public at a subsequent election."[5] A much more realistic picture of this relationship is presented by Aberbach et al., who view politicians and bureaucrats as policymakers whose inputs into the policy process are different but complementary. It is precisely because the theoretical dichotomy is unrealistic that debate currently rages over how to make the bureaucracy accountable and responsive.

In sub-Saharan Africa, concern over the relative imbalance of power between bureaucrats and politicians produced measures that gradually eroded civil service autonomy. This autonomy, part of the heritage from the colonial era, was therefore lost. The bureaucracy was gradually politicized. G. Mutahaba, who has analyzed the consequences of this loss of autonomy and increased politicization of the civil services, notes that sub-Saharan bureaucracies lost both their efficiency and effectiveness as a result of politicization.[6]

Democracy and bureaucracy promote values that sometimes come into conflict. For example, democracy stands for representation and accountability, while the fundamental values of bureaucracy are efficiency, economy, and effectiveness. In order to realize its values, democracy emphasizes universal suffrage and regular elections; bureaucracy uses rules and regulations, rationality, and expertise. Tensions between the two arise from the way each approaches the policymaking process, and from the inputs they bring into the process. For example, politicians bring legitimacy and political support, while civil servants generally bring expertise and information. It is not surprising, therefore, that in societies where democracy has become an important part of the political culture, there should be concerns about the prospect of nonelected officials taking over the role of elected representatives.

Bureaucracy also creates a dilemma for democracy in the sense that "bureaucracy is a threat to, but also indispensable for democracy."[7] The threat usually arises where the bureaucracy becomes too powerful, where it develops the capacity to exempt itself from control by politicians and thereby avoids democratic accountability.

Democracy also creates a dilemma for bureaucracy because the rules and regulations it formulates are often "contradictory, and put the bureaucracy in a double bind. By such rules, bureaucracy is expected to be both independent and subservient, both responsible for its actions and subject to ministerial responsibility, both politicized and non-politicized, at the same time."[8] As a result, the conflict between bureaucracy and democracy is almost inevitable.

☐   *The Development of Bureaucracy in Botswana and Its Role in
the Political Process*

When Botswana attained independence from Britain in 1966, it inherited a
relatively small civil service modeled along the lines of the British civil
service. The major principles inherited at independence were civil service
autonomy, neutrality, and permanent, career tenure.

The principle of civil service neutrality means that civil servants will
not be directly involved in the political process of policymaking. This is to
be left to politicians. Civil servants are expected to execute orders from any
political superior, irrespective of his or her political persuasion. Thus, the
role of the civil servant is purely advisory. As an observer puts it, "the top
civil servants in particular are expected to be nothing but the minister's
mind by giving the minister all the advice and technical assistance he needs
to arrive at the policy decisions." Political neutrality is not to say that
administrators will not "play politics with respect to their own programs
and budgets, but rather they rarely become involved in macroscopic policy
debates. A necessary element in giving the needed professional advice is
thus a sense of neutrality—withholding oneself from the final decision."9
By the same token, neutrality and impartiality also go hand in hand with
autonomy. A bureaucracy remains a separate tool at the disposal of any
party that assumes political office, and therefore has to be, by nature, permanent.

Botswana's civil service has been modeled along the same principles,
though in practice neutrality and autonomy are relative concepts. Since
independence, the official view in Botswana has been that policymaking is
the domain of politicians and civil servants should stay out of it. Likewise,
implementation was to be left to bureaucrats. However, in practice the civil
service, not the political leadership, has dominated policymaking. As
Isaksen correctly notes, "the tradition established was that the largely
European civil service provided expertise and organizational talents and the
politicians mobilized support at the polls."10 This tradition, established at
independence, has remained largely unbroken. The only major difference is
that the civil service contains far more Africans today than it did at independence. The bureaucracy is still "expected to perceive problems, come
up with ideas, take initiatives and gain administrative and political support
for those initiatives. There is, however, an absence of political sifting of
ideas and initiatives which makes the initiator or 'perceiver' critically
important for the direction of policies within the fixed limits."11

There are few empirical studies of the policymaking process in
Botswana, fewer still of the interactions between civil servants and politicians. One of the best is Picard's 1980 case study of the formulation
process of the Tribal Grazing Land Policy (TGLP). This study "focuses on
the relationship between the bureaucracy and the political process and the

extent to which the bureaucracy as a class are both actors in the formulation of public policy and major beneficiaries of the policy they have helped to formulate."[12] Picard's major theme is that because of self-interest on the part of the bureaucracy, it is both a participant and beneficiary in the policy process. Consultation conducted during the TGLP formulation process was nothing more than a formal exercise aimed at giving legitimacy to a policy that had already been decided.

Molutsi and Molomo have also contributed to the discussion of this issue.[13] They argue that the bureaucracy is much more involved in policy-making than has been assumed. The top civil service initiates discussion of issues and, where it deems necessary, commissions studies that lead to proposals. What normally follows are public debates in different ministries as each seeks its "share of the public expenditure pie and attempts to reorient the responsibilities of others. Interministerial committees become arenas in which decisions are made."[14] A closer examination of the formulation process of other policies, such as the Self Help Housing Agency (SHAA), Financial Assistance Policy (FAP), and many others, reveals the extent to which the bureaucracy is influential in initiating policy and determining its final content. Usually, by the time the policy goes out to be scrutinized by the political leadership and the general public, its major form and content have been thoroughly defined.

There are a number of reasons why this particular tradition has emerged and lasted. First, when Botswana attained independence in 1966, the bureaucracy was the only developed organ of the state. As in many other developing countries, the bureaucracy monopolized both administrative and technical skills, and hence, it automatically acquired the right of determining what went into plans and projects; it even monopolized the formulation of the development plan. Politicians, especially at the local level, tend to be poorly educated. Brought into policy discussions (often highly technical) at a late stage, they often lack the capacity to influence policy in any significant way. According to Democracy Project research (conducted in 1987), the political leadership is relatively less informed and less educated. "The average number of years of formal education for councillors in the Democracy Project's recent survey was 8.4 and 11.3 for members of parliament . . . sixty per cent of council civil servants said most councillors did not understand position papers and that as a result debates were often dominated by better educated, nominated councillors (nominated had an average of 10.8 years of formal education)."[15]

After the discovery of diamonds in the early 1970s the bureaucracy underwent a tremendous expansion in both scope and complexity of its functions. It therefore expanded qualitatively and quantitatively. For example, in the first ten years following independence, twenty-six new ministries and several public enterprises were set up. This growth in numbers and budget produced a powerful civil service that "in the absence of any other organized bargaining group and [given] the small size of the private sector, managed to increase its share of the national product in the form of continued salary increases."[16]

☐ *Explaining Bureaucratic Autonomy in Botswana*

How did Botswana's bureaucracy manage to retain its autonomy when other sub-Saharan African bureaucracies lost theirs shortly after independence? In seeking to answer this question, we must contrast Botswana's history with that of other sub-Saharan countries. Stephen Morrison's essay in this volume analyzes the development of Botswana's state ethos. Here I will simply point out a few important factors that contributed to bureaucratic autonomy in Botswana.

Botswana, unlike many sub-Saharan countries, did not have a violent struggle for independence. The country was a British protectorate whose primary importance to Britain was as a safeguard for its passage to the north of Africa. As an observer neatly summed it up, "Britain's presence in the territory was minimal, and consequently, no effective colonial machinery was introduced in the territory."[17]

Due to this lack of a violent struggle for independence (at least as compared to colonies such as Kenya or Zimbabwe), clashes between the colonial civil service and the nationalistic forces were barely minimal if at all present. Consequently, after independence, the civil service was not necessarily viewed with hostility and suspicion as has happened in many other African countries that experienced settler colonialism. This is further demonstrated by the fact that Botswana never engaged in a rapid Africanization of the civil service immediately following independence. Up to today, qualifications still play a primary role when people are considered for work. If there is a vacancy, and no qualified citizen of Botswana is available to take the post, an expatriate is hired. Contrary to what happened in a number of African countries, the postindependence government in Botswana never made it a priority following its assumption of power to attempt to neutralize the civil service.

Another respect in which the lack of a violent struggle for independence has shaped administration in Botswana is in the lack of radical ideology. "Slogans are absent and a matter-of-fact style is evident in the government's documents and statements and in the way government business is conducted."[18] This lack of radicalizing as a driving force for formulation of development policy influenced the way the Botswana bureaucracy operates in two respects. First, it limited interference on a day-to-day basis from politicians. This of course gave civil servants latitude to do their work. Ideology did not become the driving force in policymaking, nor in actual day-to-day planning.

The second respect in which the lack of ideology has affected the style and nature of administration has been in the way in which the so-called "We shall run while others walk" style of policymaking has been absent.[19] This style of policymaking (described by Goran Hyden) is primarily characterized by quick decisionmaking where pros and cons of various alternatives are not adequately examined before a decision is arrived at. Under this style of decisionmaking, administrative capacity is not necessarily a major consideration when projects are planned. As a result, the bureaucracy finds itself with far more work than it is actually capable of executing.

This style of policymaking has not been common in Botswana, though of course it has indeed happened that at times the bureaucracy has found itself given more than it could effectively handle. Compared to countries like Zambia or Tanzania, however, where ideology has been a strong factor in development, Botswana has been an exception. Its financial planning has been conservative, its general development policy pragmatic; these are features it does not share with many countries in the region.

■ Bureaucracy and Democracy in Botswana

Contrary to conventional theory and official thinking, in Botswana the bureaucracy and not the political leadership has been the dominant actor in policymaking. At independence, the largely European civil service was the only organ with the skills and expertise to make policy. Because of this power vacuum at that time, the bureaucracy managed to grow and become a powerful institution in Botswana's political landscape. This institution also managed to enjoy far greater institutional autonomy than its counterparts elsewhere in the region. We attributed this partly to the unique history of this country, which made it possible for the political leadership to have no immediate reason for clamping down on the civil service and neutralizing it, as has been the case elsewhere in Africa following independence. This has indeed been beneficial to the country because Botswana's bureaucracy has remained one of the most effective and corruption-free in Africa. This effectiveness has also been good for democracy because it has meant that Botswana has been able to move slowly away from the traditional feudal system to a liberal democratic system. This relationship between democracy and bureaucracy is testimony that a strong and independent bureaucracy is indispensable for democracy. Indeed, in conformity with Migdal's thesis, a strong and independent bureaucracy has proved indispensable for development.[20]

Some might ask, "Why should it matter that civil servants are formulating policy?" After all, they have the skills and the know-how. "Isn't it good for the country that the civil service is the dominant actor here?"

Botswana's good economic performance gives credibility to this kind of logic. In a liberal democracy, however, the people's elected representatives are supposed to formulate public policy. The electorate casts its vote on the basis of the various policy platforms presented. Elections are one avenue through which the accountability of the leadership can be effected. Therefore, whenever nonelected officials dominate policy the democratic process has been hijacked. The critical question is, and will remain for quite some time, "How can Botswana build and maintain a strong and independent bureaucracy without jeopardizing its democracy?"

Botswana has begun to see rising tension on this issue. As noted by Molutsi after attending the Botswana Democratic Party National Council meeting, "ministers are under pressure from the party rank and file to control civil servants. Ministers were strongly criticized for failing to implement past party resolutions demanding curtailment of civil servants' power."[21] Concerns such as these may come from more and more groups other than party activists.

In addition, a new breed of better educated and experienced politicians has begun to enter the political scene. As politicians of this caliber enter the policymaking arena, two things are likely to happen. First, there is likely to be much more tolerance, understanding, and cooperation between this breed of politicians and civil servants. There could be less tension between the two because of similarities in experience, qualifications, and outlook. The second possibility is that tension could rise as politicians slowly move into a domain that bureaucrats have come to consider wholly their own. This could particularly be so where either party feels that its interests (professional, material, or otherwise) are at stake.

What are the possibilities for change? How can democracy and bureaucracy be harmonized? We need to review two important points here. First, tensions between democracy and bureaucracy are inevitable; this is precisely why, in older democracies, the issue is still a matter of concern and is largely unresolved.

Second, the tensions may take various dimensions depending on the sociopolitical context and of course the level of development of the particular country. In Botswana, therefore, this situation of the relative imbalance of power between the various organs of the state has effectively meant that the bureaucracy has grown in some kind of a power vacuum where it has not been subjected either to much challenge, or even control. In Botswana, there is a lack of popular organizations that can effectively channel the demands of their members into the political process. Though they have begun to have some impact, the private media are still relatively small and hampered by a number of problems. This situation (of small and undeveloped media and ineffective interest groups) no doubt limits the effectiveness of the entire democratic process. Botswana's democracy is still young and in the process of being institutionalized. Where other necessary democratic institutions are either lacking, or generally ineffective (as in

Botswana), the need for measures for preventing abuse of power is even greater because, as Finer observes, "sooner or later there is abuse of power when external punitive controls are lacking."[22]

These two points therefore lead to the following question: How can these tensions be best managed to ensure that the effective operation of the democratic system is not hindered? There is no easy answer here. This chapter has argued that the problem of bureaucratic dominance is determined by several factors. Efforts to deal with it have to reflect this reality. The first requirement is to admit that the issue indeed requires discussion and research.

Even though politicians have raised concerns now and then, their concerns have remained isolated and uncoordinated. It is also not uncommon to hear civil servants claim that they do not formulate policy. The issue must enter public debate in its own right and efforts must be made to ensure that existing measures aimed at checking bureaucratic power are strengthened. It also means that new measures must be sought to reinforce existing ones. This issue needs to be taken seriously by all who are interested in building effective and sustainable democratic systems in developing countries.

■ Notes

1. Nimrod Raphaeli, Jacques Roumani, and A. C. MacKellar, *Public Sector Management in Botswana* (Washington, D.C.: World Bank, 1984), 1.

2. Joel Aberbach, Robert Putnam, and A. B. Rockman, *Bureaucrats and Politicians in Western Democracy* (Cambridge, Mass.: Harvard University Press, 1981), 5.

3. Ibid.

4. Guy Peters, *Comparing Public Bureaucracies: Problems of Theory and Method* (Birmingham: University of Alabama Press, 1988), 5.

5. Aberbach, Putnam, and Rockman, *Bureaucrats and Politicians,* 5.

6. G. Mutahaba, *Reforming Public Administration for Development: Experiences from Eastern Africa* (West Hartford, Conn.: Kumarian, 1989).

7. Eva Etzioni-Halevy, *Bureaucracy and Democracy: A Political Dilemma* (New York: Routledge and Kegan Paul, 1983), 87.

8. Ibid.

9. Donald Rowat, *Global Comparisons in Public Administration* (Ottawa: Carleton University, 1981), 114.

10. J. Isaksen, *Macro-Economic Management and Bureaucracy: The Case of Botswana* (Uppsala, Sweden: Scandinavian Institute of African Studies, 1981), 32.

11. Ibid., 33.

12. Louis Picard, "Bureaucrats, Cattle and Public Policy: Land Tenure Changes in Botswana," *Comparative Political Studies* 13, no. 3 (October 1980): 313–356.

13. Patrick Molutsi "The Ruling Class and Democracy in Botswana" and Mpho Molomo, "The Bureaucracy and Democracy in Botswana," in John Holm and

Patrick Molutsi, eds., *Democracy in Botswana* (Gaborone: Macmillan, 1989), 103–116 and 237–243.

14. Patrick Molutsi and John Holm, "Developing Democracy When Civil Society Is Weak: The Case of Botswana," *African Affairs* 89 (July 1990): 327.

15. Patrick Molutsi, "The Ruling Class and Democracy," 108.

16. Dolf Noppoen, *Consultation and Non-Commitment in Botswana: Planning with the People of Botswana,* (Leiden, Netherlands: African Studies Center, 1982), 54.

17. Raphaeli, Roumani, and MacKellar, *Public Sector Management,* 12.

18. Ibid., 13.

19. Goran Hyden, "Administration and Public Policy," in Joel Barkan and J. Okumu, eds., *Politics and Public Policy in Kenya and Tanzania* (New York: Praeger, 1977), 96.

20. Joel Migdal, *Strong States and Weak Societies* (Princeton, N.J.: Princeton University Press, 1988).

21. Molutsi, "The Ruling Class and Democracy," 109.

22. H. Finer, "Administrative Responsibility in Democratic Societies," in F. Rourke, ed., *Bureaucratic Power in National Politics* (Boston: Little Brown, 1978), 418.

8

Governance and Environment in Botswana: The Ecological Price of Stability

Rodger Yeager

This chapter explores an increasingly serious confrontation between the demands of political legitimacy and the requirements of environmental protection in modern Botswana. The study originates in a field survey of natural resource issues facing eastern and southern Africa.[1] Part of an ongoing research program in sustainable resource utilization, the survey has sought to identify priority areas for further investigations in Botswana, Kenya, Somalia, Sudan, Tanzania, and Zimbabwe. A long-term goal of this effort is to cooperate with African researchers in helping supply governmental decisionmakers and administrators with information, analysis, and policy recommendations relating to land use, natural resources, and environment.

Fieldwork has revealed many of the most critical and least resolved obstacles to sustainable economic development in the six survey countries. Overcoming these constraints depends on a delicate balancing of discrete and often contradictory technical, socioeconomic, and political requisites. In Botswana, policy compromises must consider the profound impact of people and cattle on the land, its soil and water resources, and its indigenous flora and fauna.

It would be comforting if African natural resource problems could be treated instrumentally, where rational problem solving coexists with and moderates political expediency. In Africa, however, such concerns are thoroughly politicized. Although virtually unique to the continent in terms of its democratic tendencies, Botswana's policy system shares at least one trait in common with its counterparts in other African countries. Here as elsewhere governing structures are still evolving in directions mandated by leaders in highly personalized, rather than strongly institutionalized, positions of power.[2] Constituting Botswana's political elite, these leaders maintain, enhance, and sometimes lose their preferred status through intricate and easily disrupted patronage networks that link them with peers, subordinates, and society at large.

Problems of African natural resource conservation and sustainable resource utilization involve compelling political issues. Such issues must receive attention if policy solutions are to be found before human catastrophes become pervasive in this ecologically fragile continent. By examining such factors in a country noted for its political openness, the following analysis seeks to shed light on a neglected and yet vitally important question of African development: In what ways can technically objective policy requirements be squared with the political uncertainties inherent in African policymaking and administration? In Botswana, a mutually beneficial fulcrum must be found to balance the private-interest-serving goals of a nascent democracy with the need for public control over a semicommercialized cattle culture that is inexorably depleting the country's land, water, and indigenous living resources.

■ Botswana: A Modern Pastoral Democracy?

Located almost entirely in southern Africa's arid and semi-arid zones, Botswana receives very little rainfall. Nevertheless, the country's economic performance has enabled its leadership to buy protection against drought and also to purchase one of Africa's few constitutional democracies. Diamond production began in the early 1970s and, despite occasional slumps, quickly rose in value from 79 million pula (US $42.3 million) in 1978 to 554 million pula (US $296.4 million) by 1985. Between 1965 and 1989, agriculture declined from 34 percent to 3 percent of total output, and industry, including mining, increased from 19 percent to 57 percent.[3] Made possible by mining revenues, Botswana's foreign exchange reserves reached nearly US $3 billion by 1989, establishing a world record 19.5 months of import coverage.[4] Nevertheless, since 70 percent of the labor force remains agricultural and over 75 percent of the total population is still rural, Botswana's leaders continue to view cattle as crucial to the national economy. Similarly, they see the country's pastoral culture as essential to its political unity and its democratic form of government.[5]

Botswana is typically offered as a model of effective and publicly responsible governance for the rest of Africa. In one interpretation, Botswana is ruled by "a paternalistic government dominated by an organizational bourgeoisie [that] is becoming more accountable and more involved with institutional structures of social compromise."[6] As this assessment implies, central executive agencies have been singled out for special commendation, and their political moderation and administrative proficiency are also held responsible for the government's consistently congenial relations with foreign aid donors.[7]

On the other hand, the political and administrative elite remains strongly committed to a latter-day colonial effort to promote a formal livestock sector, but one in which success is still measured more in numbers of head than in terms of herd quality and sustainability. To facilitate an eventual transition from cattle culture to beef industry, postindependence legislation has removed control over land use from traditional chiefs, headmen, and *makgotla* (village assemblies; *"makgotla"* is the plural of *"kgotla"*). Rangeland management is now vested in district councils, land boards, and, to a limited extent, village development committees, all supervised by central government ministries led by the Ministry of Local Government and Lands.[8] These institutions have assumed responsibility for the allocation of land and for the oversight of water and range use, but have generally forsaken the time-honored Tswana practice of balancing stocking rates with environmental carrying capacities. The resulting tendency toward ever-increasing cattle numbers mostly benefits large-scale ranchers, many of whom are also senior officials in the central government and the ruling Botswana Democratic Party.[9]

Land-tenure and land-use legislation, resource planning, and foreign development assistance have all been mobilized in support of this structural "mobilization of bias" toward cattle. As E. E. Schattschneider once pointed out: "All forms of political organization have a bias in favor of the exploitation of some kinds of conflict and the suppression of others because *organization is the mobilization of bias*. Some issues are organized into politics while others are organized out."[10] In Botswana, mechanisms to preserve and extend a highly unequal distribution of cattle ownership are structured into the public policy process, as are social welfare measures intended to compensate for this inequality and to maintain mass support for the regime.[11] Effectively organized out of contention are policy alternatives of environmental protection and resource conservation that, if selected, might threaten the cattle-based hegemony.

On the other hand, despite considerable mineral wealth at its disposal this elite has managed to maintain its links with society and to avoid Africa's postcolonial crises of instability, authoritarianism, and underdevelopment. Although as much as 60 percent of all cattle is owned by only 5 percent of wealthy Batswana, about 50 percent of the rural population owns at least a few animals. Many of the remaining poor enjoy access to borrowed stock through the persistence of the *mafisa* cattle-sharing tradition.[12] A mixture of freehold, leasehold, and communal land rights, together with subsidized borehole drilling, ensure the availability of sufficient range and water to enable large and small herds to disperse across the countryside.

Buoyed up by mining revenues, Botswana's paternalistic governing system thus functions as a kind of modern African pastoral democracy in a setting of relative social accord, rapid if highly unbalanced economic growth, and widening but still manageable socioeconomic inequality. The system will face two substantial challenges in its efforts to achieve economic diversification and distributional equity. It may be prevented from reaching these goals by yet another African crisis, one the policy elite has created (with foreign help) as a by-product of its other successes.

■ Public Policy and Loss of Ecological Control

I have suggested elsewhere that Botswana's record on land and resource policy forms a melange of "righteous motives and unintended consequences."[13] By providing for leased ranches where stocking rates would be regulated, the landmark Tribal Grazing Land Policy (TGLP) sought to protect the quality of grazing on tribal commons while encouraging producers to raise higher-grade cattle within ranch boundaries. Instead, grazing conditions on communal lands have worsened as large-scale TGLP ranchers release their excess stock there and drill additional boreholes. This has created a situation of extreme ecological imbalance: "Where water points have been developed for livestock, there is little or no control of the numbers of animals which are watered. As a result, the surrounding landscape is so seriously overgrazed that desertification has developed for a radius of several kilometers around the water point."[14]

The more than thirty statutes and still other executive orders directly relating to land use and resource conservation have proved inadequate in addressing the livestock problem. For example, a system of locally zoned Wildlife Management Areas (WMAs) was authorized to lessen conflict between cattle and indigenous wild species, and also to encourage rural economic diversification through multiple resource uses, including an expansion of the country's tourist and hunting safari industries. This ambitious plan would add 8 percent to the 17 percent of land area already given over to national parks and game reserves. Some district authorities have approved WMAs, but actual management plans have remained stalled in national debate for more than a decade.[15]

As another instance, in 1983 the government solicited advice from the UN Environment Programme (UNEP) on how to encourage both development and resource conservation. The UNEP mission arrived at fifteen major recommendations, with four pertaining to cattle. While most were approved, funded, and implemented, these four were rejected.[16] The UNEP study did, however, lead to a 1984 follow-up conference requested by the Ministry of Local Government and Lands, which produced another series of proposals calling for resource conservation, pollution management, economic diversification, and livestock control.[17] Some of these suggestions have since been acted upon, but again not those addressing the livestock issue.

The domestic elite has skillfully orchestrated the efforts of educational institutions, nongovernmental organizations (NGOs), and international trading and assistance partners on behalf of this short-sighted approach to sustainable development. The Department of Environmental Science may have the fastest-growing academic program at the University of Botswana. The Kalahari Conservation Society, the Botswana Society, the Forestry Association of Botswana, and *Thusano Lefatsheng* (Helping Each Other on Earth) are among Africa's most active conservation-oriented NGOs. The European Economic Community, the World Bank, and several bilateral donors have supported environmental education and public service. Nevertheless, the political leadership has remained remarkably aloof from the deeper issues of resource conservation and environmental protection. While avoiding policy options that involve reducing the cattle population, Botswana's politicians are inclined to allow other conservation agendas to be defined by expatriate advisers and NGO representatives. Senior officials have also tended to insist that acceptable alternatives emerging from the agenda setting process must be funded through supplemental foreign aid contributions. Justifying his position on the basis of drought-related fiscal pressures, Vice President Mmusi announced to a 1984 Botswana Society symposium on environmental management that

> Government has a lot of priority projects in the pipeline which are presently, and in the future, to be completed with donor finance. In spite of Government's determination finally to come to grips with the environmental problems which this country presently suffers, these environmental projects will not be permitted to re-order these priorities. Donors will therefore be expected to make additional finance available for the environmental projects.[18]

Foreign assistance has been requested to help mitigate the effects of too many cattle on a finite commons, but foreign assistance has also aggravated the problem. In addition to maintaining a heavily subsidized quota on beef exports, the EEC has financially assisted in the construction of controversial veterinary cordon fences and in the development of commercial abattoirs. The World Bank's credit services to commercial ranchers, offered through three livestock development projects, have proved equally controversial.[19] Until the well-publicized disapproval of international conservationists reached its peak in the late 1980s, bilateral donors tended to avoid active involvement in either beef production or resource conservation.

In the midst of these actions and inactions on behalf of the cattle industry, the potential for environmental disaster has become more apparent to international and local interests alike. Nearly one-third of Botswana's three million cattle were lost to a drought that lasted most of the 1980s. Surviving herds were forced to contend with declining biomasses of nutritious forages and with encroaching desert sands. Human control over the pastoral ecology became increasingly threatened,[20] as overgrazed land increased from 1.15 million hectares (2 percent of Botswana's total area) in 1975 to over 8.6 million hectares (15 percent) in 1984. By 1986, more than 5.8 million additional hectares had been severely overgrazed, bringing the total amount of livestock-degraded land to about 14.5 million hectares— fully 25 percent of the country.[21] Referring to the rangeland survey that had produced these grim statistics, an international consulting firm concluded that "rains alone will not restore this land."[22]

Prompted by an unfolding scenario of permanent loss of ecological control, the political elite in 1983 endorsed the formulation of a fresh approach to sustainable development through resource conservation. Whether this new policy line will be permitted to address a root cause of resource depletion and environmental destruction—domestically and internationally subsidized overstocking of cattle—remains an open question.

■ Toward a Meaningful Conservation Policy?

Botswana provides a major exception to conventional wisdom associating African political and economic failures with wasted development assistance. The popularly elected government is unique in Africa for its stable and widely responsive patronage system, for the economic growth rate it has fostered,[23] for its perennially cordial relations with aid donors, and for its integration of noncitizens (African as well as non-African) into the public agenda setting and policymaking processes. As demonstrated by foreign involvement in environmental affairs and the livestock economy, the domestic leadership has enjoyed the luxury of expressing an appropriate level of concern while at the same time exercising what Picard has identified as "a 'veto' at that point at which a particular policy [is] perceived as a threat to the social and economic order."[24] Time is running out for this strategy.

In 1980, during the first year of Botswana's most recent drought, UNEP announced its World Conservation Strategy (WCS). With staffing assistance from the International Union for Conservation of Nature and Natural Resources (IUCN), UNEP has since encouraged member states to adopt their own national conservation strategies (NCSs) under the general WCS principle of "conservation for development." Specifically, governments have been urged to incorporate resource conservation programs into national development plans, instead of continuing to rely on crisis intervention responses to demographic, ecological, and environmental stresses. The Botswana government authorized the development of an NCS in 1983, and included this directive in its 1985–1991 development plan.[25]

For the country's conservationists and their international colleagues, the ensuing period has been one of intense preparation, deferred gratification, and diminished expectation. An NCS coordinating group was attached to the Ministry of Local Government and Lands, under the leadership of the director of town and regional planning assisted by an expatriate adviser supplied by the IUCN. According to the group's operating procedures, a set of NCS proposals would be presented to the government only after in-depth consultations had been completed with potentially affected parties at all levels of society.[26] It was also intended that, as the NCS neared readiness for submission to the president, cabinet, and Parliament, further research would be conducted on how it might be funded and implemented in the context of the national development plan.

Between 1985 and 1987, extensive discussions were held with members of the National Assembly and House of Chiefs, with ministerial officials, with district council and land board representatives, and with chiefs, headmen, and *makgotla*. District officers were requested to obtain as much additional input as possible from private sources. Local information was compiled and supplemented by a consultant retained by the U.S. Agency for International Development (USAID).[27] USAID also funded a proposed land use plan for the Ngamiland region and a national biological diversity assessment,[28] in addition to including Botswana in its newly devised Regional Natural Resources Management Project for southern Africa.[29]

Continuing its support of the conservation debate, the local office of the UN Development Programme sponsored an NCS seminar organized by the Botswana Society.[30] In terms of further bilateral assistance, the Norwegian aid agency NORAD helped finance a grassroots environmental education project, and the Swedish International Development Authority (SIDA) offered large-scale assistance to the University of Botswana so that it could fulfill a Ministry of Local Government and Lands request for a large increase in the number of environmental science graduates to meet the anticipated staffing needs of the NCS.[31]

Those involved hoped that a draft NCS would be sent to the president by the end of 1987 and that, following parliamentary approval, implementation would begin in 1988. Indeterminate delays were encountered, and by the beginning of 1988 a new NCS senior adviser estimated that the document would be submitted to the national executive in May and to Parliament in June or July.[32] By May 1989, however, only twelve of twenty-four chapters had been written, and fears were openly expressed that the NCS had encountered serious differences of opinion on the issues of overgrazing and localization of land-use regulation. It was also doubted that, even if completed in 1989, the strategy would be acted on in a general election year.[33] These forebodings seem to have been justified; Botswana's National Conservation Strategy was neither approved nor rejected in 1989, nor in the period since.

In the meantime new boreholes have been drilled, followed by a steady movement of cattle farther into the buffer zones of national parks and game reserves. In one recent observation, "livestock expansion into the eastern Kalahari has been dramatic over the past 15 years, such that the whole area is now covered by boreholes spaced less than 8kms apart. Assessment of the environmental and social impact of this development remains an important issue."[34] This is in contrast to a recommendation contained in the second consultation draft of the NCS, that "encouragement should be given to game utilization on all land where productivity can be increased or environmental damage reduced."[35] In addition to overgrazing and wildlife depletion, still unresolved and increasingly pressing NCS issues include deforestation and overexploitation of other veld products, soil and water loss, and urban residential and industrial pollution.

At root, the critical question of who will control access to scarce and diminishing resources remains. Persisting in the colonial effort to convert cattle, land, and water from permanent community assets into disposable private commodities, Botswana's elite has helped bring about a "tragedy of the commons."[36] Unless ecological balances are restored, rural inequality and poverty will widen and deepen, problems of forced urbanization and unemployment will worsen,[37] and the regime's political base of support will recede and finally vanish in cities and countryside alike.

Permanent relief cannot be expected from the mining industry. In recent years, diamonds have generated 80 percent of export earnings and 50 percent of GDP, yet a diamond market that allowed for an 11.3 percent economic growth rate during the 1980s[38] has already leveled off, persuading the director of the Bank of Botswana to predict a 4 percent average growth rate for the 1990s.[39] This could mean near-zero per capita growth in GDP, and unemployment already stands at about 30 percent of a rapidly expanding workforce. Opportunities for mining and industrial diversification will likewise be limited by shortages of investment capital, by uncertain mineral markets, and by a lack of competitiveness with South African products. In short, Botswana's social, economic, and political future will not cease to depend on the land and its renewable resources, but rather will turn on the question of whether public policy can balance environmental exploitation with resource conservation.

One mechanism for a recovery of ecological control was identified in early discussions of the NCS:

> There is need for decentralisation, with communal zoning of land and a level of decision-making and administration to be vested in the communities. It is believed that communities would take a much greater interest in the conservation of natural resources if they believed they held the responsibility for seeing to their proper use, and had the power to apply sanctions when necessary.[40]

Botswana's democracy will be challenged to share public responsibility for protecting a severely threatened pastoral commons. This, in turn, will require a greater sharing of wealth and power.

■ Requirements for the Pastoral Democracy

In some respects, Botswana's political leadership has demonstrated a public service equivalent to Hemingway's definition of courage: "grace under pressure." Partly as a result of South African military harassment, the government was forced to increase its defense budget from zero in 1972 to more than 12 percent of total expenditures by 1989. During the same period, and while other African governments were cutting their social welfare budgets, Botswana increased its educational expenditures from 10 to 20 percent of total expenditures.[41] Impressive as they are, such achievements were made possible by windfall profits from diamond sales and were not extended to the equally important areas of economic diversification and resource conservation. A task that can no longer be ignored in the 1990s is redressing these omissions with fewer net assets. Although population growth is expected to fall below 3 percent in this decade, the educational system already produces nearly twice as many graduates as can find employment, Botswana once again confronts the challenge of drought, and the rural land-use crisis continues to intensify and become more permanent.[42]

For economic diversification and resource conservation to work, yet another issue will have to be addressed, one that is as sensitive to the elite as the future status of cattle: the political and economic empowerment of the rural poor, many of whom are increasingly disenfranchised women and remote area dwellers including the San (Bushmen) and other neglected minorities. As has emerged from discussions on the proposed National Conservation Strategy, a necessary starting point is that at which actual performance departs from intended policy outcome in land-use management.

Under the present "dual zone" concept of the TGLP, commercial lands may be relatively well cared for, but little real attention is paid to communal lands where the environmental damage is most evident. In this regard, it is important not to confuse communal land tenure with de facto nonownership of land. In the latter situation, where responsibility for maintaining soil and water resources is not firmly set, overgrazing and other forms of misuse often occur.

Where communal systems are permitted to operate, land-use decisions will reflect agricultural carrying capacities at given levels of technology, because they must in order to ensure the survival and welfare of land users. Traditionally, in Botswana, institutional mechanisms for environmentally rational decisionmaking and conflict resolution were embodied in the land-allocating chiefs, in chiefly appointed overseers of stocking rates, and in the *makgotla*. Their essential functions were later transferred to local councils, boards, and committees. Serving principally as leasing and servicing agencies for commercial farmers and ranchers, these newer structures have

been captured by the modern elite and by many co-opted traditional authorities as well. The price of this power shift is now manifest on the severely
overgrazed communal ranges. Ironically, the sheer magnitude and scope of
the problem might open new opportunities for environmentally and also
politically rational policy reform.

Botswana's resource dilemmas have received much research attention
over the years.[43] From this outpouring, five policy recommendations,
which may become more feasible from a political standpoint as the country
moves closer toward human-ecological collapse, can be distilled:[44]

1. Restore the resource-conserving qualities of communal land tenure
by enabling rural communities to regain control over the pastoral commons
and to manage it within limits imposed by the environment. This action
alone could reduce inter-ethnic and intra-ethnic suspicions about the real
motives behind resource policy, as illustrated in heavy local resistance to
the TGLP in Kweneng and Ngwaketse.

2. As part of support to the villages, strengthen existing pasture recovery and management systems, and extend them to the presently overex-
ploited communal grazing areas.

3. Provide a larger number of rural employment options, for men and
women alike, in arable and irrigated agriculture and in nonfarm activities,
including enterprises—retail trade, wildlife tourism, and small-scale textile
manufacture—that already show promise. Alternative employment opportunities may be particularly critical to the relatives of male labor migrants.
Forty-three percent of farms in Botswana are run by women with families.
These farms earn less than those managed by men, in part because women
own only one-third as many cattle and therefore lack draft animals.[45]

4. Implement measures to distribute cattle more evenly among
rural dwellers, in areas capable of being made environmentally safe for
livestock production.[46] Convert highly fragile ecosystems to less intrusive
uses, for example sustainable wildlife utilization in its many possible
forms.[47]

5. When considering local government reforms, learn from and (where
possible) incorporate traditional institutions that once promoted caution in
the allocation of land, water, and other scarce natural resources.

Agricultural privatization, eulogized in the current idiom of foreign aid
and now embraced by most African governments, has encouraged rural
impoverishment and environmental degradation in modern Botswana. At
the same time, solutions to these particular tragedies of the commons turn
less on questions of public versus private ownership of the land and its
riches. They turn more on the relative security, efficiency, and flexibility of
public and private development agencies, and on the degree of opportunity
left open for rural dwellers to influence events affecting their lives. In
short, natural resource conservation and rural development together require

that "a farmer [be] treated like a somebody."[48] Botswana's elite and the international development community possess considerable unrealized potential for achieving this fundamental change in attitude.

■ Prospects for a Democratic Reform of the Commons

The political leadership has not totally abandoned the development needs of its constituents in the economically marginal rural areas, as evidenced in the Ministry of Agriculture's Arable Lands Development Programme, begun in the 1970s, and in the Communal First Development Areas sequel to the TGLP, initiated on a pilot basis in 1980.[49] For its part, the Ministry of Local Government and Lands is heavily committed to training district council and land board personnel.[50] In general, however, Holm's conclusion of a decade ago remains valid today: "Botswana's liberal democratic government has made rural development a low priority for budget allocations and has given rural people very minimal control over the resources allocated."[51]

A widely dispersed and politically quiescent population has allowed this situation to persist. Frequent visits from politicians, and the close attention they pay to supplementing local patronage (with social and physical infrastructure and with drought relief), have helped hold down demand. Meaningful opposition has arisen only recently, and mostly within class-oriented urban communities.

Under these circumstances, national leaders have not felt compelled to decentralize decisionmaking power as a condition of maintaining their own legitimacy; but this status quo is no more sustainable than the patronage rewards that preserved it in the past or the livestock strategies that have undermined concern for communal grazing areas. Depending almost entirely on uncertain international market forces and on foreign aid agendas that now emphasize conservation as well as privatization, patronage revenues may begin seriously to shrink while a growing formal-sector class demands more and more subsidization. Competing factions have already appeared in the Botswana Democratic Party, which is also receiving its first major challenge from another party, the Botswana National Front. Intra-elite competition may increasingly become a zero-sum affair, as a steadily deteriorating commons heightens the need for survival benefits to be distributed among the poor majority. Under stress from such pressures, the regime could break down; alternatively, it might become more authoritarian. Reversing the present world trend toward greater pluralism in governance might further reduce foreign aid and investment—a reaction now being experienced in Kenya.

At least a partial escape from this unhappy scenario lies in supplementing corporatist governing relationships with more fully participatory structures at all levels of society, and likewise in attempting more resolutely to

restore the pastoral commons under a promulgated, internationally supported national conservation strategy. Most importantly, this new rationality
dictates that political authority, economic incentive, and environmental
responsibility be devolved upon local institutions, both traditional (e.g., the
makgotla) and modern (e.g., cooperative societies, district councils, land
boards, and perhaps even party "freedom squares," which currently serve
only as electoral campaign organizations). The ultimate reality is that only
through such reforms can sustainability be returned to Botswana's polity,
economy, and human ecology.

■ Notes

1. The survey was designed to initiate a collaborative African Research
Program in Strategic Policy Issues of Environmental and Natural Resource
Conservation and Biodiversity Management, administered by the African-
Caribbean Institute and financially supported by the Ford Foundation, the U.S.
Agency for International Development, and the UN Environment Programme. For
analyses of the initial outputs of this program, see Rodger Yeager et al., *Africa's
Conservation for Development: Botswana, Kenya, Tanzania, and Zimbabwe*
(Hanover, N.H.: African-Caribbean Institute, 1987), and Rodger Yeager, ed.,
Conservation for Development in Botswana, Kenya, Somalia, and Sudan (Hanover,
N.H.: African-Caribbean Institute, 1990).

2. See Robert H. Jackson and Carl G. Rosberg, *Personal Rule in Black Africa*
(Berkeley: University of California Press, 1982).

3. World Bank, *World Development Report 1991* (New York: Oxford
University Press, 1991), 209.

4. Ibid., 239.

5. "Pastoral democracy" is a phrase originally used by I. M. Lewis in refer-
ence to political relations among northern Somali herders. I. M. Lewis, *A Pastoral
Democracy: A Study of Pastoralism and Politics Among the Northern Somali of the
Horn of Africa* (London: International African Institute and Oxford University
Press, 1961).

6. John D. Holm, in National Democratic Institute for International Affairs,
Democracies in Regions of Crisis (Washington, D.C.: NDIIA, 1990), 106. See also
Jack Parson, *Botswana: Liberal Democracy and the Labor Reserve in Southern
Africa* (Boulder, Colo.: Westview, 1984), and Richard Vengroff, *Botswana: Rural
Development in the Shadow of Apartheid* (Rutherford, N.J.: Fairleigh Dickinson
University Press, 1977).

7. Examples of this praise are found in Nimrod Raphaeli, Jacques Roumani,
and A. C. MacKellar, *Public Sector Management in Botswana: Lessons in
Pragmatism,* World Bank Staff Working Papers, no. 709 (Washington, D.C.: The
World Bank, 1984).

8. Annual budgetary allocations reflect the administrative importance of the
Ministry of Local Government and Lands. Between 1984 and 1991, 16 to 17 percent of all recurrent and development expenditures were projected for this ministry,
representing a greater proportion of total annual budgets than for any other agency
except the Ministry of Education. Republic of Botswana, *National Development
Plan, 1985–91* (Gaborone: The Government Printer, December 1985), 73–74.

9. See John D. Holm, "Botswana: A Paternalistic Democracy," in Larry

Diamond, Juan Linz, and Seymour Martin Lipset, eds., *Democracy in Developing Countries*, vol. 2, *Africa* (Boulder, Colo.: Lynne Rienner, 1988), 203.

10. E. E. Schattschneider, *The Semisovereign People* (New York: Holt, Rinehart and Winston, 1960), 71. Schattschneider's emphasis.

11. It may be instructive to note that the Botswana Democratic Party has begun to encounter significant electoral competition in Botswana's rapidly growing urban areas. As Parson explains elsewhere in this volume, urban voting follows class interests and may also reflect the discontent of impoverished rural migrants. Neither the working class nor the alienated poor are well served by the mobilization of bias maintained by the BDP's pastoral elite.

12. For analyses of *mafisa* in its modern form, see O. Gulbrandson, *On the System of Mafisa* (Gaborone: Rural Sociology Unit, Ministry of Agriculture, 1977), and T. Hertel, *The System of Mafisa and the Highly Dependent Agricultural Sector* (Gaborone: Rural Sociology Unit, Ministry of Agriculture, 1978). For additional reasons why inequality of cattle ownership has failed to generate widespread rural opposition to the regime, see Jack Parson, "Legitimacy, Succession, and Sources of Opposition in the Botswana Polity, 1956–1987," (Paper presented at the Thirty-First Annual Meeting of the African Studies Association of the United States, Chicago, October 1988).

13. Rodger Yeager, "Democratic Pluralism and Ecological Crisis in Botswana," *The Journal of Developing Areas* 23 (1989): 385–404.

14. Charles E. Bussing, *National Conservation Strategy: District Issues and Potential Projects* (Gaborone: USAID/Botswana and Department of Town and Regional Planning, Ministry of Local Government and Lands, December 1987), 9. See also S. Sandford, *Keeping an Eye on TGLP* (Gaborone: University College of Botswana, 1980), and L. Wiley, *TGLP and Hunter-Gatherers: A Case of Land Politics* (Gaborone: University College of Botswana, 1981).

15. The nongovernmental Kalahari Conservation Society has assumed an active role in keeping this discussion alive. See, for example, Kalahari Conservation Society, *Which Way Botswana's Wildlife?* Proceedings of a symposium of the Kalahari Conservation Society (Gaborone: KCS and National Museum, 1983); and Kalahari Conservation Society, *Sustainable Wildlife Utilisation: The Role of Wildlife Management Areas*, Proceedings of a workshop organized by the Kalahari Conservation Society in conjunction with the Department of Wildlife and National Parks (Gaborone: KCS and Department of Wildlife and National Parks, 1988).

16. UN Environment Programme, *Report of the UNEP Clearing-House Technical Mission to Botswana, 3 November–11 December 1983* (Nairobi: UNEP, 1984). For further reference to the rejected proposals, see Yeager, "Democratic Pluralism," 402.

17. Alec Campbell and John Cooke, eds., *The Management of Botswana's Environment*, The Botswana Society's workshop organized on behalf of the Botswana Government (Gaborone: The Botswana Society, 1984).

18. Ibid., 8.

19. In response to mounting criticism of the first two projects, the World Bank added support for land management activities to the third. Forty-one percent of total funding was allocated to credit services for ranchers and 26 percent to land-use planning. See World Bank, *Botswana National Land Management and Livestock Project: Staff Appraisal Report*, Report no. 5471-BT (Nairobi: Eastern and Southern Africa Projects Department, Southern Agriculture Division, The World Bank, 1985). Not all of the multilaterals have been preoccupied with increasing beef production. While the EC and the World Bank were heavily subsidizing the

cattle industry, the local office of the UN Development Programme began supporting the public debate on environmental and ecological issues. According to local
reports, UNDP's resident representative was later compelled to leave the country
after he took certain initiatives without first receiving approval from the political
leadership.

20. For an enlightening, although perhaps overstated, account of an African
ecological control-loss disaster at the turn of this century, see Helge Kjekshus,
*Ecology Control and Economic Development in East African History: The Case of
Tanganyika, 1850–1950* (Berkeley: University of California Press, 1977).

21. World Resources Institute, *Draft Proposal to the Government of Botswana
for the Development of Wildlife Utilization in Botswana* (Washington, D.C.: WRI,
October 3, 1988), 2–3.

22. Ibid.

23. According to World Bank estimates, between 1965 and 1989 Botswana
averaged the world's highest annual growth in per capita GNP, 8.5 percent. World
Bank, *World Development Report 1991*, 204–205 and 271.

24. Louis A. Picard, "Rural Development in Botswana: Administrative
Structures and Public Policy," *The Journal of Developing Areas* 13 (1979): 300.

25. Botswana, *National Development Plan, 1985–91*, 94–96.

26. Samuel Butterfield, *The N.C.S. Methodology and Background Material*
(Gaborone: Ministry of Local Government and Lands, 1985). This widely consultative approach had earlier been employed in the formulation of the Tribal Grazing
Land Policy and other policies having to do with natural resources and rural land
use.

27. Bussing, *National Conservation Strategy*, 7–39. Topics of local concern
included degradation and loss of vegetation, soil erosion, wildlife depletion, water
availability, littering and waste disposal, and the relationship of population growth
to the environment.

28. Ngamiland District Land Use Planning Unit and Kalahari Conservation
Society, *Proposed Land Use Plan for Ngamiland Statelands* (Gaborone:
Department of Surveys and Lands, Ministry of Local Government and Lands,
October 1987); and Lee Hannah, Gary Wetterberg, and Leroy Duvall, *Botswana
Biological Diversity Assessment* (Washington, D.C.: Office of Technical Resources,
Bureau for Africa, USAID, September 1988).

29. At its project paper stage of approval in mid-1989, this effort's stated purpose was "to demonstrate the technical and economic viability of community-based
wildlife management on marginal lands in Southern Africa by increasing employment and community income in target areas of Botswana, Zimbabwe, and Zambia."
U.S. Agency for International Development, "Summary of USAID/SADCC
Regional Natural Resources Management Project," Project no. 690-0251
(USAID/Botswana, Gaborone, 1989, Mimeo), 1.

30. John Cooke and Alec Campbell, eds., *Developing Our Environmental
Strategy*, Proceedings of a seminar organized on behalf of the Botswana
Government (Gaborone: The Botswana Society, 1987).

31. Author interview with John Cooke, head of the Department of
Environmental Science, University of Botswana, Gaborone, May 1989.

32. Ralph Cobham, "NCS Progress: Consensus Before the Action," *Kalahari
Conservation Society Newsletter* 19 (March 1988): 8.

33. Author interviews with informants in and out of government, Gaborone,
May 1989.

34. Jeremy Perkins, "Eastern Kalahari Cattleposts," *Kalahari Conservation
Society Newsletter* 24 (June 1989): 5.

35. Quoted in World Resources Institute, *Draft Proposal*, 3–4. This recom-

mendation is in keeping with the goals of USAID's Regional Natural Resources Management Project. Instead, however, "farmers and RADs [remote area dwellers] . . . referred to the drastic reduction and possible westward retreat of wildlife populations over the past seven years." Ibid.

36. Garrett Hardin, "The Tragedy of the Commons," *Science* 162 (December 13, 1968): 1243–1248.

37. At 10.1 percent between 1980 and 1989, Botswana's average annual urbanization rate was exceeded in only two other countries, Mozambique and Tanzania. World Bank, *World Development Report 1991*, 264–265.

38. Ibid., 207.

39. Cited in Colleen Lowe Morna, "Botswana: Diamonds Buoy Economy," *Africa News* 31 (May 15, 1989): 6.

40. Cooke and Campbell, *Developing Our Environmental Strategy*, 35.

41. World Bank, *World Development Report 1991*, 225.

42. In a comparative historical context, large expanses in the southwestern United States have not yet recovered from the cattle boom of the 1880s.

43. A sampling of this research is reported in S. F. Eicher, *Rural Development in Botswana: A Select Bibliography* (Washington, D.C.: African Bibliographic Center, 1980); F. I. Henderson and J. B. Opschoor, *Botswana's Environment: An Annotated Bibliography* (Gaborone: University College of Botswana, 1981); and R.M.K. Silitshena, "Research and Training Trends and Needs in the Field of Natural Resource Conservation in Botswana," in Yeager et al., *Africa's Conservation for Development*, 66–70.

44. These recommendations are more fully elaborated in my forthcoming paper on the interaction of traditional and modern governing organizations in Botswana.

45. Mayra Buvinic and Sally W. Yudelman, *Women, Poverty and Progress in the Third World*, Headline Series, no. 289 (New York: Foreign Policy Association, 1989), 25.

46. Odell has pointed to the political rationality of this reform, in that

group ranches with relatively few participants will almost always run into difficulties. Schemes, however, to improve grazing conditions and access to water, and to allow for improved management of resources for entire communities, or programs which provide the same for all who wish to participate, without depriving non-participants of the use of grazing areas to which they traditionally enjoyed access, will receive widespread support (M. L. Odell, *Planning for Agriculture in Botswana: A Report on the Arable Lands Survey* [Gaborone: Institute for Development Management, and Planning and Statistics Division, Ministry of Agriculture, 1980], 21–22).

47. See Agnes Kiss, ed., *Living with Wildlife: Wildlife Resource Management with Local Participation in Africa*, World Bank Technical Paper no. 130, Africa Technical Department Series (Washington, D.C.: The World Bank, 1990).

48. *World Development Forum* 4 (1986): 1.

49. For descriptions of these programs, see Botswana, *National Development Plan, 1985–91*, 180 and 184.

50. The ministry's training effort also focuses on two technical positions created during the 1970s, district officer (lands) and district officer (development). These specialists preside over district development committees and in turn are supervised by the district commissioners.

51. John D. Holm, "Liberal Democracy and Rural Development in Botswana," *African Studies Review* 25 (1982): 84.

9

Foreign Policy Decisionmaking in an African Democracy: Evolution of Structures and Processes

James J. Zaffiro

Botswana's foreign policy has served the country well. Surrounded by hostile, white-minority-ruled regimes, economically dependent upon foreign aid and South African imports and infrastructure for its very survival, stricken by the worst drought in living memory, and counted among the poorest countries on earth, this former British protectorate had little hope for long-term viability at independence in September 1966.

Botswana did have a number of advantages, however, even then. Notable among them was the enlightened leadership of its first president, Sir Seretse Khama. It was Khama who almost single-handedly in those early years established the credibility and legitimacy of this new state in international politics.[1] His speeches provide a rich and essential record of the pre-independence roots of Botswana's foreign policy.[2]

What is missing, and what these speeches by themselves cannot provide, is a record of the evolution and growth of the *process* of foreign policy decisionmaking: not the "what" of policy but the "how and by whom," or what Boyce has referred to as the machinery of foreign policymaking and diplomacy, the procedures and institutions for handling external relations.[3]

This chapter analyzes the evolution of structures and processes[4] of Botswana's foreign policymaking, understood broadly as the pursuit of vital national interests beyond a state's borders. Focus is on key decisionmakers, particularly the president, close advisers, cabinet ministers, employees of the Department of External Affairs, and others within ministries having foreign policy responsibilities.

The presidential management styles of both Seretse Khama and his successor, Quett Masire, were (and are) characterized by a particular willingness to seek out and accept expert information and advice before making major decisions. This has nurtured wide elite participation in policymaking and implementation. Reliance on expert advice is a trademark of elite political culture in Botswana.

Governmental structures and foreign policy decisionmaking processes have remained remarkably consistent, as have policy goals and patterns of international behavior, most of which were set before independence and have endured since. Continuity in foreign policy processes and output also owes much to the values and goals shared among members of the first generation of the country's national political and economic elites. Common experiences and training shaped their preference for broad, decentralized organizational and decisionmaking systems, as well as ways of seeking and using information and advice in foreign policymaking.

Given the limited organizational resources and institutional infrastructure available for foreign policy decisionmaking throughout the postindependence period,[5] personal qualities of character and style in Sir Seretse Khama and Sir Quett K. J. Masire remain central to understanding the process of policy decisionmaking. This does not diminish the importance of examining subpresidential systems, particularly as sources of information and advice to top decisionmakers. As talk of the next presidential succession increases amid major domestic, regional, and international changes, the evolution and growth of foreign policy structures and processes take on added significance.

In Botswana the president is by far the most visible, active foreign policy decisionmaker. Important matters of national interest, particularly high level summitry, are handled personally. The minister of external affairs is often present but in a supporting role. At the same time, however, even a cursory examination of bilateral relations with the United States strongly suggests that significant foreign policy responsibility is delegated by the president to other key ministers: important aid and development agreements are often negotiated, signed, and implemented between top Ministry of Finance and Development Planning officials and USAID or embassy officials.

■ Domestic Influences on Foreign Policymaking

The changing domestic political and economic context has begun to alter elite perceptions of Botswana's national interests; timeworn strategies for their pursuit are changing, too. Demographics are particularly critical. One recent estimate predicted that the country's population will double from the current 1.3 million to 2.6 million by 2011. Urban population will leap to 923,000, from its present 245,000.[6]

Noteworthy aspects of a remarkably stable elite polity include unbroken political stability since independence; existence of a de facto one-party state; weak, divided, and poorly organized opposition parties; an efficient, expatriate-dominated bureaucracy; a frustrated, underemployed, foreign-educated professional cadre;[7] and a tradition of civilian control of the military.

Salient socioeconomic features include growing unemployment, absence of major foreign debt, diverse and willing foreign aid donors, rapid but narrowly based, mineral-led economic growth, and widening class inequalities. In 1991 Botswana experienced its first budget deficit since 1982, due to continued growth in government expenditure as revenues from diamonds declined.

■ The British Colonial Legacy and Foreign Affairs

One should not underestimate the impact of the colonial legacy on foreign policy decisionmaking structures and processes in the postindependence era, particularly the role of British authorities and outside advisers to the new government.

Unlike departing French colonial administrations in West Africa, British authorities in Bechuanaland played a minimal direct role in shaping foreign policymaking institutions and structures prior to independence. In 1961, shadow ministries were set up within the Executive Council. Some of their policy concerns embraced foreign affairs, but external relations remained constitutionally reserved for the Office of the Queen's Commissioner.[8]

The practical emphasis of British preparation lay mainly in providing specialized training and rapidly developing new administrative machinery for conducting foreign policy. Bechuanaland had only eight known university students in 1960. Within the civil service in 1962 there were only four Batswana (out of a total of 155) in administrative and professional grades, fifteen (out of 206) at the technical grade, and only twenty-two (out of 182) at the middle-level executive grade.[9] To paraphrase Ayi Kwei Armah, foreign service candidates were not yet born.

On the eve of independence the nucleus of a diplomatic service was established; it comprised a handful of civil servants, many of them teachers (some unmatriculated), all of them rushed to Oxford or London for a crash program of academic training and brief attachments to British embassies.[10] Candidates were selected, sometimes at great sacrifice to the government departments thus robbed, with help from Britain's Colonial Office, Foreign Office, and new Overseas Development Ministry. Out of the resulting cadre emerged Botswana's diplomatic service. Its central founding members included two future foreign ministers, Archibald Mogwe and Gaositiwe Chiepe.[11] Influential roles were played by A.J.A. Douglas, who had been chief secretary in the mid-1950s,[12] and Queen's Commissioner Sir Peter Fawcus; both worked closely with Seretse Khama and Quett Masire just prior to independence in setting up an administrative structure, as well as in initiating important contacts with the US and Scandinavian governments and foundations.[13]

Basic goals and foreign policy interests for the soon-to-be-independent nation began to emerge even before Seretse Khama became prime minister in 1965. As early as November 1963, Fawcus outlined a foreign policy based on strict neutrality, nonracialism, and economic relations with South Africa, "with whom we must trade if we are to live"; he also asserted his determination that the territory "shall not become a mere pawn in international politics or an instrument for any action against other territories." The policy of granting asylum to persons "who if they return to South Africa would face loss of liberty"[14] was also first advanced by the Queen's commissioner, later embraced by Seretse Khama and his new party. Efforts to attract foreign aid and expatriate advisers also began prior to independence and early successes owe much to the personality of the future president and the effectiveness of his representatives.[15]

In 1969, John Syson of the Ariel Foundation was brought in by President Khama to restructure the foreign affairs machinery, with help from David Anderson of the Ford Foundation and Robert Edwards of the Maxwell School of Syracuse University in the early 1970s. Syson also served as the president's political adviser and speech writer until 1974, greatly upgrading the effectiveness of the Office of the President (OOP) in dealing with political aspects of foreign affairs.[16]

■ Presidential Leadership and Foreign Policymaking

Foreign policy decisionmaking in Botswana remains a process dominated by a small, essentially executive elite and managed from the Office of the President, as it has been since 1965. In nearly every important respect, the president is at the center of the structure and dominates the process. Enjoying a degree of access to both traditional and charismatic legitimacy, Khama explicitly rejected both in favor of a regime and a foreign policy based on legal-rational, utilitarian grounds.[17] Following his death in 1980, Khama's successor inherited a booming, diamond-driven economy and a legal-rational claim to lead and shape foreign policy.

Seretse Khama's persona and political presence informed the government machine, even though much decisionmaking authority was left with the higher civil service. No personality cult developed. Other ministers and advisers shared the spotlight. He insisted upon constitutionally correct procedures, especially in relations between civil servants and ministers.[18]

Nonetheless, personal diplomacy was the main channel for the conduct of Botswana's foreign policy. Personal links at the presidential and top ministerial level were cultivated by Seretse Khama with great skill and care. His ability to work with others, provided he saw an opportunity for securing some of his own underlying goals, was a feature of Seretse's approach to foreign policymaking and the key element of his operating style. Notable examples include his fruitful and enduring partnerships with Queen's Commissioner Sir Peter Fawcus (1959–1965), Quett Masire (1958–1980), and later with fellow Frontline presidents Nyerere and Kaunda (1966–1980).

As prime minister in the March 1965 transition government under Queen's Commissioner Sir Hugh Norman-Walker, Khama increasingly became the focus of government. He sometimes felt constrained by constitutional restrictions placed on foreign policy development. As a member of the Legislative Council and Executive Council, he had gone abroad in an official capacity (at Norman-Walker's behest) to gain information and knowledge. Official contacts were also encouraged with newly independent Zambia and with the other High Commission Territories. Pre-independence international contacts centered more upon attracting foreign aid than upon establishing diplomatic relations.

Twenty-five years after independence is a good time to ask whether the process remains a presidential operation with front men (and a woman, the minister) in the Department of External Affairs around to take the political hits. Is the legacy of Seretse Khama so pervasive today, a decade after his passing, that his operating style has become the model for all subsequent presidents in structuring foreign policy decisionmaking? Even if the answer for the current leader is a clear and resounding "yes," the question remains with respect to President Masire's successor, whose identity will probably emerge in advance of the next scheduled national elections in 1994.

Since Seretse Khama's death in 1980, his successor, Sir Quett Masire, has kept foreign policy basically unaltered while "continuing to adapt to the changing circumstances of [our] time."[19] Like his predecessor, Masire has repeatedly stressed that Botswana's foreign policy springs from a combination of the constraints of geopolitical position and a strict adherence to four basic national principles: democracy, development, unity, and self-reliance, which together are designed to achieve social harmony (*Kagisano* in Setswana).[20] He speaks of a policy that derives from "our national ethos of mutual accommodation, tolerance and forbearance" because foreign policy is inseparable from the domestic scene to which it is firmly anchored. The domestic as well as the international environment has an impact on policy formulation.[21]

Dr. Masire inherited the presidency already possessing useful foreign policy management and decisionmaking skills derived from previous careers in education, journalism, and party organization.[22] He has grown tremendously in international stature since becoming president a decade ago. Opposition party leaders acknowledge his statesmanship.[23] He has gradually grown into a more visible leadership role on foreign policy matters, particularly those affecting the Southern African Development Coordination Conference (SADCC) region.[24] He travels extensively and consults frequently with other leaders of the Frontline States. His direct and unassuming leadership style sets him apart from the more charismatic, flamboyant style of his predecessor, as well as from most other African heads of state. He has done well as foreign policy spokesperson for Botswana. Whether he has had as great a hand in charting the course of foreign policy as Sir Seretse is doubtful. Masire was part of the generation of moderate nationalists who helped bring the country to independence without major conflict or bloodshed. He does not enjoy Khama's traditional legitimacy, but he is a better coalition builder and bureaucratic manager.

A future president, particularly if the contest grows sharp for the mantle of leadership within the ruling party, may well try to distinguish himself by a significant change of course in foreign policy. A successor may assume a more direct, personal role in foreign policy decisionmaking than the cabinet consultation and civil service design and implementation approach of Khama and Masire. Lack of experience and the entrenched, "indispensable" quality of top foreign affairs bureaucrats, however, will most likely cushion the transition and help maintain essential continuity as well as content in policy processes.

■ The Public Service and Foreign Policymaking

It has been argued that the government of Botswana has begun to acquire corporatist characteristics. Top civil servants dominate policymaking. Interministerial committees provide the arenas in which many decisions are made. Overseeing the whole process is the Ministry of Finance and Development Planning, with its budget and spending powers. Political parties are referred to as a policy vacuum. Public opinion and affected groups have no hand in drafting policy as "civil servants retain this function for themselves."[25]

How much do the rules and behaviors governing this bureaucratic/elite political culture vary when it comes to *foreign* policymaking? Is foreign policy special, reserved for the president and his own personal advisers? Are top civil servants from the ministries of finance and development planning and of external affairs, and from the Office of the President, the only ones permitted to participate? Within the cabinet, are younger ministers and assistant ministers playing a more active foreign policymaking role, or are permanent secretaries and assistants still dominant? How does the president attempt to structure this new politico-bureaucratic competition? Does he even try? To whom does the president turn for trustworthy information and advice on foreign policy decisions? Indeed, to whom do MPs, ministers, and indeed, top civil servants themselves turn? To expatriates? These questions must be investigated from inside the policy arena.

Information and advice are key resources in foreign policy decision-making. Recent scholarly work on the nature and future development of democracy in the country provides some suggestive clues as to why participation in foreign policymaking is limited in Botswana. Holm and Molutsi speak of civil servants who look upon politicians as interfering in the policymaking process. They also find that many politicians at the national level, both members of the BDP and others, lack the information base or expertise to exercise effective control over the government bureaucracy. Finally, the superior educational backgrounds of top civil servants make them thoroughly intimidating.[26]

These patterns and trends were identified with respect to democratic participation and domestic policymaking. How much more important they are in the case of foreign policymaking can only be conjectured at this point, but the secretive, sensitive nature of foreign affairs presupposes this dynamic even in Western pluralist democracies. In this respect, Botswana's uniquely democratic character, however defined and to whatever degree accepted, may not be such a significant differentiating factor in accounting for the shape and evolution of the state's particular foreign affairs structures and processes since independence.

The Office of the President, which contains a department of external affairs, information, and broadcasting, as well as the Botswana Defence Force, has functioned as a surrogate ministry of foreign affairs since the year before independence. At independence foreign affairs was a small operation run by a handful of people in OOP. There was no minister of foreign affairs until the early 1970s, and no separate permanent secretary. President Khama retained the external affairs portfolio until 1974. Expatriate advisers to the president, including John Syson and Phillip Steenkamp, played important roles.[27] Europeans also played important roles in the Ministry of Finance and Development Planning, particularly Quill Hermans and Peter Landell-Mills.[28]

The 1966 Transitional National Development Plan contained just one paragraph on external affairs, maintaining that "a country with such scant resources as Botswana cannot afford to maintain embassies in all capitals of the world [but] nevertheless it is necessary to have representatives in key places to safeguard the nation's interests." It was proposed that diplomatic missions be opened in London, Washington, and New York (UN), with a roving ambassador in Africa. Each "would be restricted to the most modest establishments considered practical."[29]

The first National Development Plan, covering the 1968–1973 period, still had only one paragraph on external affairs. It spoke of three missions rather than four, with the ambassador to the United States also serving as representative to the UN. The roving ambassador for Africa was based in Lusaka and no further expansion was foreseen during the plan period.[30]

The second National Development Plan (1970–1975), in a brief single paragraph, simply restates earlier information but also offers the important stipulation that "the negotiation of external aid is the responsibility of the Ministry of Finance and Development Planning."[31]

By the third plan period (1973–1978), visible growth in the foreign affairs sector was apparent. Until 1972, foreign affairs had been the exclusive domain of a small cadre of civil servants and expatriate advisers in OOP and Finance. As Botswana's diplomatic connections began to multiply, the need for a separate Department of External Affairs was acknowledged. In that year a secretary for external affairs was appointed and provided with a small but full-time support staff. It was proposed to expand the number of foreign missions by the end of the plan period "to deal with Botswana's continued growth in international contacts."[32] Staff in existing missions were also expanded.

By 1975, with the addition of new diplomatic missions in Brussels and Stockholm, and intensifying activity in Africa and Europe generally, the small agency and its staff were upgraded to ministry status (with name and locus unchanged: Department of External Affairs, Office of the President). Archibald Mogwe became the country's first designated minister of external affairs in the 1974 postelection cabinet.

The 1976–1981 National Development Plan explicitly states that "the External Affairs Department of the Office of the President is responsible for the formulation and implementation of foreign policy." A minister had been designated because of "increasing diplomatic contacts and the increasing need for high-level diplomatic representation at international meetings."[33]

By 1984, estimated staff, both at home and abroad, was fifty-seven.[34] Today it numbers close to a hundred. The sixth National Development Plan (1985–1991) says "the Department [of External Affairs] represents Government in the major international organizations of which Botswana is a member and serves as the lead Government department in promoting friendly relations with other countries."[35]

A division of labor has been institutionalized in foreign affairs, between pure diplomacy and representation on the one hand, and aid, trade, development, and national security aspects of foreign affairs on the other. Other ministries, particularly mineral affairs, commerce and industry, and finance and development planning, take lead roles in these more sensitive bilateral and multilateral "high politics" issues. Thus, to understand the dynamics of the process of foreign policy decisionmaking in Botswana it becomes necessary to look beyond the more visible foreign affairs bureaucratic structures.

In a state where developmental aid is such a crucial component of a successful foreign policy, top public servants in other ministries and departments across the government also play a key role. Many negotiate and sign major international agreements and carry out projects that involve foreign policy in spirit, if not explicitly in name. The Department of External Affairs has the task of coordination, although in practice both the Office of the President and Finance and Development have assumed a share of this function, partly due to staff and resource limitations within the department and partly a result of bureaucratic politics and turf-protecting at the ministerial and permanent secretary levels. Personal friendships and networks of trust, both at home and abroad, are also important in the foreign policy process. This includes informal advisers with no formal role in the OOP structure or public service.

■ Department and Minister of External Affairs

The Department of External Affairs, in the Office of the President, has a mixed functional and regional structure, with a political and economic bureau and small bureaus for the United Nations, Americas, Europe, Africa, and the EEC specified in the current structure of central government.[36] Notably absent in this scheme is Asia. With Japan becoming a significant donor of bilateral aid and with Botswana's 1991 decision to establish its first Far Eastern diplomatic mission in the People's Republic of China, this may be expected to change.[37]

External Affairs has pledged to increase the number of missions abroad and to strengthen its overworked diplomatic staff, which is stretched thin by multicountry accreditations (for example, the Brussels mission is responsible for relations with all twelve EC states).[38]

The department has functioned as a ministry at budget time, with Minister Chiepe, instead of the minister of presidential affairs, presenting proposed estimates to the National Assembly as a separate package for debate and Committee of Supply authorization. Recent years have seen notable growth in funds for foreign relations. Budget figures for 1979 show that P1.183 million (US $591,000), or approximately 1.3% of the recurrent expenditure, was allocated to foreign affairs.[39] By 1984 the figure had grown to P2.97 million (US $1.48 million).[40] For the 1988/89 financial year nearly US $6 million was allocated.[41] A new mission in Windhoek, Namibia, opened in 1991, and there are plans to purchase more properties for other overseas missions (to avoid high rents). Plans call for opening of additional foreign missions "in order to increase the Department's capacity to further Botswana's interests, at an estimated cost of US $4.2 million."[42]

External Affairs has called for more local training, either an in-house training course or one handled by the University of Botswana or Institute of Development Management (IDM). A number of retired diplomats work at or consult for IDM.[43] Currently foreign service officers are sent abroad for training to Oxford University, the London School of Economics, and Columbia University, as well as to training seminars and courses at universities and institutes in several Commonwealth countries.[44] As the number of foreign missions expands during the National Development Plan VII period (1991–1996), and as the size of Botswana's major missions grows, with addition of commercial attachés and secretaries, it may soon become economically viable to institute a regular program of home-based training for diplomats.

In the early postindependence years, ambassadorial appointments were out of necessity drawn from the small pool of university-educated elites in the top ranks of government service, the academic community, or the tiny commercial sector. By the 1980s the pool of candidates had grown somewhat as more and more university students graduated and officials gained experience. The current ambassador to the United States was formerly a district commissioner and permanent secretary in the Ministry of Local Government and Lands.[45] As is the case in most African diplomatic communities, experienced and politically trustworthy elite members are moved from sector to sector, ministry to ministry, as need dictates.[46] Politics and regionalism sometimes play a role in appointments, such as that of Kgosi Linchwe II of Mochudi as Botswana's ambassador to Washington in the 1970s.

As is generally true of permanent secretaries throughout the government, the permanent secretary for external affairs, currently Sam Mpuchane,[47] is the key departmental link with the president and cabinet and department at home and abroad. Many, if not most, of the major routine decisions are made by him working closely with the minister of external affairs and directly with the president. Another important connection is between Mpuchane and the permanent secretary to the president. Before the establishment of a separate Department of External Affairs, the president's secretary served in this pivotal role. Festus Mogae and L. M. Mpotokwane, as close advisers to President Masire, have been key players in the foreign policy decisionmaking process. Another important player was Charles Tibone, an outspoken permanent secretary during the 1970s.

Top civil servants are the key decisionmakers on matters of policy implementation. When a crisis arises, or in cases where broad lines of policy or long-established policy positions are open for reinterpretation or replacement, the cabinet plays a greater role, as the president searches for consensus.

On matters of national security policy the department works closely with the Office of the President, the Defence Council, and the Botswana Defence Force (BDF), playing more of a coordinating than a decisionmaking role. It is the official spokesman of government in times of crisis, as was the case on government pronouncements following the 1985, 1986, and 1988 South African Defence Force (SADF) raids on Botswana.

Ambassadorial appointments are made by the president on the advice of senior department and public service officials.[48] Currently Botswana has eight diplomatic missions with ambassadors or high commissioners, most accredited to several states and international organizations. The number of resident missions continues to grow, from ten in 1986[49] to fourteen in 1990. The number of nonresident missions accredited to Botswana has also grown, from twenty-two in 1979, to thirty-six in 1983,[50] to over forty as of 1990. Botswana is also a member of many international organizations, including the OAU, UN, Associate Member of the EC, SADCC, SACU, and the Nonaligned Movement. Indeed External Affairs played a major role in the 1980 founding of SADCC, which is headquartered in Gaborone.

■ Cabinet Politics and Foreign Policy Decisionmaking

Following his victory in the 1984 general elections, President Masire reshuffled the cabinet. After ten years as minister of external affairs, Archie Mogwe swapped posts with Minerals and Water Resources Minister Dr. Gaositwe Chiepe.[51] A strong, activist foreign minister, Mogwe had fought for larger budget allocations and staffing for his department, particularly during the 1980s as the country's international commitments and interests multiplied and diversified. It was Mogwe who called upon other ministers to begin taking responsibility for representation at international conferences and in staffing to cover foreign affairs issues of direct interest to their ministries. In the absence of such support his department was compelled to draw from its own limited manpower resources to provide appropriate representation. Multiple accreditations, plus the hobbling effect of an "unrealistically low" manpower percentage growth rate (3.2 percent per annum), had made it nearly impossible for foreign missions to meet these needs.[52]

At times Mogwe seemed to be speaking definitively on the nature and goals of the country's foreign policy.[53] His strong criticism of US policy in southern Africa, which won him few friends in the Reagan administration, may have been somewhat reflective of policy differences within the cabinet. Since the reshuffle, his promarket individualism and tough negotiating skills have been put to good use in the Ministry of Mineral Resources, particularly in managing the country's booming diamond sector.

Dr. G.K.T. Chiepe, a teacher prior to party, diplomatic, and government service, is more measured and subdued in her style.[54] She has emphasized cooperation and coordination on foreign policy matters between ministries. She works well with President Masire and enjoys his respect and trust. A team player rather than a flamboyant individualist, Chiepe has distinguished herself by her dignified, effective manner representing the country in key international forums such as the United Nations—particularly during the Security Council debate following the June 1985 South African military raid on Gaborone. Her credibility within the cabinet is best exemplified by the frequent travel and important nondiplomatic assignments she is called upon to perform by the president in the areas of education, employment, and development.

As the government's chief spokesperson, Dr. Chiepe has proven effective in arguing the government's case. She has been ably served by Department Secretary for External Affairs Jeffrey Garabamono and his replacement, Sam Mpuchane. Mpuchane has been described by one outside observer as "the brains behind foreign policy."[55] He works closely with Chiepe and President Masire, particularly on especially sensitive matters, such as bilateral meetings with South African officials.

A number of other key individuals in the cabinet are influential in foreign affairs. The former director of personnel, Ponatshego Kedikilwe, was brought out of early retirement and named assistant minister in Finance and Development Planning. By 1985, following some undisclosed disagreement and friction involving Minister of Presidential Affairs and Public Administration Daniel Kwelogobe, Kedikilwe was brought over to OOP as his replacement; Kwelogobe was shifted to Agriculture.

During his five years at the helm, Kedikilwe proved a tough civil servant who served as enforcer for a number of unpopular government decisions, including the deportation by presidential order of people on a list furnished by the South African Security Services following the June 1985 SADF raid on Gaborone. Kedikilwe also spoke out harshly and repeatedly against private press investigative reporting of circumstances surrounding the raid. Described as "cool, efficient, and tough," he was considered by some as the second most influential man next to the president, and included as a member of a foreign policy inner circle of ministers and advisers, along with the new vice president, Festus Mogae, and former BDF Commander (now Minister of Presidential Affairs) Major General Mompati Merafhe, Police Commissioner Simon Hirschfeld, and his brother, who heads the Intelligence Services.[56] Agriculture Minister Daniel Kwelogobe remains influential, particularly within party circles, although his transfer from Presidential Affairs in 1984 was seen by many as a demotion.

Whether an inner cabinet exists as a defined entity and makes foreign policy decisions independent of the full cabinet remains a matter for speculation. Henderson reports that Seretse Khama worked with the full range of cabinet colleagues, allowing everyone, even assistant ministers, to speak out. He believes that the cabinet thus developed a significant decisionmaking capacity, even though it relied heavily on civil service advice.[57] This model has most likely carried over to the Masire cabinet. In important meetings, such as during the September 1990 official visit of Namibian president Sam Nujoma to Gaborone, Mogwe, Kedikilwe, and General Merafhe were included in official mentions as important participants.[58]

Other ministers are gaining some influence on foreign policy matters of special concern to their area. This process is well along for Commerce and Industry, inasmuch as the scale of foreign trade and of foreign desire to invest in Botswana has grown beyond the capacity of External Affairs to coordinate and manage it with its own limited diplomatic personnel. Commercial attachés have been named to five overseas posts.[59]

As formerly nonpolitical elites filter into top ranks of cabinet, what are the implications for Botswana's foreign policy decisionmaking processes? More participants? Less consensus among decisionmakers? A foreign policy at long last more self-consciously responsive to electoral pressures than to external geostrategic and economic ones, as has been the case since independence in 1966? Are changing domestic conditions causing top leaders to view foreign policy as a less closed, isolated area of the overall government policy process? Is foreign policy decisionmaking becoming more political as the number and skills of top players increase and as the range of their competing interests becomes more diverse?

New players arriving in the policy arena find traditional intraparty adversaries already contending there. As the 1994 election season approaches, these personality conflicts may spill over into consensus areas of government and party policymaking, including foreign policy. Basic foreign policy interests and goals will need to be adjusted accordingly. If this involves questioning traditional goals, then personality conflicts will be intensified by basic policy disagreements.

■ The Diplomatic Service

In Botswana, as is true across Africa, top positions in the diplomatic service and public service on the home front are shuffled frequently. The Public Service Commission has selected talented top administrators from government departments with little or no foreign affairs training and experience and thrust them into top ambassadorial assignments. This happened in 1989 when the director of Information and Broadcasting, Mrs. Margaret Nasha, was named Botswana's new high commissioner to the United Kingdom. Similarly, career diplomats have on a number of occasions been called from service abroad or from the Department of External Affairs to take charge of Information and Broadcasting.[60]

The government has also rewarded party loyalists with diplomatic assignments, as was the case in 1984 when a junior BDP MP stepped down from Parliament and was given the post of ambassador to the Nordic countries (and later the post of high commissioner to the United Kingdom), which allowed the president to use his Specially Elected prerogative to nominate former Vice President Peter Mmusi to Parliament after his defeat in the Gaborone North constituency.[61] Interviewed by the private press on his return to party politics in 1989, the displaced legislator revealed that his appointment to the Foreign Service "was a purely political matter. In my case the president simply decided on the matter and informed me. Even the Ministry [Department] of External Affairs did not have to recommend me."

Staff shortages and training needs create difficulties for the Department, which in the face of growth in overseas missions has often been hard pressed to shift top people from headquarters to ambassadorial posts or bring home ambassadors to fill top administrative posts in Gaborone.[62] As further expansion looms, one would expect even more borrowing from Peter to pay Paul to fill ambassadorial assignments; this was the case in 1989 when Botswana's UN ambassador was called home to represent the country in Namibia.[63] Younger and younger officers are reaching the top ranks of the service; future arrivals may also be less and less experienced, unless a major training and recruitment effort is launched soon. Over the past decade a concerted effort has been made to provide better training and support to Botswana's diplomats abroad. Biennial heads of mission conferences have been sponsored by the government. Such conferences afford junior diplomats opportunities to meet with the president, the minister of external affairs, and representatives of other ministries to discuss common problems and to interact with colleagues and support staff from headquarters of the Department of External Affairs.[64] These meetings are useful ways of briefing representatives on crucial new policy areas, such as the environment.

■ National Assembly and Foreign Policymaking

Since independence the legislative role in foreign policy decisionmaking in Botswana has been limited usually to discussion or debate of policies already decided in cabinet or carried out by the president, the Department of External Affairs, or other ministries. Under the constitution, the National Assembly has treaty ratification powers in the foreign affairs area but these have not been used in practice. There is no constitutionally defined role for the legislative branch in foreign policy decisionmaking, except for a limited power of the purse within the ranks of ruling party MPs.

Moreover, Parliament has limited information and no research staff to support involvement in or even informed debate of foreign policy by members.[65] Recent calls for a greater foreign policy role are in large measure a function of growing general desire for more autonomy and a larger governing role by the National Assembly. Since 1988 MPs have repeatedly called upon the government to detach administrative responsibility for the National Assembly and the House of Chiefs from the Office of the President and to provide new facilities.[66] These demands come most strongly from younger, better educated, and ambitious back-benchers of the ruling party, as well as from opposition members.[67]

A new Parliament building, complete with office space and a library, should go a long way toward solving space problems. The larger and thornier issue of an underdeveloped legislative branch, sheltered under the budgetary and administrative wing of the Office of the President and treated as just another government department, remains for a future government to resolve. This is especially vexing for a country that regularly proclaims its exceptional status as a genuine representative African democracy.

The Minister of External Affairs has regularly briefed Assembly members on major foreign policy issues and during periods of crisis (for example, following SADF raids).[68] President Masire and Minister Chiepe have stated repeatedly the importance of collective responsibility and regular interparty consultations on security, defense, and foreign policy concerns "where the country has to present a united front to the rest of the world and against potential enemies."[69] Opposition leaders have at times taken pains to correct perceptions of their disagreement with government on key foreign policy matters, such as the signing of a Nkomati-like nonaggression pact with South Africa in the mid-1980s.[70]

Foreign affairs issues are not very prominent in the written and oral question reports of Botswana's *Hansard*. Not surprisingly, most questions tend to focus upon domestic economic concerns. Many MPs of the ruling Botswana Democratic Party (BDP) speak in support of government foreign policy positions: by contrast, ever since the early days following independence, opposition parties have had little to say on foreign policy in their manifestos, programs, and speeches.[71]

Two opposition party MPs who have, however, used question time and annual budget debates to raise foreign policy issues are Dr. Kenneth Koma of the Botswana National Front (BNF) and Motsamai Mpho of the Botswana Independence Party (BIP). Koma has called for turning of External Affairs into a full-fledged ministry, more language training for diplomats, the promotion of External Affairs staff to ambassadorial posts, and more frequent foreign policy briefings for the opposition.[72]

Members generally support the government on foreign policy across party lines. This was strikingly demonstrated in the aftermath of the June 14, 1985, SADF raid on Gaborone. President Masire met with leaders of all opposition parties within days of the raid[73] and Minister of Home Affairs Kgabo publicly thanked the opposition for standing with the government in the face of the crisis.[74]

Some members have called upon the department to request more money for expansion of its activities abroad.[75] A few BDP members outside of the cabinet have been more vocal in the debates on foreign policy matters than their colleagues. One actually called for the establishment of a Parliamentary Foreign Affairs Committee with provision for opposition representation and staff support. This idea has some support among the younger, better educated MPs. Greater legislative involvement in foreign affairs is likely if the country remains stable and prosperous following the 1994 elections.

■ The Military and Foreign Policy

Botswana did not even have an army until 1976, when threats to territorial security from neighboring white-ruled states finally prompted President Khama to accept its necessity.[76] From the beginning civilian control over the military has been a cardinal principle from which leaders in government and the Botswana Defence Force command have never deviated.[77] Both the constitution and the BDF Act of 1977 are clear on this point.[78] President Masire has called for the BDF to be professional and concerned with the security of the country and its citizens.[79]

The president is commander in chief of the armed forces. His power extends to determining the composition of a civilian Defence Council, which provides that the BDF commander serve as *ex-officio* member. This group has been rumored to function as an inner cabinet on national security matters, with participants coming mainly from top civil servants in the foreign affairs sector and trusted senior ministers with experience in foreign policy, like Archibald Mogwe. Under the terms of the Botswana Defence Force Act, the president also appoints not only the commander but also the top officers. Brigadier Ian Khama, son of the late president, and Lieutenant Colonel Moeng Pheto are examples. These men have made the paramountcy of the defense mission of the Botswana military quite clear in public statements when the issue of military influence in foreign affairs or national policy in general has been raised.[80] For his part, President Masire has on rare occasions dramatized his leading role in this area by putting on a BDF uniform and presiding at a military parade, an action that seems strangely out of place in a state so self-conscious of its civilian democracy and so careful to guard its political legitimacy.[81]

The president also determines functions and roles for the military forces besides national defense; for example, he can commit BDF troops to international peacekeeping bodies, or assign them to internal peacekeeping duties to supplement the police in case of domestic unrest. There is no minister of defense in the government, but with the first commander of the BDF now in the cabinet and presumably on the Defence Council, these presidential powers may be shared to a much greater extent, at least at the consultative level, than has previously been the case.

President Masire may be making a conscious effort to bring together BDF commanders with higher-grade permanent secretaries in public service and government ministers as the elite political culture continues to evolve toward 1994. Likewise, by consciously choosing to keep External Affairs and the BDF under one roof, President Masire is using the Office of the President as an organizational elite melting pot, thereby increasing the likelihood of future harmony between foreign policymakers and their subordinates. Legitimacy, stability, and more effective policy should result.

The presence in the cabinet of the most experienced, trusted senior representative of the military sends a clear signal to the party, the military, and particularly to presidential aspirants that continuity and stability remain crucial components of the next leadership transition and beyond. This may also be viewed in light of continuing talk of an eventual political career for Ian Khama. Married, installed as nominal chief of the Bamangwato, and commander of the BDF, all at a relatively young age, he is more and more a serious contender for eventual national leadership. To many, his eventual entry into political life seems a matter of "when" and "how," rather than "if."

The budget of the BDF, like that of External Affairs, remains under control of the Office of the President and is regularly presented to the National Assembly by the minister of presidential affairs. The budget underwent a dramatic growth spurt during the 1980s, rising by over 600 percent, as arms acquisition and training, including the development of an air arm,[82] were stepped up to counter the threat of further South African military incursions.

Compared to other African states with far less severe security threats, Botswana spent relatively little on defense until recently. The 1986–1987 defense budget was $7.81 million and the 1979–1985 National Development Plan allocated an additional P72 million ($35 million) to defense.[83] By 1987–1988, approximately $27.5 million, or about 4 percent of the budget, was allocated to the BDF.[84] Botswana's 1989 defense allocation rose sharply, by 57 percent, to $58 million.[85] Recruitment was stepped up[86] and soldiers were even raising fruits and vegetables to save taxpayers money.[87] The 1991–1992 request of P76.4 million ($38.2 million) represents a 29 percent increase over the previous year and accounts for 56 percent of the total Presidential Affairs Ministry request.[88] With the military threat from the SADF receding somewhat since the coming to power of F. W. de Klerk and the release of Nelson Mandela, projected levels of growth in defense spending are probably being revised further downward.

■ **External Influences on Foreign Policymaking**

Finally, in addition to the domestic patterns and trends discussed above, Botswana's regional position has improved dramatically in the wake of diamond-driven economic growth, changes in South Africa, growth of SADCC, and Namibian independence. The 1980s bequeathed striking opportunities for foreign policy adaptations to a changing regional environment.

A list of important regional issues and challenges for Botswana foreign policy in the 1990s must certainly include: (1) coming to terms with a majority-ruled South Africa, economically as well as politically, (2) the foreign exchange surplus at home, (3) Namibian independence, (4) addition of two new members to SADCC, (5) reconstruction of and reconciliation with postwar Angola and Mozambique, and (6) increasing foreign aid to southern Africa from new sources, particularly Japan and Germany, and diminishing aid from old ones, including Britain and the United States.

Botswana suddenly finds itself in a post–Cold War world. It may also soon find itself with a neighbor to the south under new majority rule. As regional and international environments change, it seems reasonable to assume that new vital national interests will emerge, in some cases replacing long-standing others.

If these change sufficiently rapidly and differ significantly from prevailing interests, then the structure and process of foreign policy decision-making will have to change as well. Given the volatility of key personalities and the evolving character of the national elite culture, it should not automatically be assumed that such changes will enhance, or even preserve, present levels of administrative democracy.

■ Notes

I wish to thank the Research and Development Committee of Central College, Counsellor Cecil Manyuela of the Botswana Embassy in Washington, D.C., and Professors Willie Henderson and Richard Dale for encouragement and suggestions. Views expressed are those of the author.

1. See Willie Henderson, "Seretse Khama: A Personal Appreciation," *African Affairs* 89, no. 354 (January 1990): 27–56, for an excellent study of leadership traits, management style, and personal history surrounding the political career of Botswana's first president.

2. See Willie Henderson, "Seretse Khama and the Institutionalization of the Botswana State," in Willie Henderson, ed., *Botswana: Education, Culture and Politics* (Edinburgh: Centre for African Studies, 1990), 217–242. For key statements by Seretse Khama, see "We Shall Not Be Attached to Any One Camp, Says Khama," *Mafeking Mail and Protectorate Guardian* (Mafeking, South Africa), April 23, 1965, 7; and Gwendolen M. Carter and E. Philip Morgan, eds., *From the Frontline: Speeches of Sir Seretse Khama* (Bloomington: Indiana University Press, 1981), for a major sampling of his foreign policy speeches.

3. Peter J. Boyce, *Foreign Affairs for New States* (New York: St. Martin's, 1977), 2, 5.

4. See James A. Caporaso et al., "The Comparative Study of Foreign Policy: Perspectives on the Future," *International Studies Notes* 13, no. 2 (Spring 1987): 40. Structure: "a compound of activities sufficiently stable . . . [over time]"; a process: "a smoother unfolding of events over time [including longer time-frame decision-making]." Ibid.

5. See Maurice A. East, "Foreign Policy-Making in Small States," *Policy Sciences* 4, no. 4 (December 1973): 491–508.

6. *Consumer Markets Abroad* (Ithaca, N.Y.: 1989), 15.

7. See Sam Kauffmann, "Young Professionals Stifled in Botswana," *Christian Science Monitor*, April 22, 1991, 12.

8. Letter to the author from Sir Peter Fawcus, former Queen's Commissioner for Bechuanaland, January 6, 1991.

9. Louis A. Picard, *The Politics of Development in Botswana* (Boulder, Colo.: Lynne Rienner, 1987), 85.

10. Boyce, *Foreign Affairs*, 28.

11. Letter to the author from A.J.A. Douglas, CMG, May 7, 1989. Douglas was chief secretary in the protectorate under Sir Peter Fawcus prior to independence; see also Henderson, "Seretse Khama: A Personal Appreciation," 44.

12. Letter to author from Alan H. Donald, formerly chief information officer in the Bechuanaland Protectorate, 1960–1966, April 24, 1989.

13. Author interview with Sir Peter Fawcus, London, April 1, 1989.

14. See Edwin S. Munger, *Bechuanaland: Pan-African Outpost or Bantu Homeland?* (London: Oxford University Press, 1965), 84–85, and his address to the Bechuanaland Protectorate Legislature, November 1963.

15. Anthony Sillery, *Botswana: A Short Political History* (London: Methuen, 1974), 164.

16. Letter to the author from Neil Parsons, March 12, 1990.

17. Lawrence Frank, "Khama and Jonathan: Leadership Strategies in Contemporary Southern Africa," *Journal of Developing Areas* 15, no. 1 (January 1981): 197.

18. Henderson, "Seretse Khama: A Personal Appreciation," 55.

19. Q.K.J. Masire, "Botswana Foreign Policy Perspectives," *Development Dialogue* (Uppsala, Sweden), nos. 1–2 (1984): 1.

20. "Botswana's Foreign Policy Spelt Out," *Daily News* (Gaborone), May 8, 1984, 3.

21. "Our Foreign Policy Should Be As It Is," *Daily News*, August 22, 1986, 1.

22. "Profile: President Quett Masire," *Africa*, no. 109 (September 1980): 40–41.

23. "Masire: A True African Statesman," *Daily News*, September 12, 1990, 3.

24. See Johannes Pilane, "Masire: Africa's Great Statesman," *Daily News*, February 2, 1987, 1, for Namibian praise of Dr. Masire.

25. Ibid., 10.

26. John D. Holm and Patrick P. Molutsi, "Monitoring the Development of Democracy: Our Botswana Experience" (Paper presented to the Annual Meeting of the African Studies Association, Atlanta, Georgia, November 2–5, 1989), 2.

27. Author interview with Cecil Manyuela, Counsellor, Embassy of the Republic of Botswana, Washington, D.C., July 13, 1989.

28. Letter to author from Professor Willie Henderson, May 30, 1990.

29. Republic of Botswana, *Transitional Plan for Social and Economic Development* (Gaborone: The Government Printer, 1966), 41, par. 242.

30. Republic of Botswana, *National Development Plan, 1968–73* (Gaborone: The Government Printer, August 1968), 69, par. 10.3.

31. Republic of Botswana, *National Development Plan, 1970–75* (Gaborone: The Government Printer, September 1970), 125, par. 10.21.

32. Republic of Botswana, *National Development Plan, 1973–78, Part I* (Gaborone: The Government Printer, 1973), 319, sec. xvi.

33. Republic of Botswana, *National Development Plan IV, 1976–81* (Gaborone: The Government Printer, May 1977), 249.

34. James H. Polhemus, "Botswana's Role in the Liberation of Southern Africa," in Louis A. Picard, ed., *The Evolution of Modern Botswana* (London: Rex Collings, 1985), 233.

35. Republic of Botswana, *National Development Plan VI, 1985–91* (Gaborone: The Government Printer, 1985), 347.

36. Ibid., fig. 1.1.

37. "China Appreciates Decision," *Daily News*, May 10, 1991, 1.

38. "External Affairs Pledges to Increase Foreign Missions," *Daily News*, March 30, 1987, 2.

39. Richard Dale, "Botswana and the International Political System," in Louis A. Picard, ed., *The Evolution of Modern Botswana* (London: Rex Collings, 1985).

40. Jowitt Mbongwe, "External Affairs Budget Reflects 11% Increase," *Daily News*, March 20, 1984, 2.

41. "Chiepe Requests Over P11m for Her Ministry," *Daily News*, March 20, 1989, 3.

42. Botswana, *National Development Plan VI, 1985–91*, 347; and Part II, 1.5: (EX 01), Mission Buildings.

43. For example, E. L. Setswaelo and M. Modise, both are also former directors of information and broadcasting; letter to the author from Professor Ranwedzi Nengwekhulu, IDM, Gaborone, June 29, 1989.

44. Author interview with Hon. Mrs. Margaret Nasha, Botswana high commissioner to Great Britain, London, April 2, 1989.

45. "DC's Are Not Governors," *Daily News*, September 21, 1988, 6.

46. See "Two More Diplomatic Missions May Be Opened," *Daily News*, January 30, 1989, 3.

47. "Mpuchane Talks to Norwegian Journalist," *Daily News*, January 13, 1983, 1; Mr. Mpuchane was the former Botswana high commissioner to the United Kingdom.

48. Author interview with Mr. Cecil Manyuela, Counsellor, Embassy of Botswana, Washington, D.C., July 1989.

49. "Botswana Houses More Diplomatic Corps," *Daily News*, December 3, 1986, 1.

50. Republic of Botswana, Ministry of Finance and Development Planning, *National Development Plan V, Vol. II* (Gaborone: The Government Printer, May 1985), 16–20.

51. "New Cabinet Is Announced," *Daily News*, September 14, 1984, 1.

52. "Magang's Request for Commercial Attaches," *Daily News*, March 28, 1983, 2.

53. See "The Western Five Have Failed—Mogwe," *Daily News*, November 17, 1983, 1; and "Mogwe Says the U.S. Delayed Namibian Independence," *Daily News*, January 25, 1983, 1.

54. See "The View From the Eye of the Storm," *MacLean's* 93 (March 3, 1980) 40, for a personal interview with Dr. Chiepe when she was minister of mineral resources.

55. See "Botswana Team Goes to Pretoria for Security Discussions," *Daily Gazette* (Gaborone), February 6, 1986, 1; "Gaborone and Pretoria Discuss Bilateral Issues," *Daily News*, September 19, 1988, 1.

56. See *Africa Confidential* (London) 26, no. 21 (October 16, 1985), reprinted in *Mmegi wa Dikang* (Gaborone), November 9, 1985, 4.

57. Henderson, "Seretse Khama: A Personal Appreciation," 54.

58. "Botswana, Namibia Condemn Iraq," *Daily News*, September 10, 1990, 1–3.

59. Larona Sedimo, "Commercial Attaches Will Increase," *Daily News*, January 30, 1989, 3.

60. See James J. Zaffiro, "Broadcasting in Post-Independence Botswana: The First Twenty Years" (Paper presented to the African Studies Association Annual Meeting, Chicago, October 30, 1988).

61. "Matlhabaphiri Awaits Primaries," *Mmegi wa Dikang*, February 11–17, 1989, 5; and "President Confirms Press Speculation," *Daily News*, May 9, 1989, 1.

62. See "Rasebotsa Posted to Zambia," *Daily News*, February 3, 1984, 4; "Mpofu Appointed Ambassador," *Daily News*, February 16, 1987, 1; "Garebamono Is New Admin. Secretary," *Daily News*, July 5, 1989, 4.

63. Desmond Montshiwa, "Masire Commended for Releasing Legwaila to Serve in Namibia," *Daily News*, July 28, 1989, 4.

64. See "Come Home, Meet, Find Common Ground—Masire," *Daily News*, May 22, 1991, 1.

65. "MP's Must Be Enlightened on Foreign Relations," *Daily News*, December 10, 1987, 3.

66. Johannes Pilane, "MP's Want Parliament Autonomous," *Daily News*, March 10, 1988, 3.

67. Larona Sedimo, "Parliament Is a Supreme Body," *Daily News*, April 13, 1988, 3.

68. Kwapeng Modikwe, "House Briefed on SA's Aggression," *Daily News*, March 30, 1988, 1.

69. See "Why Botswana Democracy Works," *Daily News*, May 11, 1984, 1; "Lack of Collective Responsibility Can Bring Down Government," *Daily News*, February 17, 1986, 1–2; and "Botswana's Democratic System Is Dynamic and Elastic," *Daily News*, October 28, 1988, 4.

70. See "Koma Refutes Press Report," *Botswana Guardian*, May 4, 1984, 1; and "BNF Harbours No Coup d'Etat Ideas," *Daily News*, June 29, 1987, 5.

71. Botswana Peoples' Party, *Thulaganyo* (Francistown: BPP, 1967), 1, 7–9.

72. "BNF Concerned About Quality of Ambassadors," *Daily News*, March 21, 1989, 3.

73. "Dr. Masire to Meet Party Leaders," *Daily News*, June 21, 1985, 1.

74. "SA Should Respect Our Policy—Kgabo," *Daily News*, August 5, 1985, 1.

75. "External Affairs Pledges to Increase Foreign Missions," *Daily News*, March 30, 1987, 2.

76. See Richard Dale, "The Creation and Use of the Botswana Defence Force," *Round Table* (London), no. 290 (April 1984), 216–235.

77. See Mompati S. Merafhe, "The Role of the Army in a Society," *Sethamo* (journal of the BDF) (Gaborone), nos. 1–2 (1981): 4–5; Larona Sedimo, "Soldiers Relied Upon as Protectors," *Daily News*, August 23, 1989, 1.

78. *Constitution of Botswana* (Gaborone: The Government Printer, 1972), Part III, sec. 49(2)(3); Botswana Defence Force Act No. 13 of 1977, in *Government Gazette* (15) 27, April 15, 1977, A109–187.

79. Jowitt Mbongwe, "Govt. Wants Effective BDF," *Daily News*, May 18, 1984, 1.

80. "Ian Khama: Security Is Paramount," *Financial Mail* (Johannesburg), March 5, 1982, 1059; Moeng Pheto, "Formation of Botswana Army: Where National Security Starts," *BDF Newsletter*, nos. 2–3 (1980): 8–9.

81. *Daily News*, April 20, 1983, 1; and April 27, 1983, 4.

82. Keshholofetse Phetlu, "Everything Done to Equip Air Arm," *Daily News*, November 9, 1983, 1; "Army Needs Effective Leadership," *Daily News*, February 17, 1983, 2.

83. *Africa Contemporary Record* (1986–1987): B642.

84. U.S. Department of State, *Botswana* (Washington: USGPO, 1988), 1.

85. As reported in *Southscan* (London), February 22, 1989; see also *Mmegi wa Dikang* (Gaborone), February 18–24, 1989, 3.

86. "Careers in the Botswana Defence Force," *Mmegi wa Dikang,* December 3, 1988, Careers Supplement, 1.

87. "BDF Praised," *Daily News,* September 5, 1989, 4.

88. "BDF Seeks a P30.5 Million Increase," *Daily News,* March 7, 1991, 3; "BDF Gets 56% of Allocated Funds," *Daily News,* March 7, 1991, 5.

PART 3

BOTSWANA IN A CHANGING SOUTHERN AFRICA

10

Botswana as a Hostage to High Politics? Twentieth Century Conflict with South Africa and Zimbabwe

Richard Dale

Ever since the 1960s, much of the literature on Botswana and also on South African foreign relations has asserted that Botswana (like Lesotho and Swaziland) is a South African hostage. This may gratify those who find apartheid appealing and discourage others who find it appalling. Still, the hostage metaphor is analytically flaccid, static, and intellectually slothful because it does not really grapple with the conceptual or empirical issues. It is more fruitful to visualize the relationship, as thoughtful students of Botswana have done, as an asymmetrical interdependence, recognizing the imbalances between the two partners. But does that characterize a whole host of issues, or just a few? We need to determine the range or extent of imbalances with distinct partners so that, for instance, we can ascertain whether state A is much more dependent upon state B than the converse with respect to issue areas X, Y, and Z. If we conduct this analysis over time, we can judge whether the asymmetry is becoming more or less pronounced for any issue or cluster of issue areas.

The fascination with the regional power of South Africa, and the moral indignation of outsiders with the unsavory application of that power in a form that has come to be called destabilization, has obscured the significance of Zimbabwe as Botswana's next most important neighbor. Much less is written about Botswana and Zimbabwe than about Botswana and South Africa, yet the same range of questions can be posed. In what dimensions can Botswana be regarded as Zimbabwe's hostage (and vice versa); that is, what is the range and extent of the asymmetry? Has the shift from minority to majority rule in Zimbabwe changed the asymmetry? If so, what might this portend for Botswana's relations with South Africa following the demise of minority rule in Pretoria?

Although we acknowledge that Botswana's relations with these two powerful states are a blend of cooperation and conflict, in this chapter we confine ourselves to the patterns of conflict, realizing that there is no clear dividing line between cooperative and conflictual behavior. The one can fade out and blend into the other, so that conflict resolution can lay the groundwork for subsequent cooperation. We examine Botswana's relations first with South Africa and then with Zimbabwe (before and after independence), paying close regard to specific conflict issues. We show that where Botswana and Zimbabwe are concerned, pockets of residual conflict remain in most of the selected issue areas. Regime change does not necessarily insure conflict abatement.

We shall explore three issues: political status and territorial integrity; refugee influx, management, and burden sharing; and military security against armed attack. These three issues constitute a cluster; moreover, they are important issues of the sort that political scientists usually regard as "high politics," for they involve the integrity and security of the nation-state.[1] Thus we examine the topic of Botswana as a hostage to high politics with particular reference to its two most powerful neighbors, South Africa and Zimbabwe.

The rationale for the first issue is that Botswana might never have become a separate political entity had it been absorbed by its southern and eastern neighbors. The country's escape from this fate (fairly recent in historical terms) leaves its leaders concerned about its international status and territorial integrity, both of which were at risk for much of this century. The second issue area is not what one ordinarily thinks of as a national security matter and hence high politics. However, decolonization in southern Africa (a turbulent, often violent process in which white minority rule has been supplanted by African majority rule) has produced vast numbers of refugees. Host states, in turn, have sometimes treated the refugees as security risks, fearing social disruption unless they can be controlled (made politically and militarily docile) or removed (dispersed throughout the region or continent). In brief, in the Southern African context this means that refugees often become targets of violence. The frequency or amount of violence seems to be positively related to the amount of space separating them from the border with their home nation-state.

The third issue area, the military balance between neighbors, follows logically from the refugee factor. Unlike most other African Commonwealth states, Botswana had no military force until a decade after independence. Only when Southern Rhodesian border violations became frequent and destructive did Botswana develop a military capability. Since that time, the military has been concerned with warding off external attacks, which the attacking states often claimed were designed to destroy the capabilities of, or undercut the morale of, insurgents operating from Botswana. The line between refugee and insurgent was sometimes nebulous.

■ Political Status and Territorial Integrity

□ South Africa

During the nineteenth century, the term Bechuanaland came to be a qualified term. There was British Bechuanaland and the Bechuanaland
Protectorate (BP). Now, in the twentieth century, there is the Republic of
Botswana and the Republic of Bophuthatswana. What is the difference
among these terms? Are the differences significant? What is now the
Republic of Botswana was once the BP, and the transition to independence
did not change the area or boundaries. The international boundary between
the BP and British Bechuanaland was the Molopo River. British
Bechuanaland, in turn, was a distinct territorial entity, a crown colony,
from 1885 until 1895, when it was absorbed into the Cape Province of
South Africa. Portions of the crown colony reemerged as part of the archi-
pelago of Bophuthatswana in 1977, when that area was granted independence by the Pretoria regime. There is consequently a Tswana diaspora,
with Setswana speakers living in the Republic of Botswana, the Republic
of Bophuthatswana, and the remainder of South Africa. There are roughly
four times as many Setswana speakers in South Africa (2.7 million) as in
Botswana (0.7 million). Botswana, then, is the product of British decolonization, while Bophuthatswana is the result of apartheid or of the territorial dismemberment of South Africa. The former enjoys widespread, international recognition, while the latter, says its spokesmen, "still slaves to
convince the world of its validity."[2]

In its original formulation at the time of the creation of the Union of
South Africa in the aftermath of the Anglo-Boer War, the transfer of the BP
and the other two High Commission Territories (Basutoland and
Swaziland) to South Africa was intended to be a relatively straightforward
affair. It was part of a larger expansionist mood that included Southern
Rhodesia, and it was provided for in Articles 150-151 of the 1909 Act of
Union and in the Schedule to the Act.[3] Unlike the possible incorporation of
Southern Rhodesia by the Union, the transfer of the HCTs entailed the consent of the British government (King-in-Council) and some attention (ill
defined) to the wishes of the inhabitants of the three territories. Formally,
the South African Parliament was to request the King-in-Council to transfer
the territories.[4] Over time, the British Parliament served as the principal
forum for public consideration of the topic, as well as the focus for interest
group efforts to block the transfer. The British government considered the
transfer on a number of occasions, but was essentially dilatory, telling the
South African government that the time was not propitious for a transfer.[5]

Because the dispute over transfer of the HCTs has been adequately
covered elsewhere,[6] we concentrate here on three interesting particulars of
that prolonged debate. First, during the mid-to-late 1930s, the South

African government added functionalism to its array of foreign policy tools. It was anxious to provide capital and technical skills to the neighboring HCTs in order to create the proper groundwork and to cultivate African elite opinion for the subsequent transfer. Seeing this for what it was, the Batswana wanted nothing to do with Pretoria's Trojan horse. Years later, South African foreign policy toward Southern Africa still betrays functionalist proclivities.[7]

Second, there is evidence that during the 1950s, when territorial apartheid was being considered and debated by the National Party establishment, the transfer issue was subsumed by the larger domestic goal of building apartheid. Thus the grand design, set forth in the Tomlinson Commission Report, made reference to the inclusion of the BP and its merger with the Tswana African homelands in the Union to create an entity known as the "Tswana block." Although Dr. Hendrik F. Verwoerd, then minister of native affairs, indicated that such a merger was outside the mandate of the commission, it did underscore the government's interest in ethnic amalgamation.[8]

Third, South Africa claimed to be a better, more generous surrogate colonial power than Britain. This idea, a sort of competitive colonialism, seems to have been Dr. Verwoerd's particular contribution to the doctrine of apartheid; he announced it in 1963. His hubris impressed neither the British nor the Batswana, who subsequently discussed the matter in their legislature in Lobatse. Tactlessness aside, Dr. Verwoerd's challenge did highlight South Africa's desire for international recognition as the region's leader, on the one hand, and Britain's basic parsimony as a colonial power, on the other. The yearning for recognition still persists, and there is no a priori reason to think it will die along with apartheid.[9] Nevertheless, the 1963 challenge was really South Africa's last hurrah for territorialism, and the matter faded away. It formally ended after the South African constitution was amended in 1969 to delete sections 150 and 151 of the South Africa Act of 1909.[10]

Following the independence celebrations, which the South African foreign minister attended, Botswana's relations with South Africa were cordial and correct, yet distant because Botswana would not exchange ambassadors with South Africa. Only one independent African state, Malawi, has done so.[11] The primary reason was President Khama's reluctance to subject Botswana's representative in Pretoria to the pervasive system of racial discrimination in South Africa.[12] Consequently, diplomatic activities are conducted through other channels, ranging from telephone calls to official ministerial visits between Gaborone and Pretoria.[13] This saves Botswana the odium of formal diplomatic exchanges that might imply legitimacy for apartheid.

South Africa, still lacking even a semi-official presence in Botswana (such as a trade mission, as in Swaziland and Zimbabwe), is anxious to have such a post if only to assist those South Africans who have been held in Botswana on security charges.[14] Conversely, Botswana has a semi-official mission in South Africa, known as the Botswana Labor Office, recognized by both governments in a 1973 bilateral treaty. Even though this office, located in Roodeport in the Witwatersrand, was created ostensibly just to serve the many Batswana migrant workers there, it actually functions as the Botswana Consulate in South Africa, handling tasks that routinely would be carried out by diplomatic and consular agents.[15] This suggests that low politics[16] can sometimes shade into high politics.

At the highest levels of statecraft, Botswana, like all other members of the Organization of African Unity, condemns the South African system of separate development. This means, in particular, that it has not recognized the incorporation of remnants of British Bechuanaland into the Republic of Bophuthatswana, notwithstanding the cultural and ethnic affinity between the two neighbors. Botswana, moreover, will not enter into any territorial merger with Bophuthatswana nor recognize it (or any of the other ethnic states granted independence by South Africa) as a member of the Southern African Customs Union.[17]

Beginning in 1987 there developed a protracted wrangle over Botswana's railway that directly involved Botswana, Bophuthatswana, and South Africa. This second transformation of low into high politics occurred when the Bophuthatswana authorities required engine crews of the National Railways of Zimbabwe, which operated the railways for Botswana, to obtain Bophuthatswana visas before traversing twenty-two kilometers of Bophuthatswana's territory in order to link up with South African train crews at Mafeking. Neither Zimbabwe nor Botswana accepted this, and the matter was resolved by having the South African crews change at Rakhuna halt, located ten kilometers inside Botswana, where the Chinese constructed a turning loop, a freight terminal, and locomotive shunting facilities at the cost of P2 million. The ruckus that Bophuthatswana caused was seen as a gambit to force Botswana to grant it diplomatic recognition. It did not do so.[18]

☐ Zimbabwe

South Africa and its system of territorial fragmentation through separate development were not the only territorial concerns for the people of BP and their colonial governors. If, following the terminology of certain Africanists, South Africa can be described as a subimperial power[19] (relative to Britain and Western European industrial states), then it would be logical to designate Southern Rhodesia as a subsidiary of South Africa. Southern Rhodesia too had its territorial claims on the BP, which it pressed on the imperial power, often to the annoyance of the South African government. The Rhodesian factor, as Dr. Q. Neil Parson has correctly pointed out, is far too often neglected in the study of the history of Botswana.[20]

For the British the BP was an early strategic, rather than economic, asset: a land corridor through which expansion could proceed northward.[21] They needed such a passageway because they were blocked in the northwest by German South West Africa and in the northeast by Portuguese Mozambique. Through the BP they could advance the British route from Cape to Cairo, and the pioneer column moved through the BP and into Southern Rhodesia in 1890. This was followed, in 1897, by an extension of the railway from Mafeking (site of the BP's administrative headquarters until 1965), to Bulawayo; the route, which ran along the eastern perimeter of the BP, was the sole rail line joining Southern Rhodesia with South Africa from 1897 until 1974, when a connecting line was built to link Beit Bridge in Transvaal Province with Rutenga in Southern Rhodesia.

An 1895 visit to London by the three Batswana chiefs (Khama, Batheon, and Sebele), who met Queen Victoria and Colonial Secretary Joseph Chamberlain, helped keep Cecil Rhodes' British South Africa Company (BSAC) at bay. Rhodes claimed that the BSAC charter permitted the incorporation of the BP. However, the failed 1895 Jameson raid from the BP into the South African Republic (Transvaal) had so tarnished the reputation of Rhodes and his BSAC that the British government would not transfer the BP to them.[22]

In 1909, having acquired three parcels of land reserved for white farmers in eastern BP, the BSAC once again raised the issue of incorporation. Four years later, the BSAC brought up the matter once more, but this time South African Prime Minister Louis Botha took exception to what he regarded as Rhodesian poaching. The most persistent pressure for incorporation came from white residents in the BP, who raised the matter in the segregated local council (European Advisory council) in Mafeking. Sometimes the matter surfaced in the parliamentary debates in Salisbury, and it even showed up during question time in the British House of Commons. The various petitions and debates customarily focused on the transfer to Southern Rhodesia of one or more of the contiguous eastern white farming blocs (known as the Gaborone, Tuli, and Lobatse blocs) and the Tati district around Francistown.[23]

Compared with the provisions in the 1909 South Africa Act, there was little or no imperial or territorial attention or thought given to the wishes of the Batswana in these areas, possibly because the authorities in London— who presumably would need to approve such transfers—perceived the white Southern Rhodesian establishment as less harsh in their treatment of Africans than the South Africans, particularly the Afrikaners. British policy toward the Africans was inconsistent. Although they deferred to African opinion in the BP, they pushed ahead with the Central African Federation (of the two Rhodesias and Nyasaland) without much heed to African sensibilities. British officials seem to have excluded the BP in their planning of the Federation, possibly because people in the BP appeared to be only mildly interested in such a territorial arrangement.[24]

What is noteworthy about the Southern Rhodesian attempts to add all or contiguous parts of the BP is that they angered the South African government, which considered the Southern Rhodesians interlopers. The dispute centered on which took precedence, the BSAC Charter or the 1909 South Africa Act. As we indicated earlier, Prime Minister Louis Botha had shown his displeasure with these competing claims. Sometimes the Rhodesians muted their claims, focusing them on northern BP, that is, roughly that portion north of the twenty-second degree south latitude. With the breakup of the Federation in 1963 and the subsequent drift into the unilateral declaration of independence (UDI) in 1965, Southern Rhodesia no longer expressed an interest in partial or piecemeal incorporation, so the matter faded away. There were tensions between the BP and Southern Rhodesia during the UDI period, but they concerned refugee flows and territorial trespassing, not territorial aspirations.[25]

■ Refugee Influx, Management, and External Burden Sharing

□ South Africa

Refugees have followed in the wake of counterinsurgency campaigns, police sweeps, and threats to life and limb. As was the case earlier with the founding of the BP, the territory has served to channel refugees northward, thereby reducing the security threat of retaliation by the sending nation and also decreasing the drain on scarce financial, housing, and food resources. Our concern here is with those persons designated (by the host government) as political refugees, that is, those who are deemed by host state authorities to be fleeing imminent or probable threats to their lives and liberties. In this sense, the refugees in Botswana are persons at risk relative to the nation of origin. Should they be repatriated, it is believed that they would be subject to arrest and likely imprisonment for crimes that carry no penalty or stigma in the host country. Those who have committed crimes in the country of origin that are also punishable in the host country can be extradited to the country of origin, provided there is an extradition treaty between the two states.[26]

During the colonial period, Botswana received a number of refugees, beginning with the German-Herero war in Namibia early in this century, when these pastoral people fled across the Kalahari following their defeat at the battle of the Waterberg in northern Namibia in 1904. They traveled to the area around Ghantsi and to Mahalapye, and they remained in Botswana. Observers expected them to return to Namibia once it became independent, but that did not happen. Other rural refugees had come from Angola, which is separated from Botswana only by the narrow Caprivi Strip of Namibia.

The Angolans were apolitical and wanted to avoid being caught up in the battles for Angolan independence. These refugees settled in the north at Etsha and were granted Botswana citizenship.[27]

These two examples are the exception rather than the rule in refugee policy, particularly compared with the South Africans. The Herero and Angolan cases represent the sedentary approach to refugee management because, as essentially rural dwellers, these refugees adjusted easily to the tempo and style of the majority of Batswana, who are rural, not urban, residents. The South African refugees, however, tended to be from urban backgrounds, were more politicized, were often better educated, and were less tolerant of constraints on their freedom of travel and political activities than the rural Angolans and Herero. The South African refugees were more conscious of relative deprivation than the rurally oriented ones.[28]

During the 1960s African nationalists increasingly challenged the South African white establishment. Political violence became more common, especially after the nationalists realized that passive resistance and moral suasion were not yielding the expected political dividends. Increasingly they saw the HCTs as safe havens to which to flee or from which to continue their fight against apartheid. As in Newtonian physics, there was an equal and opposite reaction: the South African government tightened border and aircraft departure regulations, attempting to keep the nationalists and their white South African allies from departing through the back door. Correspondingly, the British authorities in the HCTs tried to manage the flow of refugees in the interest of local peace and good order. In essence, this meant the British immobilized the South African refugees politically and insured that they left the HCTs. The BP was the best positioned of the three HCTs because (after 1964) it bordered (at Kazungula) on a majority-ruled state, Zambia. Basutoland was an enclave surrounded by South Africa, while Swaziland abutted Mozambique, then under Portuguese control. It was with good reason, then, that the small ferry that plied between the BP and Zambia at Kazungula was nicknamed "the freedom ferry."[29]

There were no radical alterations to Botswana's refugee policy in the independence era. The policy shifts were essentially incremental and designed in part to comply with continental and international conventions regarding refugees. In 1969, Botswana accepted (with some reservations) the 1951 United Nations Convention Relating to the Status of Refugees, which the British government had made applicable to the BP in 1960. Shortly after independence the National Assembly adopted the Refugee (Recognition and Control) Act as the basic framework law, thus institutionalizing the task of screening refugees, granting asylum to some, and monitoring their activities. The task, under the aegis of the Office of the President, involved officials from the Department of Immigration and from the Special Branch of the Botswana Police Force. The government also cooperated with the office of the UN High Commissioner for Refugees (UNHCR), which successfully encouraged the government to improve its refugee legislation to benefit the refugees.[30]

As refugees continued to enter Botswana, the government relied increasingly on the UNHCR and an international nongovernmental organization, the Lutheran World Federation (LWF), to share the burden of refugee management and support. Refugees stayed not only in urban areas but also in refugee camps at Selebi-Phikwe and Francistown, and by 1977 the LWF had assigned staff to the Office of the President to help minister to the refugee population's material needs. After the Soweto unrest in 1976, young South African secondary-school students began to cross the Botswana border. In 1978 an additional refugee camp at Dukwe (133 kilometers northwest of Francistown) was established, and by 1980 the Dukwe camp took over the work of the other two camps; its operations continued for more than a decade. Much of the funding for Dukwe came from the UNHCR, while the government and the LWF were responsible for day-to-day operations.[31]

Maintenance of a resident refugee population can challenge any government's economic and security capabilities, and the authorities at Dukwe were anxious that the inhabitants become self-supporting. Not all refugees, however, lived at Dukwe; the remainder were located in the major urban centers in the east. Many South African refugees have been very reluctant to move to remote areas such as Dukwe, where they are isolated even if out of reach of South African commando teams (whose operations are examined in the next section). South African police and intelligence operatives have been interested in the identity and activities of those South African refugees who are active members of anti-apartheid or African nationalist organizations, and these people are often at risk in urban settings. Since 1963, with the passage of the Prevention of Violence Abroad Act, the Botswana government has made it a criminal offense to use its territory as a base for launching attacks on neighboring states.[32]

Ever since the initial projection of South African police power into Southern Rhodesia to assist in counterinsurgency warfare, the South African government and its security managers have made frequent use of a forward line of defense when combatting the *Umkhonto we Sizwe* (Spear of the Nation), the military arm of the African National Congress (ANC). The line of defense, in short, is pushed as far as possible beyond South African territory. In addition, the Pretoria regime has tried to keep white farmers from leaving their border area farms with the 1979 Promotion of the Density of Population in Designated Areas Act. The security reason for this legislation was that unoccupied farmland would afford an inviting infiltration route from Botswana into the Transvaal.[33]

☐ *Zimbabwe*

The situation concerning Zimbabwean refugees differs from that concerning South African ones because Zimbabwe achieved independence under majority rule in 1980. South Africa is still under white minority rule. Prior to Zimbabwe's internationally recognized independence, Botswana was dealing with a white minority regime lacking in legitimacy as far as the British (and almost all the rest of the world) were concerned. Unlike the situation in South Africa, Botswana had no continuous unofficial contact with Southern Rhodesia except for those authorities responsible for the operations of the Rhodesia Railways. Botswana's Southern Rhodesian diplomacy was principally railway diplomacy. As long as the Union Jack flew over the BP, the British determined the BP's response to the Smith regime's UDI of November 1965. After its independence in September 1966, Botswana continued the modest sanctions the British had imposed upon Southern Rhodesia, and the Khama government asked the United Nations for a special waiver in the applications of economic sanctions, fearing that Southern Rhodesia could retaliate quickly and effectively against its fragile economy, including the railway. Under the circumstances, Botswana offered asylum to Zimbabwean nationalists, yet it was in no position to wreak significant economic injury upon the Smith regime.[34]

The Smith government inflicted some damage upon Botswana when its security forces violated the territorial integrity of Botswana on several occasions. The violations prompted the intervention of the United Nations Security Council and the subsequent creation of the Botswana Defence Force (BDF) in 1977. Increasingly the population of the Dukwe camp came to reflect the turbulence on the eastern, as well as the southern, frontier, with the number of refugees from Southern Rhodesia increasing. At the end of 1979, on the eve of Zimbabwe's independence, Botswana was host to an estimated 20,000 refugees from Southern Rhodesia. This reflects the intensity of the fighting against the regime in Salisbury. The Botswana government expressed its need for international help to handle the influx, and it attempted to fly some of the refugees to safety in Zambia. By contrast, its police and BDF arrested ZIPRA (Zimbabwe People's Revolutionary Army) guerrillas who traversed Botswana territory while traveling from their base camps in Zambia to Southern Rhodesia.[35]

Once Zimbabwe became independent, the Zimbabwean refugees returned home voluntarily. By 1981 there were only 94 Zimbabwean refugees in the Dukwe camp, but the numbers jumped to 601 the next year and skyrocketed to 4,181 by 1985.[36] This sudden influx was indicative of the volatile political situation in Matabeleland in western Zimbabwe, in which the Zimbabwe African National Union (ZANU) government attempted to establish its authority over Zimbabwe African People's Union (ZAPU) partisans.[37] The situation deteriorated and became tense, especially when Joshua Nkomo, the ZAPU leader, fled to Botswana in 1983, and the Harare authorities alleged that Botswana was permitting ZAPU to use the refugee camp as a base for attacking Zimbabwe, a charge the Gaborone regime denied. The Zimbabweans accused South Africa of using the Dukwe camp as a recruiting site to form a super-ZAPU group that would stage raids against Zimbabwe, attempting to destabilize it.[38]

Subsequently there was a rapprochement between the two major political leaders, Nkomo of ZAPU and Robert Mugabe of ZANU, which had a salutary effect upon the refugee situation. Nkomo revisited Botswana in 1988 and met with the Zimbabwean refugees, urging them to return home. Most of them were willing to do so, and the Botswana government closed down operations at the Dukwe camp. Official 1990 Botswana refugee statistics made no mention of the number of refugees from Zimbabwe among the 691 who were classified as refugees, so there is reason to believe that the number is small (because 395 of the 691 were from Angola and South Africa) or, alternatively, that they are no longer recognized as political refugees.[39]

■ Security Against Armed Attack

□ South Africa

Two striking features of the British decolonization of Botswana are that the country had neither an army nor defensive alliances with the British when it became independent in 1966. When the Union Jack was replaced by the blue, white, and black flag of Botswana, the Khama government faced two principal military powers on its borders: the South Africans and the Southern Rhodesians. Only a month before the BP became the Republic of Botswana, the insurgency had begun in Namibia, following the ruling of the International Court of Justice at the Hague that sustained the South African position there. Thus, on its western flank Botswana faced the South African Police Force (and subsequently the South African Defence Force [SADF]); it was hemmed in on the east by the Southern Rhodesian armed forces, and on the south by the SADF. The South Africans had by far the most formidable military forces in Africa, while the Southern Rhodesian military was small, but fairly impressive by African standards.

What is remarkable is that the South Africans waited nearly twenty years before unleashing their military power against Botswana. Botswana had no army until 1977, although it did have a paramilitary security force called the Police Mobile Unit configured along infantry lines. Because the development of the BDF has already been covered elsewhere,[40] we can concentrate on the South African elements of Botswana's security concerns. From the South African perspective, Botswana offered a counter-ideology to that enshrined in the doctrine of apartheid, which found race to be an organizing principle for economic and sociopolitical life. President Khama made much of Botswana's nonracialism, which demonstrated to the region, continent, and world that there was a viable alternative to apartheid. Such a policy attracted outside attention, respect, and assistance.[41]

Although the South Africans were clearly upset when the Soviets established an embassy in Gaborone and provided the newly established BDF with a small inventory of arms and military hardware—only after the United States declined to do so—there was a rather low level of South African threat perception with respect to Botswana. The BDF was no match for the SADF. Following the SADF raid on Maputo in January 1981, Botswana's President Masire expressed his concern that South Africa was anxious to have some pretext for attacking Botswana. He objected to the violation of Botswana's airspace by South African Air Force flights from the Transvaal to Namibia, and he was disturbed that the South African government was unwilling to accept adequate responsibility for those instances in which SADF soldiers in the Caprivi Strip of Namibia had either trespassed on Botswana territory or had fired their weapons into Botswana. He was equally troubled about the possibility that Pretoria would fabricate charges of attacks by the BDF on South Africa or Namibia. South Africa, he observed, was very subtle and sophisticated in its application of pressure on Botswana.[42]

Once the South African government signed nonaggression treaties with Swaziland in 1982 and Mozambique in 1984, the Pretoria regime was keen to add Botswana to the list. South Africa had been interested in negotiating these treaties with its African-ruled neighbors since 1970, but it had no success until an accord was secretly arranged with Swaziland. The Gaborone authorities indicated they had no interest in agreeing to such a treaty and thought that they had the ANC's operatives in Botswana well under control. After the Nkomati agreement between South Africa and Mozambique was concluded, ANC operatives lost their base of operations in Mozambique and shifted their personnel to Botswana. As far as the South Africans were concerned, however, the Botswana government was not adequately monitoring the allegedly hostile activities of the ANC activists in Botswana. The South Africans had had a history of launching cross-border attacks, which were designed to interdict or cripple command and control mechanisms the ANC had developed to coordinate the work of headquarters and militants.[43]

On June 14, 1985, the SADF struck at Gaborone in an early morning commando-type raid that damaged or destroyed a number of structures and killed twelve civilians, of whom four might have been linked with the ANC. The BDF and the Police Force were caught by surprise and offered no resistance to the attack. The foreign minister of Botswana traveled to New York to put the nation's case before the United Nations Security Council, which then severely censured South Africa. South Africa paid no reparations or damages; rather, the SADF returned to attack the outskirts of Gaborone in May 1986. Using helicopters, the SADF troops fired at a BDF barracks in Mogoditshane; this time the BDF returned fire. The South Africans killed one person and wounded three, including a BDF soldier. Survey research undertaken by South Africa in 1982, 1984, 1986, and 1988 indicates that such cross-border raids were most strongly supported by the conservative elements in the white electorate.[44]

There were two further SADF raids in 1988, and the Botswana police were able to capture two SADF commandos during the second raid in June. As in the past, the South African government continued to insist that it would concentrate on ANC sanctuaries outside South Africa. The commandos, tried and convicted under the terms of the 1986 National Security Act, received ten-year prison sentences. Since then, there have been several unsuccessful attempts to free them. By the close of 1989, however, the South African minister of defense indicated that cross-border raids were a thing of the past. The Batswana were dubious, while two able American scholars indicated that South Africa was no longer capable of pursuing policies of destabilization; its reservoir of power was too low to support such policies.[45]

☐ *Zimbabwe*

It was the depredations and cross-border forays of the Smith regime that convinced the Botswana government that the time had come to create an army. Botswana had no defensive alliances and no powerful patron state to protect it. The initial threat to its security came from the eastern perimeter during the conduct of the guerrilla war in Southern Rhodesia. When it placed its case before the United Nations Security Council in 1976–1977, Botswana provided an inventory of these border violations. Special Southern Rhodesian commando units crossed the border to kidnap a ZIPRA official in Francistown in 1974, to destroy a ZIPRA house in Francistown in 1976, and to put the freedom ferry at Kazungula out of action in 1979. The BDF and the Southern Rhodesian forces engaged in battle, and the BDF took some heavy casualties in a 1978 hot pursuit operation near Kazungula.[46]

Once the liberation war ended and Zimbabwe became an independent, majority-ruled state, the situation improved; there were no further difficulties until 1983, when a number of border incidents and firefights between the BDF and the ZNA (Zimbabwe National Army) took place. These clashes, however, did not result in any long-term estrangement between the two Commonwealth neighbors and were resolved through bilateral channels, such as the Defence and Security Commission. The Zimbabwean perception was that Botswana offered shelter for ZAPU dissidents, a charge Botswana denied. In the world of high politics, the Zimbabwean allegation is remarkably similar to the one the South African regime continuously made against Botswana. In both cases, Botswana was cast in the role of negligent host to highly politicized refugees bent on destabilizing or overthrowing the government of the country whence they fled. The two cases differed, however, on the extent of legitimacy of the regimes from which the refugees fled.[47]

■ The Direction of High Politics

This brief survey of selected aspects of high politics involving Botswana and its two most powerful neighbors suggests that issue areas of high politics are not discrete entities in practice. In the case of Botswana, refugee flows and management meld into security politics. The relationship would seem to be dynamic and interactive; causality does not necessarily flow from refugee generation to security anxiety. Because of its general weakness, Botswana has had to locate extraregional sources of funds, supplies, equipment, and expertise. This is most apparent in terms of the help the UNHCR and the LWF have provided to transport, house, feed, care for, and educate refugees. Its own material resources were too meager to do the job, but with international assistance it managed well—so well that Sir Seretse Khama was awarded the Nansen medal for service to refugees.[48]

In terms of the territorial aspects of high politics, the principal problem now is the status of Bophuthatswana and whether, in postapartheid South Africa, there would be a territorial amalgamation of Setswana-speakers. The most likely outcome would be the territorial reabsorption of Bophuthatswana and all the other homelands into South Africa.[49] At present, there are no pending boundary claims, and Botswana has no irredentist ambitions. There has been some concern expressed recently about the accuracy of Botswana's border with Namibia along the Caprivi Strip, but the attorney general and the minister of external affairs made it clear that the matter would be settled by treaty with Namibia. The imbroglio over whether Botswana has a common border with Zambia at Kazungula has died down, and there are no more South African objections to constructing a bridge connecting Botswana with Zambia.[50] In the very long run, the reincorporation of Walvis Bay into Namibia would facilitate the construction of a trans-Kalahari railway line; this would provide Botswana and Zimbabwe access to the Atlantic Ocean at Walvis Bay.[51] In this case, as we noted earlier with respect to the railway line traversing Bophuthatswana and the functions of the Labor Office in Roodeport, there is a commingling of high and low politics.

Finally, there is the security aspect of high politics. The altercation between Botswana and Zimbabwe in 1983–1984 suggests that regime consolidation, as in Zimbabwe, can contribute to the efflux of refugees and that there are security risks and challenges connected with ethnic migrations. Much has been made of the ascendancy of the military within the South

African polity, especially during the premiership of P. W. Botha. Botswana, in the midst of the Zimbabwean liberation war, found it necessary to develop a military establishment in order to contain Southern Rhodesian forces in northern Botswana. Since 1977, Botswana has been able to draw upon the resources of several advanced military powers to train its soldiers and pilots and to provide weapons and standard military equipment. This has been an expensive operation in terms of present funds and in opportunity costs. The South African intrusions have led to the enactment of the 1986 National Security Act, which represents an erosion in some civil liberties. Consequently Botswana has become less secure than it was in the late 1960s, it has proportionately less to spend on development activities, and its citizens have witnessed a slight decline in the quality of their civil liberties. Thus high politics has extracted high costs from the citizens of Botswana. Southern Africa can be turbulent, dangerous, and expensive.

What conclusions may we draw regarding the extent to which Botswana is truly a hostage to its larger neighbors, South Africa and Zimbabwe? From the perspective of territorial high politics, now that Botswana has become independent and a member of continental and global organizations, such as the Organization of African Unity, the Commonwealth of Nations, and the United Nations, there is no current conflict with Zimbabwe. Both are internationally recognized states and enjoy common membership in a number of international and regional governmental organizations. Neither entertains irredentist notions about the other, although earlier in the century colonial Zimbabwe's authorities did have territorial ambitions regarding Botswana, particularly the northern part. But these authorities were unwilling to press their claims in London at the expense of South African claims. Both Zimbabwe and Botswana had been territorial desiderata of South Africa in this century, a position clearly set forth in the 1909 South African constitution. White Zimbabwean self-determination in 1922 put an end to that aspect of South African expansion, while British paternalism, international opinion, and an accelerated retreat from empire terminated South African plans for the transfer of Botswana to Pretoria's realm.

In the domain of territorial legitimacy, South Africa is Botswana's hostage. Not only has Botswana (like other members of the Organization of African Unity, except Malawi) refused to exchange ambassadors with South Africa but also Botswana will not sanction the territorial by-products of apartheid even if they are kith and kin. Such is the case with Bophuthatswana. It is true that there are a number of technical interactions—low politics—between Botswana and Bophuthatswana but they are carefully handled in such a way as to preclude the hint or suspicion of diplomatic recognition. Botswana, along with all the other OAU members, stands between Bophuthatswana and international legitimacy and respectability. So does Zimbabwe, but the ethnic bonds are much stronger between Botswana and Bophuthatswana than between Bophuthatswana and Zimbabwe.

Because of the great disparity in size, levels of modernization, technical and tactical skills, patterns of deployment and force projection, combat skills, and experienced leadership, Botswana is distinctly the hostage of both South Africa and of Zimbabwe in the military field of high politics. Should there be a series of mutual and balanced reductions of armed forces in southern Africa with the independence of Namibia, the end of the civil war in Angola, and the dismantling of apartheid and the demise of cross-border SADF raids, then Botswana will be at less of a military disadvantage. It is doubtful that Botswana will return to the halcyon days of the 1960s and early 1970s, when its national security needs were met not by an army but by a constabulary called the Police Mobile Unit.

Finally, in the realm of high politics affecting refugees, Botswana is less of a hostage than it once was with regard to Zimbabwe in the colonial and early postcolonial period. Dukwe camp has ceased operations. In the case of South Africa, the great influx of refugees has ended and Botswana no longer plays a significant role as a transit camp to points further north. Yet Botswana lacks an extensive monitoring capacity to make sure that its hospitality is not being abused and that it does not become a staging area for attacks on the Transvaal. This point was really the core issue in South Africa's attempts to persuade Botswana to sign an Nkomati-type nonaggression agreement. Botswana's role as South African hostage with regard to political asylum depends upon the questions of political stability and legitimacy in South Africa as the source of the refugees. Yet, as Zimbabwe showed, a shift toward majority-rule regimes is not enough in itself to assure neighboring states that the flow of refugees has ceased. In the future Botswana could be a haven for dissident South Africans, Zimbabweans, and perhaps even disgruntled Namibians.

■ Notes

I wish to record my gratitude to the American Philosophical Society (Philadelphia), the Earhart Foundation (Ann Arbor, Michigan), and Southern Illinois University at Carbondale for travel and other types of support for this research. The Office of the President in Gaborone kindly provided several research permits over the years to facilitate the in-country aspects of the work, of which this chapter is a part. I only am responsible for the data and interpretations presented in this chapter.

1. High politics tends to focus on "matters of security, particularly the strategic interests of states." Paul R. Viotti and Mark V. Kauppi, *International Relations Theory: Realism, Pluralism, Globalism* (New York: Macmillan, 1987), 592.

2. Anthony Sillery, *Founding a Protectorate: History of Bechuanaland, 1885–1895* (The Hague: Mouton & Co., 1965), 20 and 43; Richard P. Stevens,

Historical Dictionary of Botswana (Metchuen, N.J.: Scarecrow, 1975), 28; Louis A. Picard, *The Politics of Development in Botswana: A Model for Success?* (Boulder, Colo.: Lynne Rienner, 1987), 5 (for statistics) and 276; and *Bophuthatswana Historical Notes* (Mafeking, South Africa: Bophuthatswana Director of Information, Department of Foreign Affairs, 1987), 6 and 7 (for quotation).

3. There is a sizeable literature on this topic, although some of it is dated. Two of the best studies, based on the Public Record Office and Botswana National Archives materials, are Ronald Hyam, *The Failure of South African Expansion, 1908–1948* (London and Basingstoke: Macmillan, 1972), and Harold H. Robertson, "From Protectorate to Republic: The Political History of Botswana, 1926–1966" (Ph.D. diss., Dalhousie University, 1979), respectively.

4. For the text of the relevant portions of the 1909 Act, with accompanying constitutional commentary, consult Henry J. May, *The South African Constitution,* 3d ed. (Cape Town and Johannesburg: Juta & Co., 1955), 19–21 and 626–627.

5. Hyam, *The Failure,* 77.

6. For a summary of the topic, consult Richard P. Stevens, "The History of the Anglo-South African Conflict over the Proposed Incorporation of the High Commission Territories," in Christian P. Potholm and Richard Dale, eds., *Southern Africa in Perspective: Essays in Regional Politics* (New York: The Free Press, 1972), 97–109 and 352–354.

7. Hyam, *The Failure,* 145–150; Charles Rey, *Monarch of All I Survey: Bechuanaland Diaries, 1929–37,* ed. Q. Neil Parsons and Michael Crowder (Gaborone: The Botswana Society; New York: Lilian Barber; London: James Currey, 1988), 191, 202, 259 n. 14, and 260 n. 7; and Deon J. Geldenhuys, "South Africa's Regional Policy," in Michael Clough, ed., *Changing Realities in Southern Africa,* Research Series no. 47 (Berkeley: University of California, Institute of International Studies, 1982), 134, 150–152, and 156.

8. South Africa, *Summary of the Report of the Commission for the Socio-Economic Development of the Bantu Areas Within the Union of South Africa,* UG 61/1955 (Pretoria: The Government Printer, 1956), 181, paras. 19 and 22; and South Africa, Parliament, House of Assembly, *Debates* (hereafter cited as SAPHAD), 91, col. 5504 (May 16, 1956).

9. *Dr. H. F. Verwoerd on . . . II. The Road to Freedom for Basutoland[,] Bechuanaland[, and] Swaziland,* Fact Paper no. 107 (Pretoria: Department of Information, 1963), 11–18; Bechuanaland Protectorate (hereafter cited as BP); Legislative Council, *Official Report,* Hansard 9 (November 22, 1963), 109–123 (Quett K. J. Masire's remarks in this debate [on 119–122] were insightful and are still germane today); "British Pledges to the Protectorates: No Question of Transfer," *The Times* (London), September 5, 1963, late London edition, 10; and "The Political Scene: 'Tactless' Verwoerd Offer Caused Stir," *The Star* (Johannesburg), September 9, 1963, city late edition, 19. Joseph Hanlon, in *Apartheid's Second Front: South Africa's War Against Its Neighbours* (New York: Viking Penguin 1986), 46, suggests that South Africa wants to be regarded as the "King of southern Africa."

10. SAPHAD, 25, col. 613 (February 12, 1969) (speech of the minister of the interior on the second reading of the South Africa Act Amendment Bill).

11. Rolf Bodenmuller, *Botswana, Lesotho, and Swaziland: Their External Relations and Policy and Attitudes Towards South Africa* (Pretoria: Africa Institute of South Africa, 1973), 85; and Suresh C. Saxena, *Foreign Policy of African States: Politics of Dependence and Confrontation* (New Delhi: Deep and Deep, 1982), 96–97.

12. Seretse Khama, *From the Frontline: Speeches of Sir Seretse Khama,* ed.

Gwendolen M. Carter and E. Philip Morgan (London: Rex Rallings, 1980), 88 (speech to the ninth annual conference of the Botswana Democratic Party in Molepolole, March 28, 1970).

13. Roger Martin, *Southern Africa: The Price of Apartheid: A Political Risk Analysis*, Special Report no. 1130 (London: Economist Intelligence Unit, 1988), 36–37.

14. "SA Gets Tough on Botswana," *Mmegi wa Dikgang* (Gaborone), September 24–30, 1988, 3; Martin, *Southern Africa*, 40–41; and Gerald L'Ange, "SA, Botswana Talks on ANC in Balance," *The Star*, October 5, 1988, international airmail weekly edition, 11.

15. Athaliah Molokomme, "Mine Labour Migration from Botswana to South Africa: Some Practical Legal Issues," in Louis Molamu, Athaliah Molokomme, and Gloria Somolekae, eds., *Perceptions of Batswana Mineworkers Towards the South African Gold Mines, with Special Reference to Living and Working Conditions, Legal Issues and Trade Unions*, International Migration for Employment Working Paper no. 36 (Geneva: International Labour Organization, 1988), 41, 43–44, 51; and W. J. Breytenbach, *Migratory Labour Arrangements in Southern Africa*, rev. ed., Communications of the Africa Institute, no. 33 (Pretoria: Africa Institute of South Africa, 1979), 19–22 (for the text of the agreement).

16. By low politics we mean "those [matters] dealing with socioeconomic or welfare issues." Viotti and Kauppi, *International Relations Theory*, 592.

17. "Bop[hutha]tswana Will Not Be Recognized, States Khama," *Mafeking Mail and Botswana Guardian* (hereafter cited as MMBG), July 1, 1977, 1; "No Federation with Homelands, Says Khama," MMBG, August 30, 1974, 1; and Martin, *Southern Africa*, 14.

18. "Botswana: The Transport Weapon," *Africa Confidential* (London) 28, no. 4 (February 18, 1987): 7; "New Handover Arrangement with SATS Keeps Railway Traffic Moving," *Country Report: Namibia, Botswana, Lesotho, Swaziland* (London) (hereafter cited as CRNBLS), no. 2-1987 (May 13, 1987): 42–43; and "China Continues Railway Upgrading," CRNBLS, no. 3-1987 (August 14, 1987): 35.

19. See Kenneth W. Grundy, "South Africa in the Political Economy of Southern Africa," in Gwendolen M. Carter and Patrick O'Meara, eds., *International Politics in Southern Africa* (Bloomington: Indiana University Press, 1982), 150; and Timothy M. Shaw, "Kenya and South Africa: 'Subimperialist' States," *Orbis* 21, no. 2 (Summer 1977): 375–394. Paul R. Maylam, *Rhodes, The Tswana, and the British: Colonialism, Collaboration, and Conflict in the Bechuanaland Protectorate, 1885–1899*, Contributions in Comparative Colonial Studies, no. 4 (Westport, Conn.: Greenwood, 1980), 5–7, refers to "subimperialists" as the "men-on-the-spot" in South Africa responsible for colonial expansion.

20. Q. Neil Parsons, "The Evolution of Modern Botswana: Historical Revisions," in Louis A. Picard, ed., *The Evolution of Modern Botswana: Politics and Rural Development in Southern Africa* (London: Rex Collings; Lincoln: University of Nebraska Press, 1985), 34–36.

21. See Charles W. Gossett, "The Civil Service in Botswana: Personnel Policies in Comparative Perspective" (Ph.D. diss., Stanford University, 1986), 140–149 and 461–462, for a sophisticated analysis of the various motivations underlying the British acquisition of the BP.

22. There is no one definitive source devoted to this topic from the beginning of the BP until the end of World War II. The most useful are Q. Neil Parsons, "Three Botswana Chiefs in Britain, 1895" (African studies diploma thesis, University of Edinburgh, 1967); Maylam, *Rhodes;* Martin L. Chanock,

Unconsummated Union: Britain, Rhodesia, and South Africa, 1900–45 (Totowa, N.J.: Frank Cass and Company, 1977); and Jackson C. Chirenje, *A History of Northern Botswana, 1850–1910* (Rutherford, N.J.: Farleigh Dickinson University Press, 1977).

23. See Henderson M. Tapela, "The Tati District of Botswana, 1866–1969" (D.Phil. diss., University of Sussex, 1976), 191; and Philip R. Warhurst, "Rhodesia and Her Neighbours, 1900–23" (D.Phil. diss., University of Oxford, 1971), 397–401.

24. J. R. Stebbing, "Race Relations in the Union of South Africa: Their Influence on the Problem of the High Commission Territories" (B.Litt. thesis, University of Oxford, 1953), 244–247; "Bechuanaland Eager to Join [the Central] African Federation," *The Star*, June 1, 1950, stop press edition, 17; "Incorporation of Bechuanaland in the C.A.F. [Central African Federation] Urged," *The Star*, August 12, 1955, city late edition, 3; and J. Richard T. Wood, *The Welensky Papers: A History of the Federation of Rhodesia and Nyasaland* (Durban, South Africa: Graham Publishing Company, 1983), 146–147 and 155.

25. "Dr. Malan Tells Rhodesia Protectorates Concern Only Britain and Union," *The Star*, December 23, 1949, city late edition, 5; Southern Rhodesia, Legislative Assembly, *Debates* 31, part 2 (June 15, 1950), cols. 2125–2126 (speech of the prime minister in the no confidence debate); M. N. Smith, "We Have a Good Claim to Northern Bechuanaland," *The Chronicle* (Bulawayo, Zimbabwe), April 26, 1956, 8; Wood, *The Welensky Papers*, 49 and 155; Parsons, "Historical Revisions," 35; and United Kingdom, Commonwealth Relations Office, *Basutoland, Bechuanaland Protectorate, and Swaziland: History of Discussions with the Union of South Africa, 1909–1939*, Cmd. 8707 (London: H.M.S.O., 1952), app. 7, 129 (Prime Minister Huggins's definition of northern BP).

26. For background on this topic, consult Leon Gordenker, *Refugees in International Politics* (New York: Columbia University Press, 1987), and Jenny Zetterqvist, *Refugees in Botswana in the Light of International Law*, Research Report no. 87 (Uppsala, Sweden: The Scandinavian Institute of African Studies, 1990).

27. The two most helpful, historically grounded research studies on Botswana's refugee policy are Roger Southall, "Botswana as a Host Country for Refugees," *The Journal of Commonwealth and Comparative Politics* (London) 22, no. 2 (July 1984): 151–179, and James H. Polhemus, "The Refugee Factor in Botswana," *Immigrants and Minorities* (London) 4, no. 1 (March 1985): 28–45.

28. Christian P. Potholm analyzes the different types of refugees in his "Wanderers on the Face of Africa: Refugees in Kenya, Tanzania, Zambia, and Botswana," *Round Table* (London), no. 261 (January 1976): 85–92, while John A. Marcum explores relationships within refugee groups and between them and their patrons in his "The Exile Condition and Revolutionary Effectiveness: Southern African Liberation Movements," in Christian P. Potholm and Richard Dale, *Southern Africa in Perspective: Essays in Regional Politics* (New York: The Free Press, 1972), 262–275 and 380–388.

29. One of the earliest public references to this exit corridor was "Africa: Captain Nelson's Freedom Ferry," *Time* 83, no. 15 (April 10, 1964): 38. We are grateful to Mr. E. Brian Egner, a former BP district officer who served in the area at the time, for this reference (personal communication from Mr. Egner).

30. Louis A. Picard, "Role Changes Among Field Administrators in Botswana: Administrative Attitudes and Social Change" (Ph.D. diss., University of Wisconsin, Madison, 1977), 525–526; and Zetterqvist, *Refugees*, 49–54.

31. Zetterqvist, *Refugees*, 37–38; and *LWF/WS Botswana: 1985 Annual Report* (s.l.: n.p., n.d.), 3.

32. *LWF/WS Botswana*, 8–9; Zetterqvist, *Refugees*, 25; "Pretoria Is Invited to Identify Any ANC Bases," *Quarterly Economic Review of Namibia, Botswana, Lesotho, Swaziland* (London) (hereafter cited as QERNBLS), no. 3-1983 (September 12, 1983): 22; "Police Mount Night Swoop on Refugees," *Daily News* (Gaborone) (hereafter cited as DN), March 25, 1980, 1; Bapasi Mphusu, "SA Spying Agent Jailed," DN, July 28, 1982, 1; "Kok Is Freed," DN, July 15, 1983, 1; and BP, *Statute Law*, 47 (1963), 347–358.

33. Paul L. Moorcroft, *African Nemesis: War and Revolution in Southern Africa (1945–2010)* (London: Brassey's, 1990), 126–127; C. J. Botha, "Anticipatory Self-Defence and Reprisals Re-Examined: South African Attacks on ANC Bases in Neighbouring States: The 'Guns of Gaborone' or 'rAIDS Disease'?" *South African Yearbook of International Law* (Pretoria) 11 (1985–1986): 138–157; and Philip H. Frankel, *Pretoria's Praetorians: Civil–Military Relations in South Africa* (Cambridge: Cambridge University Press, 1984), 136.

34. For a survey of this period, see Richard Dale, "The Loosening Connection in Anglophone Southern Africa: Botswana and the Rhodesian Regime, 1965–1980," *Journal of Contemporary African Studies* (Pretoria) 2, no. 2 (April 1983): 257–285.

35. Polhemus, "The Refugee Factor," 33; "Botswana 'Alarmed' by Refugees," *The Star*, May 15, 1979, stop press edition, 2; Deon du Plessis, "Refugee Situation Critical in Botswana," *The Star*, March 20, 1979, late final edition, 6; and Brendan Nicholson, "Intense Neutral," *The Star*, April 6, 1979, late final edition, 14.

36. Zetterqvist, *Refugees*, 22; and *LWF/WS Botswana*, 3.

37. For a thoughtful, scholarly analysis of the situation, consult Richard Hodder-Williams, "Conflict in Zimbabwe: The Matabeleland Problem," *Conflict Studies* (London), no. 151 (1983): 1–20.

38. "Nkomo's Flight Heightens Tensions," *African Economic Digest* (London) 4, no. 10 (March 11, 1983): 22–24; "Diplomatic Ties to Be Established with Botswana," *Foreign Broadcast Information Service, Daily Report, Middle East and Africa* (hereafter cited as FBISDRMEA) 5, no. 106 (June 1, 1983): U8; "Refugee Influx from Zimbabwe Increasing," FBISDRMEA 5, no. 60 (March 28, 1983): U6; and Joseph Hanlon, *Beggar Your Neighbours: Apartheid Power in Southern Africa* (London: Catholic Institute for International Relations and James Curry; Bloomington: Indiana University Press, 1986), 180.

39. Keto Segwai, "Nkomo Visit Augurs Return Home," *Mmegi*, May 21-27, 1988, 4; "Zimbabwean Refugees Are to Be Repatriated," CRNBLS, no. 2-1989 (June 14, 1989): 26; "The Remaining Zimbabwean Refugees Will Have to Leave," CRNBLS, no. 4-1989 (December 22, 1989): 25; and "Refugee Community Dwindles," *Mmegi*, January 26–February 1, 1990, 2.

40. Richard Dale, "The Creation and Use of the Botswana Defence Force," *Round Table*, no. 290 (April 1984): 216–235.

41. Willie Henderson, "Independent Botswana: A Reappraisal of Foreign Policy Options," *African Affairs* (London) 73, no. 290 (January 1974): 39–41.

42. Richard Dale, "Botswana," in Potholm and Dale, *Southern Africa*, 117 and 356–357 nn. 60–61; Peter Vanneman, *Soviet Strategy in Southern Africa: Gorbachev's Pragmatic Approach* (Stanford, Calif.: Hoover Institution Press, 1990), 5–6, 8, and 73; James J. Zaffiro, "The U.S. and Botswana, 1966–1989: Foreign Policy in the Shadow of Boer and Bear" (Paper prepared for the Twenty-ninth Annual Meeting of the International Studies Association, London, March 28–April 1, 1989), 22; Hanlon, *Beggar Your Neighbours*, 136; and Wilf Nussey, "Masire Fears SA Gearing for Attack," *The Star*, December 2, 1981, late final edition, 29.

43. John de St. Jorre, "Destabilization and Dialogue: South Africa's Emergence as a Regional Superpower," *CSIS Africa Notes*, no. 26 (April 17, 1984): 2; "U.S. Official's Visit Confirmed," FBISDRMEA 5, no. 167 (August 27, 1984): U5; "Police Say Botswana Not Sanctioning ANC Acts," FBISDRMEA 5, no. 216 (November 6, 1984): U7; and Christopher Coker, "South Africa: A New Military Role in Southern Africa, 1969–82," *Survival* (London) 25, no. 2 (March–April 1983): 63–64.

44. For details on the 1985 raid and the handling of the matter in the United Nations Security Council, see Richard Dale, "Not Always So Placid a Place: Botswana Under Attack," *African Affairs* 86, no. 342 (January 1987): 78–85. For the 1986 raid, consult "Botswana Gov[ernmen]t Condemns South African Aggression," DN, May 20, 1986, 1, and "Botswana Had Done Nothing to Warrant SA Attack," DN, May 21, 1986, 1. On the links between raids and voter attitudes, see "The Latest South African Raid Causes Outrage," CRNBLS, no. 2-1988 (June 8, 1988): 26; "Reflecting the Start of the Namibia Decolonization Process," CRNBLS, no. 2-1989 (June 14, 1989): 25; and Andre du Pisani, *What Do We Think?: A Survey of White Opinion on Foreign Policy Issues No. 4* (Braamfontein: The South African Institute of International Affairs, 1988), 12–13.

45. "The Latest South African Raid Causes Outrage," 25–26; "Two South African Commandos Are Captured," CRNBLS, no. 3-1988 (September 2, 1988): 24–25; "And the Trial Starts of Captured South African Commandos," CRNBLS, no. 4-1988 (November 18, 1988): 25–26; Mesh Moeti, "Another Rescue Attempt for SA Commandos?" *Mmegi*, August 10–16, 1990, 2; Rampholo Molefhe, "Malan Says 'No More Raids'—Political Observers Sceptical," *Mmegi*, December 8-14, 1989, 1–2; and Michael Clough and Jeffrey Herbst, *South Africa's Changing Regional Strategy: Beyond Destabilization*, Critical Issues Series, 1989, no. 4 (New York: Council on Foreign Relations, 1989), 8–10.

46. Ron Reid Daly as told to Peter Stiff, *Selous Scouts: Top Secret War* (Alberton, South Africa: Galago, 1982), 167–172, 202–207, 438–444, 655–671, and 681–685; Barbara Cole, *The Elite: The Story of the Rhodesian Special Air Service*, 3d ed. (Amanzimtoti, South Africa: Three Knights Publishing, 1985), 296–304; and "15 Die After Hot Pursuit," *The Star*, March 4, 1978, international airmail weekly edition, 2.

47. Norman Chandler, "Zimbabwean Troops Deep in Botswana," *Rand Daily Mail* (Johannesburg), October 8, 1983, morning final edition, 1; "Zimbabwe Army Unit Clashes with Botswana Soldiers," *The Star*, November 14, 1983, international airmail edition, 9; Norman Chandler, "Botswana Steps Up Security Along Border," *Rand Daily Mail*, December 19, 1983, morning final edition, 5; "Talks with Zimbabwe on Border Incident Held," FBISDRMEA 5, no. 220 (November 14, 1983): U3; Botswana, National Assembly, *Official Report*, Hansard (hereafter cited as BNAOR) 78 (November 9, 1983), 9 (minister of public service and information); and "Border Incidents Continue to Damage Relations with Zimbabwe," QERNBLS, no. 1-1984 (March 5, 1984):22–23.

48. "Khama Gets U.N. Refugee Award," MMBG, April 28, 1978, 1.

49. Robert I. Rotberg, "Homelands' Demise," *The Christian Science Monitor*, March 19, 1991, 18.

50. BNAOR 74 (August 18, 1982), 184–185, 189–191, and 193–194 (speeches of the attorney-general and minister of external affairs during the committee stage of the debate on the Tribal Land [Amendment] Bill); and Louis V. Ebert III (a U.S. Department of State officer), "Some International Legal Aspects of the Botswana-Zambia Boundary Question" (M.S. thesis, George Washington University, 1971).

51. John Battersby, "S. Africa, Namibia Try for Walvis Bay Settlement," *The Christian Science Monitor*, September 21, 1990, 4.

11

A Changing Southern Africa: What Role for Botswana?

Bernard Weimer
Olaf Claus

The independence of Namibia; the end of South Africa's Total Strategy, including regional, economic, and military destabilization; and the political transition of South Africa toward a nonracial democracy have set in motion fundamental change in southern Africa, a change exacerbated by an equally fundamental change in international relations. The old dividing lines in southern Africa are bound to wither away as new problems, challenges, and conflicts emerge. What contributions can Botswana make to this process of regional change? What can its experiences offer to the neighboring countries? What new challenges does Botswana face?

■ Regional Changes

As a first step toward answering these questions, we identify some of the major regional challenges Botswana and its neighbors are likely to face:

1. The end of the East-West conflict has already had significant ramifications for southern Africa. Indeed, Namibia owes its independence and Angola the end of its fifteen-year-old war to the end of the Cold War. The Gulf War notwithstanding, there seems to be a common view emerging that military "solutions" to regional conflicts do not provide the necessary foundation for eventual development and cooperation. Rather, peaceful conditions at the international, regional, and national levels and a balance of interests among actors are imperative for regional development. On the other hand, the end of East-West tensions obviously deprives African countries of foreign policy options and may make them vulnerable to additional external pressures.

2. Sooner or later South Africa will be transformed into a pluralistic, democratic, nonracist state. Fundamental changes in the society and in the economy have already taken place. These changes will not necessarily be smooth but rather will entail economic, social, ethnic, class, and power struggles. The conflicts and struggle will not only lead to a realignment of social forces and a redefinition of national interests, but are also likely to dampen expectations concerning economic growth, potential business confidence, and, thus, the flow of credit and investment to South Africa.

New socioeconomic circumstances as well as expectations of the black majority, fueled by poverty and mass unemployment, are likely to necessitate an inward-looking economic policy, with an emphasis on social justice. Under such conditions, it is likely that South Africa might become a recipient of aid and a case for IMF/World Bank–inspired structural adjustment policies.

On a more modest scale, similar challenges will arise for South Africa's neighbors, notably with respect to social justice, job creation for an increasingly young and educated population, employment of the poor, popular participation, democratization, and the empowerment of the poor. Nevertheless, in the postapartheid period, South Africa will—in GNP terms—remain the regional economic powerhouse, albeit under difficult internal conditions. South Africa might be characterized as the region's economic giant, but a giant with clay feet. In terms of economic development, South Africa is closer to being a "semi-industrialized developing country" than an NIC.[1]

Given these circumstances, the future democratic South Africa is likely to have neither the political will nor the economic muscle to become the savior of ailing neighboring economies. All expectations and calculations to the contrary on the part of their governments and elites amount to pipe dreams.

3. With the end of colonialism and apartheid, the raison d'être of the Frontline States (FLS) alliance will disappear despite its political successes (e.g., contributions to the independence of Zimbabwe and Namibia and to the foundation of SADCC in 1980).

Probably, the FLS alliance will disappear but its experiences in consultation and conflict resolution will continue to prove valuable for SADCC, regional political cooperation, and the possible formation of a Conference on Cooperation and Security in Southern Africa (CCSSA). Such an organization is already being discussed.[2]

4. The transformation of SADCC into an eleven-member group including South Africa and from "coordinated project cooperation" to higher degrees of regional planning and integration seems to be on the agenda. This transformation might even be accompanied by a shift of some political

decisionmaking from national to regional entities. Some of the most contentious issues are trade and investment, finance, industrialization, and employment. With regard to trade, the question is whether a future regional trade regime will amount to an extension of the present SACU into a larger customs union or whether it will take the form of a regional network of bilateral preferential trade agreements. In both cases, Botswana's experiences are extremely valuable and relevant to regional decisionmaking.[3]

In their relations to donors, the SADCC members will likely experience an increasing number of political conditionalities attached to development assistance. These might include economic adjustment as well as bilateral cooperation programs. More and more, official development assistance (ODA) donors will take into account criteria such as popular participation, democratization, defense spending, and ecological issues.

5. Ecological and resource issues will also increasingly ascend to the top of national agendas and will be linked not only to development theory and practice,[4] but also to regional security.[5] An example may be the problem of water shortage. Not too far in the future, potable water might become the most valuable natural resource on a regional scale, as is already the case in Botswana and in other areas of the world. The emerging debate about use and pollution of the river systems in southern Africa cannot be avoided. The realization that ecological problems do not respect national borders will compel governments to work in tandem on "economic-ecological orders."

We can extend the list of challenges to include persistent regional issues such as labor migration, health (AIDS), drought susceptibility, etc. In contrast to other regions, not only do national governments in Southern Africa recognize these challenges but SADCC and other regional bodies acknowledge them as well. SADCC seems to have established some mechanisms and capabilities to tackle some of these challenges. Therefore, it is our contention that SADCC, possibly with a future democratic and nonracial South Africa as its eleventh member, will continue to play an important role in regional coordination, cooperation, and integration.

■ Botswana: A Success Story and Model?

In a review of Charles Harvey and Stephen R. Lewis, Jr.'s recent book on Botswana,[6] Christopher Colclough argues that Botswana "has much to teach others, both within and outside Southern Africa,"[7] and claims that

Botswana can serve as a model. He calls on scholars to examine whether Botswana's experience provides a paradigm for other states.

We do not want to add our voices to those that either advocate the transference of Botswana's achievements onto other political systems or criticize the suitability of the Botswana case as a model for others. We would rather like to look at some of the achievements and shortcomings associated with Botswana's experience. In doing so, we offer the following assessment as points of departure and comparison rather than as prescriptions. Further, we assume that historical circumstances, cultural setting, and specific natural environment are always unique and form part of the diversity on which the evolution and development of humankind depends. Therefore, one would miss the point altogether if a specific "success story" or a model of development were propagated and projected onto other countries and regions. The effects of the application of European success stories and models on the African continent underline this point. This is not to say, however, that specific experiences cannot be a point of reference and discussion for other peoples, nations, scholars, and politicians. It is, in fact, the specific experience of a large but sparsely populated country, richly endowed with resources but situated in a fragile environment and in a difficult geopolitical position, that attracts our interest and prompts us to draw from its achievements and shortcomings.

At the outset, we would like to make some general remarks. We share the rather common view that economic growth in Botswana has been impressive, not only in terms of mining sector growth and the resulting revenues, but also with regard to manufacturing. At the same time, we emphasize Colclough's contention with respect to unequal distribution of the fruits of growth that Botswana's "development record is more mixed than is sometimes claimed."[8] In other works, we have characterized Botswana as a case of "growth without development" or "growth without employment," if interpreted as an overall assessment of all sectors of the society.[9] One result of this paradox is a growing army of young unemployed, often educated Batswana, sometimes referred to as *the* political challenge, sometimes as a "time bomb."

This brings us to the analysis of political developments. Considering the present African rethinking, with its rejection of the postindependence political formula of "development first, democracy later," one must appreciate, implicitly or explicitly, Botswana's early choice of a political strategy encompassing both development and democracy. One would nonetheless have to underline Holm's and Molutsi's arguments concerning the structural weaknesses of democracy in Botswana,[10] arguments strengthened by the chapters of Holm, Parson, and Somolekae in this volume.

☐   *Achievements*

Taking into account the abject material poverty and structural dependence in which Botswana found itself at independence, one can point out major achievements. They include:

- The efficient economic management and central planning of a mining economy;
- The nationalization of natural resources and of the commanding heights of the economy (e.g., the mineral wealth and the beef industry);
- The design and implementation of successful negotiation strategies by a weak and underdeveloped economy vis-à-vis powerful states and multinational companies; and
- The reduction and diversification of dependency relations with South Africa in the context of SACU.

Successful Management of a Mining Economy
Botswana's economy, like those of South Africa, Namibia, Zambia, and, to a certain extent, Angola and Zimbabwe, is a mining economy, and, as such, Botswana's gross national product (GNP) depends on the world price of the raw materials produced. But dependency on world prices is not the only problem for mining economies. The real risk is the rent-seeking trap, whereby state elites derive profits from national resources.[11] Although in Botswana the mining sector made up 43.9 percent of the gross domestic product (GDP) in 1988,[12] it has been the only African mining economy not to fall into the rent-seeking trap.

In the future, however, Botswana must face the challenge of the postdiamond era. The economic pie will not grow as in the past, and the number of people who want and who have a right to participate in the sharing of the economic proceeds will have increased. Perhaps the reason for the presently restrained development spending of the government is to avoid further long-term financial obligations (e.g., employment in central government).

Meanwhile, as of 1990, Botswana had accumulated enough foreign exchange reserves to pay for about twenty-nine months of imports. Even so, the Ministry of Finance and Development Planning forecasts considerable reductions in future years. According to the budgetary plan for the financial year 1991/92, the government expects a mining income of approximately 1.47 billion pula; the preliminary figure for 1990/91 was 1.95 billion pula. As a consequence of this forecast, the government has reduced development spending and investment by 8 percent for 1991/92.[13]

In 1981–1982 Botswana managed to compensate for declining income from diamonds through conservative, farsighted development spending and modest, albeit insufficient, investment in industrialization and employment-creation programs. However, it is difficult to foresee similar partial solutions for the future, given the synergy of population pressures, resource limitations, and restructuring of regional and international relations.

National Control of Natural Resources and
the Commanding Heights of the Economy
Botswana's territory is divided into tribal, freehold, and state land. Other than the 5 percent freehold farmland and the privately owned land in urban areas, land is held in some form of public ownership and can only be leased. The same is true regarding mineral resources. Unlike in Namibia and South Africa, the mineral resources in Botswana are not owned by private capital or by multinational or transnational corporations. All mining enterprises must obtain mining leases to exploit the mineral resources. They are obliged to pay royalties, taxes, and dividends to the state by way of partnerships with the government. The macroplanning of the mining sector is shared between the Ministry of Mineral and Water Affairs and the Ministry of Finance and Development Planning. Moreover, the Botswana government as a partner participates in the decisionmaking process of these joint venture companies.

The Botswana government, for example, holds less than 55 percent of the shares of the DEBSWANA Mining Company but receives some 80 percent of pretax profits and controls 5.27 percent of DeBeers, the parent company, with two members on the board of directors.[14]

On the other hand, the government of Botswana has also been involved in less successful ventures, such as the Bamangwato Concessions Limited (BCL) copper-nickel mining and processing project in Selebi-Phikwe. Initially planned to open Botswana to foreign investment and to win a share of the world market, the Shashe complex project turned out to be a debt trap. The government of Botswana remained the junior partner in this joint venture of American, German, British, and South African investors and creditors.[15] This is also the reason for the effort to minimize the statal investment in the newly created Soda Ash Botswana (SAB) project.

As in the past, Botswana's strategy has been quite straightforward: it aims to attract investment by encouraging industrial development. The strategy has had a bias toward regional (southern African, including South African) investors on the basis of risk sharing, mutual interests, and benefits, which result from the rise in local employment, mining royalties, and taxes. Again, however, while boosting government income, this strategy leaves many questions with regard to redistribution and employment creation.

More or less the same can be said about investment in other industries. The government gives strong support to projects that are labor intensive, especially for rural areas (Financial Assistance Policy, Arable Lands Development Programme). Beyond this legal framework, the Botswana government itself, through the Botswana Development Corporation (BDC, created in 1970), functions as a private sector employer. As of the beginning of the 1990s, the BDC was involved in about a hundred enterprises (real estate, agriculture, industry, tourism, and trading) as shareholder or creditor.

The government also controls the beef industry, the second most important export sector, through the Botswana Meat Commission (BMC). A nationalized BMC had been an unwavering policy objective even before independence,[16] reflecting not only the specific interest of the cattle-farming lobby, but also that of the cattle-owning rural population. Stephen Morrison's chapter in this volume describes how the newly independent state of Botswana was able to balance its need to control the cattle industry while also meeting the needs of that sector.

We can therefore conclude that all the commanding heights of the Botswana economy are more or less under the direct or indirect control of the state. The Botswana experience of a mixed economy is an instance of the compatibility of sound macroeconomic central planning and economic management with the free market system.

The high degree of socialism in Botswana, in the sense of state involvement in the economy and collective ownership of resources, is stunning and, judging from the macroeconomic performance over the past two decades, refutes the notion that socialist or quasisocialist systems are poor economic performers.

Reduction and Diversification of Dependency Relations
We assume that there has been a lessening of the extremely asymmetrical interdependence that characterized the relationship between Botswana and South Africa in the 1960s and early 1970s, a change demonstrated in various aggregate indicators such as the SACU revenue pool, trade patterns, and labor migration. The reduction of Botswana's dependence on South Africa over the past twenty years is partially a result of successful policies and strategies on the part of Botswana, of the declining performance of the South African economy, and of changed international conditions (e.g., sanctions).[17]

We need only look at the declining importance of SACU to the economy of Botswana. Commentators often cite the revenue from the SACU's revenue pool to demonstrate Botswana's dependency on the customs union: on the contrary, it indicates a reduction of dependency. In the financial year 1973/74, revenue from the pool made up 50 percent of government income. Since then, this rate has declined considerably, with 13 percent in 1987/88 marking the low point. If one compares the 1984/85 rates for Botswana, Lesotho, and Swaziland, the success is even more striking: Lesotho 69.7 percent, Swaziland 63.7 percent, and Botswana 20.4 percent.[18]

One sees the same trends for Botswana in the case of the Common Customs Area (CCA). From 1980 to 1987, imports from the CCA declined from 87 to 79.6 percent. Twenty-five to 40 percent of the imports from

South Africa are in transit from overseas. This import gap was filled by imports from the EC and from other African countries (Zimbabwe). Botswana's exports to CCA countries fell from 6.6 to 4.2 percent between 1980 and 1987. This export gap (including the massive decline in exports to the United States) has been filled by the EC. However, it is interesting to mention that exports to African countries (excluding CCA) declined from 8.4 (1980) to 4.8 percent (1987).

While the significance of the customs union to Botswana has been reduced, its importance to South Africa has been rising. The South African economy depends on exports, especially of manufactured products sold to other African countries. Capital outflows compel South Africa to run current account surpluses. Erich Leistner, of the Africa Institute (in Pretoria), has estimated that the South African balance of trade surplus with member SADCC countries is presently in the range of three billion rand per annum. The net profit of the South Africa transport services was approximately 300 million rand in 1986. SADCC itself calculated the same figure to be approximately $350 million dollars in the same year.[19]

The importance of SACU for South Africa is rising with the deteriorating economic situation. The fall of the rand against the pula has had an export-promoting effect. In 1990 Botswana revalued the pula against the rand for the second time (the first reevaluation having taken place in 1989). The reduction of dependency has led to an improved bargaining position for Botswana vis-à-vis South Africa. Let us give two examples of this. First, the South Africans failed in 1988 to persuade the other members to reduce the multiplier of the revenue sharing formula (1.42) or to include the so-called independent homelands (Transkei, Bophuthatswana, Venda, Ciskei) "de jure" in the Customs Union Agreement.

Second, during the same negotiations, the BLS countries (Botswana, Lesotho, Swaziland) forced South Africa to cancel a previous arrangement with Turkey concerning a reduction of import duties on textiles. These two examples illustrate that the time when South Africa could always act without the consent of the other SACU members has passed.

Negotiation Strategies vis-à-vis Powerful
Neighbors and the Total Strategy
Another of Botswana's achievements has been the successful handling of its powerful, aggressive neighbor during the phase of South Africa's regional destabilization strategy. Given the differences in economic and military power between South Africa and Botswana it can be said that on occasions, at least in political matters, "the tail wags the dog" rather than vice versa.

A case in point is the South African attempt to link the soda ash project to the signing of an Nkomati-type nonaggression pact, clearly an attempt to coerce Botswana into playing a significant part in the Total Strategy of the Botha era. Even before Mozambique and South Africa signed the Nkomati accord in March 1984, Pretoria indicated it was also interested in signing a nonaggression pact with Botswana. Botswana, however, uncomfortable with the spirit of Nkomati, did not attend the signing ceremony on the banks of the Inkomaati River. A few days before, at the SACU consultative conference meeting where the negotiations of the soda ash project topped the agenda, the South African delegation presented a draft of a nonaggression pact with Botswana, ready to be signed.[20] It was understood that if Botswana would not sign, the soda ash project would not be allowed to fall under the "major industries protection" clause of the Customs Union Agreement. Of course, this was sheer blackmail.

The draft "Notwane Accord"[21] is more restrictive than the Nkomati accord. First, there is a mutual nonintervention clause. Article 4 states:

> The Contracting Parties undertake to respect each other's sovereignty and independence and shall in fulfilment of this duty refrain from interference in the internal affairs of each other and shall not resort to or participate, whether individually or collectively, in any coercive measures of a political or economic nature against each other.

This would have prevented Botswana from supporting or initiating UN resolutions against South Africa, such as a call for the maintenance of sanctions. In addition, the accord states that signatories should assure "that their national broadcasting organizations do not broadcast material of whatever origin that may result in or be supportive of activities contemplated in this article [Article 3]." Under Article 6, Botswana would have committed itself to transfer all data about South African refugees to Pretoria:

> The Contracting Parties shall provide each other with full particulars about their respective nationals who claim refugee status in each other's territory in order to enable them to determine jointly whether such nationals do in fact qualify as refugees in terms of the Mandate of the United Nations High Commissioner for Refugees and shall, whenever circumstances and their respective international commitments allow thereof, repatriate such persons to the Contracting Party of their nationality.[22]

This, in effect, would mean that the state from which people were fleeing could determine whether they were "criminals" or victims of persecution! For the Botswana government, this politically subtle proposal was totally unacceptable. Pretoria did not back away from its Notwane accord/soda ash project linkage until February 1985. That it did, however, must be seen as the results of the improved bargaining position of Botswana as well as skillful diplomacy. South Africa overestimated its potential for applying economic leverage (investment in the soda ash project and withholding of protection) and underestimated its own dependence on potentially cheap soda ash imports from Botswana.

The late realization on the part of South Africa that it could not force Botswana into political and security commitments through economic leverage, however, cost Botswana dearly. Richard Dale's chapter in this book describes the military raids and pressure that South Africa carried out against Botswana in the 1980s.

In sum, we can say that Botswana has valuable experience in successful negotiations vis-à-vis powerful neighbors as well as transnational enterprises. Namibia and other SADCC members could likely learn from these. Indeed, during the month before the independence of Namibia, designated permanent secretaries and directors of ministries (finance, mineral resources) of the incoming Namibian government spent some time in the offices of their future counterparts in Gaborone. Within SADCC it is being increasingly recognized that Botswana's experiences are worth studying. More and more officials from SADCC member countries have been spending time in Botswana to learn from their respective counterparts.

□ *Shortcomings*

According to a German proverb, "Where there is light, there is also shadow." Of course, Botswana provides no exception to this rule. Shadows on the Botswana success story appear to touch three major areas: first, the uneven distribution of wealth and socioeconomic opportunities, and increasing poverty; second, the neglect of, and in some cases disregard for, the heavy environmental and ecological costs attributable to agricultural practices, policies, and programs; and third, the somewhat undefined role Botswana's security system, built around the BDF, is playing and will be playing in internal politics as well as in the regional context.

Uneven Distribution of Wealth

In recent publications by Stephen Lewis, Charles Harvey, and others, much has been said about the bright side of Botswana's macroeconomic success, but relatively little attention has been given to the widening gap between rich and poor, the concentration of economic power and property, and the marginalization of an increasing number of Botswana's rather small population. It has been suggested already that Botswana could be labeled a case of "growth without development" or "growth without employment." Even less is known about the exact relationship between macroeconomic growth and planning, on the one side, and Botswana's liberal political system on the other.

Taking into account Molutsi's assertion that the bureaucracy is dominating "the political elite on the one hand and is seeking to limit popular and democratic control on the other,"[23] one could argue that the "growth without development" dilemma is primarily a result of the bureaucratic approach to "development." This point is emphasized in Holm's conclusion that it is the bureaucrats—the civil servants, not the politicians—who incorporate into their decisionmaking the interests of economic interest groups.[24] The dichotomy between impressive growth and infrastructural development and the inequality in the distribution of benefits and welfare, as well as the resulting conflict potential, seem to be directly attributable to the relative power of the bureaucratic elite, its policies and programs, planning procedures, ideologies, and external backing. It is therefore no surprise that issues such as bureaucratic power, poverty, and socioeconomic conflicts are increasingly reflected in the agenda of Botswana's political parties, the ruling BDP included.[25]

Hence, what seems to be called for is both the democratization of the bureaucracy and the empowerment of the political parties, civic associations, and grassroots organizations; the "checking and balancing" of the bureaucracy by democratic means and processes. This democratization of bureaucratic decisionmaking might have negative effects on the effectiveness of centrally organized planning, decisionmaking, and program implementation by the state and its organs. Gains, however, would be likely in a larger degree of political legitimacy in bureaucratic actions, in a higher degree of popular participation, and, eventually, in policies and programs that reflect the well-being of all strata of the Botswana society. Popular participation, political legitimacy, good governance, and accountability have become criteria for the evaluation of the political performance of African states. These criteria are not only employed by foreign donors, but also by African leaders themselves.[26] The case of Botswana seems to underline the need to apply these criteria in the broadest sense, not only to the political system but especially to the bureaucracy, as the essential and dominating part of it.

Botswana, a country with a small population, has achieved indisputable economic and political progress; it has followed a tradition of moderate policies and peaceful conflict resolution, for which it has received international recognition. If Botswana is not in a position to tackle creatively and to resolve at least some of these homegrown socioeconomic and socio-political problems, how then should its African neighbors fare, less richly endowed with assets and successes? We feel that Botswana is not only in a unique position in southern Africa but also has a moral obligation to take a lead and make a determined effort to design and implement strategies to combat poverty. These strategies ought to be based on the genuine participation of all its citizens and not solely on technocratic concepts of economic lobbies, bureaucrats, planners, and donor agencies. This certainly requires genuine dialogue and participation, not so much in Gaborone and vis-à-vis donors and statesmen abroad as with and among all groups and people at home.

We strongly advocate political reform to deepen and broaden the democratic process and—by implication—to control the bureaucratic approach to development. Reform can also strengthen local and regional government institutions, create new ones where necessary (why not introduce parliaments on the district level?), and give them a higher degree of political and economic autonomy in decisionmaking, the latter, for example, in the form of an independent tax base. In this regard, Botswana can learn from debates elsewhere in southern Africa, particularly in South Africa. Some of the conclusions and recommendations in the work of Francis Wilson and Mamphela Ramphele have a relevance for Botswana, too.[27]

Furthermore, one has to think about electoral reform in Botswana. In particular, the system of special elected members of Parliament, by which the president has the right to nominate five additional MPs (who might have previously lost their seats) seems to be incompatible with modern structures.

Ecological Consequences of Development

As pointed out by Rodger Yeager in this volume, Botswana has been criticized on occasion for not addressing environmental questions and for not designing policies to prevent or balance the negative consequences of industrial and agricultural development programs and projects on land, water, fauna, and flora.[28]

More specifically, the criticism focused on four main issues, namely, the environmental damages due to the growth of the national herd in general and to specific livestock-related projects in particular; the negative impact of cattle and veterinary fencing on wildlife migration; the environmental pollution and destruction due to the "tsetse war" and to the opening up of fringes of the Okavango Delta for cattle rearing; and, lastly, the tapping of the Okavango water system for industrial and agricultural purposes. This latter issue, which became prominent during the early 1990s, has served as a rallying point for national and international environmentalists.[29]

We do not intend to engage in a detailed discussion of these complex issues; rather, we would like to make a few observations and suggestions, which also have relevance beyond Botswana.

Firstly, economic development in general terms not only entails production and distribution of goods and services for the purpose of the well-being of people, but also inherently and inevitably it involves the transformation and eventual destruction of material taken from nature's treasury and the production and circulation of various forms of waste. This simple fact is often overlooked in the debate over the relationship between economy and ecology. In addition, the faster the process of economic transformation and growth takes place, the more waste and pollution will be produced and the more natural resources will be damaged. Critical adherents to the school of sustainable development argue that in the long run the aims of economic growth, ecological soundness of production and distribution, and social peace cannot be reconciled in a capitalist economic system, neither in the rich countries of the North nor in the poor countries of the South.[30] In the case of Botswana it seems obvious that there is a correlation between the country's impressive growth performance and its environmental problems.

On the techno-economic level, concepts for anticipating, measuring, and minimizing the environmentally detrimental effects of development projects are increasingly applied. The environmental assessment of development programs and projects have become part of project cooperation with donors. On the sociopolitical level, "green" movements and associations are mushrooming across the globe, including in southern Africa. In the case of Botswana, the Boro dredging project in the Okavango Delta became a rallying point not only for international environmentalists, but also for local people (in Maun) and the political parties in Ngamiland, including the BDP.[31] Environmental issues will increasingly appear on political agendas at the local, national, and regional levels; they will add a further dimension to the democratization process.

In the case of Botswana, one can argue that the government and bureaucracy have not yet exhausted all possibilities in environmental impact assessment, monitoring, and legislation. Even in terms of economic cost-benefit analyses, investments in certain environmental projects have not yet been appropriately appraised as genuine investments in the economic sense, with positive effects not only on the environment itself and the people living in it, but also on production and on employment creation.

In other cases, such as the tsetse eradication programs, it can be argued that their direct and indirect costs (as well as opportunity costs) may well exceed their economic benefits.[32] It can be argued that—besides their catastrophic ecological effect—such programs are inefficient and should be abandoned on economic grounds alone. The same seems to be true for certain cattle-fencing projects.

In some industrialized countries, economists have begun to complement the computation of GNP statistics with statistics concerning environmental cost factors in order to attain a clearer picture of the costs and benefits of growth-related policies and programs. Given its excellent statistical services and administration, Botswana could follow suit; statistical computation of environmental data would enable it better to gauge the true costs of certain programs and to adjust policies accordingly. The establishment of a department or even ministry for environmental and ecological affairs as well as the publication of an annual environmental survey would be appropriate steps to include an ecological dimension in development planning.

Concerning the sociopolitical level, it can be argued that the "greening" of politics will remain a feature of democratization in Botswana, requiring responses by the government, the bureaucrats, and the political parties. Already, "green" issues have been included in resolutions passed at a recent BDP congress.[33] The suspending of the Boro dredging project has been praised as a "victory for democracy" in Maun, "where the Kgotla has reasserted itself as the major forum for consultation and decision-making and forced the government to back down on the Okavango dredging row."[34] Even if this appraisal appears premature in 1992, environmental issues and problems exist; they command increasing local and regional political attention; this being so, awareness of a link between growth, environment, and equity is bound to increase. With the announcement in 1985 of a National Conservation Strategy (NCS) recommended by the UNDP under its environment program, Botswana became one of the first countries to recognize the political importance of public environmental awareness and of measures to improve the protection and management of the environment.[35] However, it appears that the NCS has remained by and large under wraps within the bureaucracy.[36] The momentum lost did not begin to be recovered until the early 1990s. Legislation concerning the NCS has been passed by the National Assembly, with specific reference to the Okavango Delta. It has been recommended that the delta "be designated a World Heritage Site and that the government join the Ramsar Convention on Wetland Protection."[37] Although this convention appears to allow operations such as the Boro dredging and would emphasize conservation rather than protection, we are encouraged that Botswana's politicians are taking steps in the right direction. With regard to perceiving the unique Okavango Delta as a World Heritage Site or, in the words of President Masire, a "God-given natural phenomenon,"[38] it would indeed be shortsighted and parochial if Botswana's government were to view the Okavango waters and the adjacent river system as "national entities," subject to exclusively national decisionmaking. The balancing of national, regional, and international interests seems to be a matter of logical necessity.

Botswana's government, in cooperation with Namibia and Angola, would earn much international praise if it took the bold step and declared the Okavango Delta and its contributing riverine system a natural heritage of mankind, a global natural common, protected under the auspices of a special international regime.

At a time when debt-for-nature swaps increasingly appear on the agenda between donors and recipients, when appraisals of the environmental impact of development projects are bound to be made compulsory, Botswana, given its natural treasures and experiences, could take a lead in southern Africa in promoting national, regional, and international research and dialogue on environment, ecology, conservation (especially concerning the Okavango), and other riverine systems in southern Africa. There, again, Botswana could learn from the greening of politics in other parts of southern Africa, notably from South Africa.

What Future Security Regime?
What Role for the Botswana Defence Force (BDF)?
The creation and expansion of the BDF from 1977 onward is easily explained. Originally it was the threat and occurrence of spillover effects of

the liberation war in former Rhodesia that caused the transformation of a Police Mobile Unit (PMU) into the BDF. Thereafter, it was the destabilization strategy and cross-border military operations of SADF that led to an expansion and buildup of the BDF. Today, the BDF is comprised of two components (an army and an air force), with 4,500 males in voluntary active military service. The equipment includes sophisticated hardware, such as ten SAM-7 batteries, thirteen combat jet aircraft, and a small fleet of transport aircraft and helicopters. The defense budget in 1990 was 93 million pula ($56.76 million).[39] In fiscal year 1990/91 the BDF was the third largest budgetary expenditure item (after the Ministry of Education and the Ministry of Works and Communication).[40] Until 1990, the threat from South Africa and the presence of the BDF in and around the capital distorted and spoiled the friendly and open character of Setswana society and seemed to have led to what is referred to as a war mentality.[41] There was probably no alternative to this. The National Security Act, passed to enable the security forces better to cope with certain aspects of South African destabilization, is still in force, although rarely applied. It appears, however, that the BDF is somehow a state within the state, not subject to democratic and public control. This state of affairs is exacerbated by an attitude of BDF personnel, who "have the impression that the army is entitled to a degree of immunity from the norms and controls under which the rest of the society lives."[42] A more open information policy concerning national and regional security issues, and more public scrutiny and accountability in financial matters, is needed. This specifically applies to what is referred to as Operation Eagle, a strictly classified project that apparently involves the construction of at least one military air base, estimated at US $600 million.[43]

Given the fundamental changes in the region toward cooperation instead of confrontation, the demobilization of parts of SADF, significant cuts in the South African defense budget, and increasing talk of a regional cooperation and security system, a number of questions arise concerning the BDF, its future role, and its place in the society:

- Who is the "enemy"?
- Why is there a need for an air force with combat aircraft and for an expensive air base? Why does the BDF have a budget of more than 100 million pula (1990/91), one of the country's largest spenders in terms of state budget expenditure?
- What is the democratic control mechanism for the security system? Why not introduce a joint defense committee, consisting of parliamentarians from both houses, including opposition members?
- Is there a case for reviewing the BDF and national security structures, including for the cutting of defense spending?

The latter could be seen as contributing to a process of military confidence-building in Southern Africa as well as in Botswana itself. A confer-ence on cooperation and security in postapartheid Southern Africa, which is presently being discussed,[44] is expected to provide valuable stimuli for the cutting of defense budgets, a reviewing of military doctrines and force pos-tures, and the restructuring of armed forces—not only in Botswana but in the whole region, South Africa in particular. What seems to be needed as a precondition for a new regional security regime, however, is a gradual "demilitarization of the mind" throughout the region. There again, Botswana, with its tradition of peaceful conflict resolution, could take a leading role.

■ Notes

1. Bernhard Weimer, "New Deal Economics, Post-Apartheid Priorities," *Indicator SA* 8, no. 3 (Durban: University of Natal, Winter 1991).

2. *Resolutions of the Sixth International Conference on Peace and Security in Southern Africa,* Arusha, Tanzania, February 25–28, 1991.

3. Bernhard Weimer, "Post-Apartheid Southern Africa: Regional Cooperation and Trade," *Internationales Afrika Forum* 27, no. 2 (1991): 167–174.

4. In this context, the concept of "sustainable development" needs special mention, as it emerged from the work of the World Commission on Environment and Development ("Brundtland Commission").

5. Michael Hough, "Security, War and the Environment," *Strategic Review for Southern Africa* (Pretoria) 12, no. 2 (1990): 1–13.

6. Charles Harvey and Stephen R. Lewis, Jr., *Policy Choice and Development Performance in Botswana* (Houndmills, Basingstoke, Hampshire: Macmillan, in association with the OECD Development Center, 1990).

7. Christopher Colclough, "Review Article," *African Affairs* 90, no. 385 (1991): 145–147.

8. Ibid., 147.

9. Olaf Claus, "Botswana: Südafrikanisches Homeland oder unabhängiger Frontstaat. Eine Untersuchung zur Bestimmung der wirtschaftlichen und politischen Handlungfreiheit 'kleiner' Staaten vis-à-vis 'mächtiger' Nachbarn" (Hamburg: Institut für Afrika-kunde, 1992). Bernhard Weimer, "Botswana: African Economic Miracle or Dependent South African Quasi-Homeland?" in Karl Wohlmuth et al., eds., *African Development Yearbook 1989* (Berlin: Research Group on African Development Perspectives, 1990), 395–419.

10. Patrick P. Molutsi and John D. Holm, "Developing Democracy When Civil Society Is Weak: The Case of Botswana," *African Affairs* 89, no. 365 (1990): 323–340.

11. See Richard Sklar, "No Perestroika without Glasnost," in *Beyond Autocracy in Africa,* Working Papers from the inaugural seminar of the Governance in Africa Program, Atlanta, Georgia, February 17–18, 1989, edited by the Carter Center of Emory University, Atlanta, Georgia, 143.

12. Republic of Botswana, Central Statistics Office, *Statistical Bulletin,* vol. 14, no. 2 (June 1989).

13. *Informationsdienst Südliches Afrika* 3 (May/June 1991): 4.

14. Claus, "Botswana," 144.

15. Raymond F. Mikesell, "The Selebi-Phikwe Nickel/Copper Mine in

Botswana: Lessons from a Financial Disaster," *Natural Resources Forum* (New York) 8, no. 3 (1984): 279–290.

16. Michael Hubbard, *Agricultural Exports and Economic Growth: A Study of Botswana's Beef Industry* (London, New York, KPI: distributed by Routledge and Kegan Paul Methuen, 1986), 143ff.

17. With special references to a theoretical framework, see Claus, "Botswana," 14–49.

18. Garvin Maasdorp, "The Southern African Customs Union (SACU)," in Erich Leistner, Pieter Esterhuysen, eds., *South Africa in Southern Africa: Economic Interaction* (Pretoria: Africa Institute of South Africa, 1988), 54.

19. Erich Leistner, "Whither South Africa: The African Perspective in Foreign Policy," *Africa Insight* (Pretoria) 18, no. 1 (1988): 3; "Southern Africa: The Market for the Future?" *Africa Insight* (Pretoria) 15, no. 1 (1985): 17–21.

20. Personal communication in Gaborone and Pretoria, May 1990 (Olaf Claus). The draft of the nonaggression pact can be found in Claus, "Botswana," 312–322.

21. We propose this term in analogy to the Nkomati Accord. The Notwane is a border river south of Gaborone, the Botswana capital.

22. Article 3, Notwane Accord.

23. Patrick P. Molutsi, "The Ruling Class and Democracy in Botswana," in Patrick P. Molutsi and John D. Holm, eds., *Democracy in Botswana,* Proceedings of a symposium held in Gaborone, August 1–5, 1988 (Athens: Ohio University Press, 1989), 113.

24. John D. Holm, "How Effective Are Interest Groups in Representing Their Members?" in Holm and Molutsi, *Democracy,* 147.

25. The BDP congress held in Palapye in July 1991 resolved, inter alia, to study the "escalating problem of poverty" and "to identify causes with a view to correcting the situation" (Radio Botswana, in English 1910 gmt, July 16, 1991, cited in *BBC Summary of World Broadcasts,* ME/1127/B/7, July 18, 1991).

26. African Leadership Forum, Report on the Results of a Brainstorming Meeting on a "Conference on Security, Stability, Development and Cooperation in Africa," Addis Ababa, 1990), 24.

27. Francis Wilson and Mamphela Ramphele, *Uprooting Poverty: The South African Challenge* (New York and London, W. W. Norton and Company, 1989).

28. See, inter alia, E. M. Veenendaal and J. B. Opschoor, *Botswana's Beef Exports to the EEC: Economic Development at the Expense of a Deteriorating Environment* (Amsterdam: 1986); Yves Galland (rapporteur), "The Disturbance of the Ecological Equilibrium in Botswana" (European Parliament Committee for Development and Cooperation, Strasbourg, 1986).

29. *Okavango Delta or Desert? A Question of Water (*London: Greenpeace, 1991); Derek James, "People Defend Botswana's Environment," *Africa Recovery* 5, no. 1 (1991): 20–21.

30. Hans-Jürgen Harborth, *Dauerhafte Entwicklung [Sustainable Development]. Zur Entstehung eines ökologischen Konzepts* (Berlin: Kissenschaftseentrum, 1989). For a critique see Sharachchandra M. Lele, "Sustainable Development: A Critical Review," in *World Development* (June 1991): 607–621.

31. Douglas Tsiako, "Boro Dredging Suspended," *News Link Africa,* January 18, 1991.

32. Ludwig Gruber, *Landwirtschaftliche Kooperation zwischen EG und Afrika im Rahmen der Lomé-Abkommen. Fallstudien zum Zucker-und Rindfleischhandel* (Hamburg: Institut für Afrika-Kunde, 1987), 208ff.

33. Radio Botswana.

34. Tsiako, "Boro Dredging Suspended."

35. Alec Campbell and John Cooke, eds., *The Management of Botswana's Environment,* Workshop organized by the Botswana Society on behalf of the Botswana government, June 5–7, 1984 (Gaborone: The Government Printer, 1984).

36. Ministry of Local Government and Lands, Department of Town and Regional Planning (Report of the Workshop on the National Convention Strategy, October 23–25, 1985). Gaborone: The Government Printer.

37. *Africa Recovery,* 20.

38. Quett K. J. Masire, "Opening Speech," in *Proceedings of the Symposium on the Okavango Delta and its Future Utilization,* Symposium on the Okavango Delta (Gaborone: The Government Printer, 1986), 1.

39. International Institute for Strategic Studies (IISS), *Military Balance 1990–1991* (London: IISS, 1991), 126.

40. "A Dangerous Dinosaur," in *Southern African Economist,* June/July 1990, 21.

41. Sandy Grant and Brian Egner, "The Private Press and Democracy," in Holm and Molutsi, *Democracy,* 250.

42. Ibid., 251.

43. *Southscan* 6, no. 9(8) (March 1991): 89; *Africa Confidential* 32, no. 10 (May 17, 1991): 8.

44. Reference is made to the recommendations of the Sixth International Conference on Peace and Security in Southern Africa, held in Arusha, Tanzania, February 25–28, 1991, and to the Workshop on Cooperation and Security in Post-Apartheid Southern Africa, held in Maputo, Mozambique, September 1–4, 1991.

Selected Bibliography

Bodenmuller, Rolf. *Botswana, Lesotho, and Swaziland: Their External Relations and Policy and Attitudes Towards South Africa.* Pretoria: Africa Institute of South Africa, 1973.

Breytenbach, W. J. *Migratory Labour Arrangements in Southern Africa.* Rev. ed. Communications of the Africa Institute, no. 33. Pretoria: Africa Institute of South Africa, 1979.

Bussing, Charles E. *National Conservation Strategy: District Issues and Potential Projects.* Gaborone: USAID/Botswana and Department of Town and Regional Planning, Ministry of Local Government and Lands, 1987.

Callaghy, Thomas. "Africa and the World Economy: Caught Between a Rock and a Hard Place." In John Harbeson and Donald Rothchild, eds., *Africa in World Politics.* Boulder, Colo.: Westview, 1991.

Claus, Olaf. "Botswana: Südafrikanisches Homeland oder unabhängiger Frontstaat. Eine Untersuchung zur Bestimmung der wirtschaftlichen und politischen Handlungfreiheit 'kleiner' Staaten vis-à-vis 'mächtiger' Nachbarn." Ph.D. diss., University of Mainz, 1991.

Clough, Michael, and Jeffrey Herbst. *South Africa's Changing Regional Strategy: Beyond Destabilization.* Critical Issues Series, no. 4. New York: Council on Foreign Relations, 1989.

Colclough, Christopher, and Stephen McCarthy. *The Political Economy of Botswana: A Study of Growth and Distribution.* Oxford: Oxford University Press, 1980.

———. "Review Article." *African Affairs* 90, no. 385 (1991): 145–147.

Dale, Richard. "The Loosening Connection in Anglophone Southern Africa: Botswana and the Rhodesian Regime, 1965–1980." *Journal of Contemporary African Studies* (Pretoria) 2, no. 2 (April 1983): 257–285.

———. "Not Always So Placid a Place: Botswana Under Attack." *African Affairs* 86, no. 342 (January 1987):78–85.

de St. Jorre, John. "Destabilization and Dialogue: South Africa's Emergence as a Regional Superpower." *CSIS Africa Notes* 26 (April 1984): 2.

Diamond, Larry, Juan Linz, and Seymour Martin Lipset, eds. *Democracy in Developing Countries.* Vol. 2, *Africa.* Boulder, Colo.: Lynne Rienner, 1988.

Duggan, William. *An Economic History of Southern African Agriculture.* New York: Sage, 1985.

Geldenhuys, Deon J. "South Africa's Regional Policy." In Michael Clough, ed., *Changing Realities in Southern Africa*. Research Series, no. 47. Berkeley: University of California, Institute of International Studies, 1982.

Gordenker, Leon. *Refugees in International Politics*. New York: Columbia University Press, 1987.

Greenpeace. *Okavango Delta or Desert? A Question of Water*. London: Greenpeace, 1991.

Grundy, Kenneth W. "South Africa in the Political Economy of Southern Africa." In Gwendolen M. Carter and Patrick O'Meara, eds., *International Politics in Southern Africa*. Bloomington: Indiana University Press, 1982.

Halpern, J. *South Africa's Hostages: Basutoland, Bechuanaland and Swaziland*. Harmondsworth: Penguin Books, 1965.

Harvey, Charles, and Stephen R. Lewis, Jr. *Policy Choice and Development Performance in Botswana*. London: Macmillan, 1990.

Holm, John D., and Patrick Molutsi. "Monitoring the Development of Democracy: Our Botswana Experience." *The Journal of Modern African Studies* 28, no. 3 (September 1990).

———. "State and Society Relations in Botswana: Beginning Liberalization." In Goran Hyden and Michael Bratton, eds., *Governance and Politics in Africa*. Boulder, Colo.: Lynne Rienner, 1992.

Hough, Michael. "Security, War and the Environment." *Strategic Review for Southern Africa* (Pretoria) 12, no. 2 (1990): 1–13.

Hubbard, Michael. *Agricultural Exports and Economic Growth: A Study of Botswana's Beef Industry*. London: KPI, 1986.

Hyam, Ronald. *The Failure of South African Expansion, 1908–1948*. London and Basingstoke: Macmillan, 1972.

Hyden, Goran. "Governance and the Study of Politics." In Goran Hyden and Michael Bratton, eds., *Governance and Politics in Africa*. Boulder, Colo.: Lynne Rienner, 1992.

International Institute for Strategic Studies. *Military Balance 1990–1991*. London: IISS, 1991.

Kalahari Conservation Society. *Sustainable Wildlife Utilisation: The Role of Wildlife Management Areas*. Proceedings of a workshop organized by the Kalahari Conservation Society in conjunction with the Department of Wildlife and National Parks. Gaborone: KCS and Department of Wildlife and National Parks, 1988.

Khama, Seretse. *From the Frontline: Speeches of Sir Seretse Khama*. Edited by Gwendolen M. Carter and E. Philip Morgan. London: Rex Collings, 1980.

Leistner, Erich. "Southern Africa: The Market for the Future?" *Africa Insight* (Pretoria) 15, no. 1 (1985): 17–21.

———. "Whither South Africa: The African Perspective in Foreign Policy." *Africa Insight* (Pretoria) 18, no. 1 (1988): 3.

Lewis, Stephen R., Jr., and Jennifer Sharpley. "Botswana's Industrialization." Discussion Paper no. 245. Brighton, England: Institute of Development Studies.

Nankani, Gobind. "Development Problems of Mineral Exporting Countries." World Bank Staff Working Paper no. 345. Washington, D.C.: World Bank, 1979.

Martin, Roger. *Southern Africa: The Price of Apartheid: A Political Risk Analysis*. Special Report no. 1130. London: Economist Intelligence Unit, 1988.

May, Henry J. *The South African Constitution*. 3d ed. Cape Town and Johannesburg: Juta & Co., 1955.

Migdal, Joel. *Strong Societies and Weak States: State-Society Relations and State Capabilities in the Third World*. Princeton, N.J.: Princeton University Press, 1988.

Mikesell, Raymond F. "The Selebi-Phikwe Nickel/Copper Mine in Botswana: Lessons from a Financial Disaster." *Natural Resources Forum* (New York) 8, no. 3 (1984): 279–290.

Molokomme, Athaliah. "Mine Labour Migration from Botswana to South Africa: Some Practical Legal Issues." In Louis Molamu, Athaliah Molokomme, and Gloria Somolekae, eds., *Perceptions of Batswana Mineworkers Towards the South African Gold Mines, with Special Reference to Living and Working Conditions, Legal Issues and Trade Unions.* International Migration for Employment Working Paper no. 36. Geneva: International Labour Organization, 1988.

Molomo, Mpho. "The Political Process: Does Multipartyism Persist Due to the Lack of a Strong Opposition?" *Southern Africa Political & Economic Monthly* 3, no. 7 (May 1990): 9.

Molutsi, Patrick P., and John D. Holm. *Democracy in Botswana.* Athens: Ohio University Press, 1989.

———, eds. "Developing Democracy When Civil Society Is Weak: The Case of Botswana." *African Affairs* 89, no. 365 (1990): 323–340.

Moorcroft, Paul L. *African Nemesis: War and Revolution in Southern Africa (1945–2010).* London: Brassey's, 1990.

Moore, Barrington, Jr. *The Social Origins of Dictatorship and Democracy: Lord and Peasant in the Making of the Modern World.* Boston: Beacon, 1966.

Lord Hailey. *Native Administration in the British African Territories, Part V, The High Commission Territories: Basutoland, the Bechuanaland Protectorate and Swaziland.* London: HMSO, 1953.

Nengwekhulu, Ranbwedzi. "Some Findings on the Origins of Political Parties in Botswana." *Pulu* 1, no. 2 (June 1978): 47–76.

———. "Class, State, Politics and Elections in Postcolonial Botswana: the 1984 General Election." In Jack Parson, Lionel Cliffe, and Ranbwedzi Nengwekhulu, *The 1984 Botswana General Elections.* University of Botswana Election Study Project, Gaborone. Manuscript.

Noppen, D. *Consultation and Non-Commitment in Botswana: Planning with the People of Botswana.* Research Report no. 13. Leiden, Netherlands: African Studies Center, 1982.

Parson, Jack. *Botswana: Liberal Democracy and the Labor Reserve in Southern Africa.* Boulder, Colo.: Westview, 1984.

———. "The Peasantariat and Politics: Migration, Wage Labor and Agriculture in Botswana." *Africa Today* 31, no. 4 (1984): 5–25.

Parsons, Q. Neil. "The Evolution of Modern Botswana: Historical Revisions." In Louis A. Picard, ed., *The Evolution of Modern Botswana: Politics and Rural Development in Southern Africa.* London: Rex Collings; Lincoln: University of Nebraska Press, 1985.

Picard, Louis A. "The Historical Legacy and Modern Botswana." In Louis A. Picard, ed., *The Evolution of Modern Botswana: Politics and Rural Development in Southern Africa.* London: Rex Collings; Lincoln: University of Nebraska Press, 1985.

———. *The Politics of Development in Botswana: A Model for Success?* Boulder, Colo.: Lynne Rienner, 1987.

Polhemus, James H. "Botswana Votes: Parties and Elections in an African Democracy." *Journal of Modern Studies* 21, no. 3 (1983): 397–430.

———. "The Refugee Factor in Botswana." *Immigrants and Minorities* (London) 4, no. 1 (March 1985): 28–45.

Republic of Botswana. *National Development Plans, 1979–1985, 1985–1991.* Gaborone: The Government Printer, 1980, 1985.

————. Statistical Bulletin 14, no. 2. Gaborone: The Central Statistics Office, June 1989.

————. *Labour Statistics 1988.* Gaborone: The Central Statistics Office, 1989.

————. *Report to the Minister of Presidential Affairs and Public Administration on the General Election, 1989.* Supervisor of Elections. Gaborone: The Government Printer, n.d.

Resolutions of the Sixth International Conference on Peace and Security in Southern Africa, February 25–28, 1991, Arusha, Tanzania.

Roe, Emery. *Development of Livestock Agriculture and Water Supplies in Eastern Botswana Before Independence: A Short History and Policy Analysis.* Ithaca, N.Y.: Rural Development Committee, Center for International Studies, Cornell University, 1980.

Samboma, Leonard M. *The Survey of the Freehold Farms of Botswana.* Gaborone: Animal Production Division, Ministry of Agriculture, 1982.

Saxena, Suresh C. *Foreign Policy of African States: Politics of Dependence and Confrontation.* New Delhi: Deep & Deep, 1982.

Sillery, Anthony. *Founding a Protectorate: History of Bechuanaland, 1885–1895.* The Hague: Mouton & Co., 1965.

Somolekae, Gloria. "Do Batswana Act Democratically?" In Patrick P. Molutsi and John D. Holm, eds., *Democracy in Botswana.* Athens: Ohio State University Press, 1989.

Southall, Roger. "Botswana as a Host Country for Refugees." *The Journal of Commonwealth and Comparative Politics* 22, no. 2 (July 1984): 151–179.

Stevens, Richard P. *Lesotho, Botswana and Swaziland: The Former High Commission Territories in Southern Africa.* London: Pall Mall, 1967.

————. "The History of the Anglo–South African Conflict over the Proposed Incorporation of the High Commission Territories." In Christian P. Potholm and Richard Dale, eds., *Southern Africa in Perspective: Essays in Regional Politics.* New York: The Free Press, 1972.

————. *Historical Dictionary of Botswana.* Metuchen, N.J.: Scarecrow, 1975.

Vanneman, Peter. *Soviet Strategy in Southern Africa: Gorbachev's Pragmatic Approach.* Stanford, Calif.: Hoover Institution Press, 1990.

Vengroff, Richard. *Botswana: Rural Development in the Shadow of Apartheid.* Rutherford, N.J.: Fairleigh Dickinson University Press, 1977.

Viotti, Paul R., and Mark V. Kauppi. *International Relations Theory: Realism, Pluralism, Globalism.* New York: Macmillan, 1987.

Wheeler, David. "Sources of Stagnation in Sub-Saharan Africa." *World Development* 12, no. 1 (January 1984): 1–23.

Wiley, L. *TGLP and Hunter-Gatherers: A Case of Land Politics.* Gaborone: University College of Botswana, 1981.

Wilmsen, Edwin. *Land Filled With Flies: A Political Economy of the Kalahari.* Chicago: University of Chicago Press, 1989.

World Bank. "Managing Development: The Governance Dimension, A Discussion Paper." Washington, D.C.: The World Bank, 1991.

————. *World Development Report 1991.* New York: Oxford University Press, 1991.

Yeager, Rodger. "Democratic Pluralism and Ecological Crisis in Botswana." *The Journal of Developing Areas* 23 (1989): 385–404.

————, ed. *Conservation for Development in Botswana, Kenya, Somalia, and Sudan.* Hanover, N.H.: African-Caribbean Institute, 1990.

Zaffiro, James J. "The U.S. and Botswana, 1966–1989: Foreign Policy in the Shadow of Boer and Bear." Paper prepared for the Twenty-ninth Annual Meeting of the International Studies Association, London, March 28–April 1, 1989.

Zetterqvist, Jenny. *Refugees in Botswana in the Light of International Law.* Research Report no. 87. Uppsala, Sweden: The Scandinavian Institute of African Studies, 1990.

About the Contributors

Olaf Claus received his doctorate from Mainz in 1991, while working in the Africa section of the Research Institute for International Affairs of the Stiftung Wissenschaft und Politik (SWP) in Ebenhausen, Germany. He is currently working as a reporter for German television.

Richard Dale is an associate professor in the Department of Political Science, Southern Illinois University. Professor Dale has written and lectured extensively on the history, politics, and societies of the southern Africa region, with particular focus on Botswana, South Africa, and Namibia. He presently serves on the editorial advisory board of *Conflict Quarterly*. Professor Dale's current research is focused on a book manuscript "Botswana's Search for Autonomy in Southern Africa."

John D. Holm teaches political science and is chair of the Political Science Department at Cleveland State University. Since 1987, he has worked on various programs of the Democracy Project at the University of Botswana. He has written numerous articles on the development and character of democracy in Botswana, and with Patrick Molutsi co-edited *Democracy in Botswana*.

Stephen R. Lewis, Jr., has been president and professor of economics at Carleton College in Minnesota since 1987. He has served as an economic consultant to the governments of Botswana and Kenya as well as the East African Community, and was a research advisor to the Pakistan Institute of Development Economics. His work includes *The Economics of Apartheid and Policy Choice and Development Performance in Botswana* (with Charles Harvey). Professor Lewis has also taught at Stanford, Harvard, and

Williams College, where he was the Herbert H. Lehman Professor of Economics.

Patrick P. Molutsi is a senior lecturer in sociology at the University of Botswana, and coordinator of the Democracy Research Project based in the university's Faculty of Social Sciences. He has published several articles on politics and society in Botswana and his latest work is "Report of the Study of Local Democratic Institutions in Botswana: The Case of Local Councils" (1992).

J. Stephen Morrison received his Ph.D. from the University of Wisconsin. For several years he worked as staff assistant for the House Foreign Relations Sub-Committee on Africa, and is currently with the United States Agency for International Development in Ethiopia.

Jack Parson was a faculty member in the Department of Political and Administrative Studies at the University of Botswana from 1973 to 1978 and is professor of political science at the College of Charleston in South Carolina. He participated in an election study in Botswana in 1974, helped direct a major study of the 1984 elections while on a Fulbright research grant in 1984–1985, and followed up on the 1989 elections during a three-month Fulbright research grant in 1990. Some of the results of this research have been published in two books and numerous articles.

Gloria Somolekae is a lecturer in public administration at the University of Botswana. She holds an M.A. in Public Policy and Administration from the Institute of Social Sciences in The Hague, and is a Ph.D. candidate in public administration at Syracuse University. Her research has focused on women's entrepreneurship, the causes and effects of labor migration from Botswana to South Africa, and small-scale business and the informal sector in Botswana.

Stephen John Stedman is assistant professor of comparative politics and African studies at the Nitze School of Advanced International Studies, The Johns Hopkins University. He has taught at Washington University in St. Louis and served as co-coordinator of Stanford University's course on peace studies. Dr. Stedman is author of *Peacemaking in Civil War* and is coauthor of *The New Is Not Yet Born: Conflict and Its Resolution in Southern Africa in the 1990s* (forthcoming).

Bernhard Weimer received his Ph.D. in political science from the Free University in Berlin. Since 1980, he has been a research fellow in the Africa section of Research Institute for International Affairs of the Stiftung

Wissenschaft und Politik (SWP) in Ebenhausen. He is currently with the Friedrich Ebert Foundation in Maputo, Mozambique.

Rodger Yeager is professor of political science, director of international studies, and adjunct professor of African history at West Virginia University. He is also affiliated with the African-Caribbean Institute of Hanover, New Hampshire, where he codirected a program supporting African research in policy problems of biological diversity management and natural resources conservation in Botswana and other eastern and southern African nations.

James J. Zaffiro is associate professor and chair of the Department of Political Science at Central College in Pella, Iowa. He has studied and written on Botswana's foreign policy and mass media. He is continuing work on a book-length study of foreign policy decisionmaking in Botswana. He has done fieldwork in southern Africa in 1983, 1985 (on a Fulbright grant), and most recently in 1991.

Index

212

About the Book

At a time when analysts speak despairingly of a lost decade of economic development in Africa, Botswana stands out as an example of successful economic performance. Indeed, Botswana attained the highest rate of economic growth in the world during the period 1965–1985; moreover, it did so as a multiparty liberal democracy, albeit one dominated by one political party.

The authors of this book examine Botswana's performance to date, seeking to understand the factors that account for its exceptional status and investigating problem areas that might endanger its achievements. They conclude by considering Botswana's prospects within a changing Southern Africa.

The SAIS African Studies Library

Tunisia: The Political Economy of Reform, edited by I. William Zartman

Ghana: The Political Economy of Recovery, edited by Donald Rothchild

Europe and Africa: The New Phase, edited by I. William Zartman

Botswana: The Political Economy of Democratic Development, edited by Stephen John Stedman